Imagining Sovereignty

*American Indian Literature
and Critical Studies Series*

IMAGINING SOVEREIGNTY

Self-Determination in American Indian Law and Literature

DAVID J. CARLSON

University of Oklahoma Press

Norman

Excerpts from the prologue to *The Power of Horses and Other Stories* by Elizabeth Cook-Lynn appear in chapter 5 and are copyright © 1990 by Elizabeth Cook-Lynn. They are reprinted here by permission of the University of Arizona Press.

An earlier version of a portion of chapter 6 appeared as "Trickster Hermeneutics and the Postindian Reader: Gerald Vizenor's Constitutional Praxis," in *Studies in American Indian Literatures* 23, no. 4 (2011). It is reprinted here courtesy of the University of Nebraska Press.

Library of Congress Cataloging-in-Publication Data

Names: Carlson, David J., 1970– author.
Title: Imagining sovereignty : self-determination in American Indian law and literature / David J. Carlson.
Description: Norman : University of Oklahoma Press, 2016. | Series: American Indian literature and critical studies series ; volume 66 | Includes bibliographical references and index.
Identifiers: LCCN 2015027984 | ISBN 9780806151977 (pbk. : alk. paper)
Subjects: LCSH: Indians of North America—Politics and government. | Indians of North America—Legal status, laws, etc.—Language. | American literature—Indian authors.
Classification: LCC E98. T77 C379 2016 | DDC 323.1197—dc23 LC record available at http://lccn.loc.gov/2015027984

Reading Sovereignty: Self-Determination in American Indian Law and Literature **is Volume 66 in the American Indian Literature and Critical Studies Series.**

The paper in this book meets the guidelines for permanence and durability of the Committee on Production Guidelines for Book Longevity of the Council on Library Resources, Inc. ∞

Copyright © 2016 by the University of Oklahoma Press, Norman, Publishing Division of the University. Manufactured in the U.S.A.

All rights reserved. No part of this publication may be reproduced, stored in a retrieval system, or transmitted, in any form or by any means, electronic, mechanical, photocopying, recording, or otherwise—except as permitted under Section 107 or 108 of the United States Copyright Act—without the prior written permission of the University of Oklahoma Press. To request permission to reproduce selections from this book, write to Permissions, University of Oklahoma Press, 2800 Venture Drive, Norman, OK 73069, or email rights.oupress@ou.edu.

Contents

Acknowledgments	vii
Introduction	3

Part I: Grounding Sovereignty Discourse

1. Colonial Contexts: Tribal Sovereignty in Western and U.S. Indian Law	15
2. The Indian Vox Populi	36
3. Collective Politics and Legal Interpretation	54

Part II: Literary Discourses of Self-Determination

4. The Pragmatics of Literary Nationalism	77
5. Elizabeth Cook-Lynn and Treaty Reading	104
6. Gerald Vizenor's Constitutional Praxis	144
7. Critical Prospects: Sovereignty in the Cahuilla Storyway	178
Notes	199
Bibliography	213
Index	223

Acknowledgments

When a manuscript finally appears in print, it has typically become the product of many hands. This one is no different. First of all, I want to acknowledge the generous support I received from the National Endowment for the Humanities; most of this book was drafted while I was an NEH Faculty Fellow in 2012–13. My former dean in the College of Arts and Letters, Eri Yasuhara, and the chair of the Department of English at California State University, San Bernardino, Sung-Heh Hyon, ensured that this was a productive year by allowing me to take a leave of absence from teaching to concentrate on my writing and research. I am grateful to both of them for the gift of time.

I have been very fortunate in recent years to find myself part of an extremely generous and inspiring community of Native American literature scholars. This community includes the anonymous reviewers at the University of Oklahoma Press, both of whom provided extremely useful and detailed commentaries on my work. I wish I could thank them by name. I *can* name and thank my editor at Oklahoma, Tom Krause, who has been an absolute pleasure to work with on this project from start to finish. A number of colleagues, both at my own institution and elsewhere, have read and commented on the manuscript, and they deserve notice. I want to thank James Mackay, Chad Luck, and Jessica Luck for their careful readings of the entire book. I have tried to take their thoughtful suggestions and incorporate them into the final product. James Mackay deserves particular praise here as well, for it was in the process of collaborating with him on a special issue of *SAIL* (focused on constitutional criticism) that I began to develop a clear sense of what this project was actually about. Thank you, James, for being a model of scholarly rigor and also a good friend. Discrete portions of the book have benefitted from many others' attention as well. Matthew Fletcher, David Stirrup, Padraig Kirwan, David Moore, Joseph Bauerkemper, Scott Andrews, Linda Lizut Helstern, Nancy Peterson, and several of the regular participants at the Native American Literature Symposium have offered me feedback and encouragement when I needed it.

Finally, I want to thank my wife, Alison Wiles, for her unwavering encouragement and patience. I also want to acknowledge my daughter, Clare, for constantly reminding me about the importance of curiosity. I eagerly anticipate the day when she is old enough to read this book and talk with me about it. I'm sure she'll ask some good questions; I hope by then I'll have even better answers.

Imagining Sovereignty

Introduction

There is no term more ubiquitous in American Indian writing today than sovereignty. Despite the proliferation of the concept's usage, though, it is strikingly difficult to pin down its specific meanings and functions. In the introduction to his 1999 collection, *Native American Sovereignty*, John Wunder offers a helpful (though not exhaustive) list of some of the different, and often contradictory, ideas frequently associated with the term. For some, he notes, sovereignty would simply mean being free from the military control of others.[1] For others, following article 1 of the 1933 Montevideo Convention of the Rights and Duties of States, sovereignty might be understood more broadly as a basic attribute of modern nation-states, which are defined as "having a permanent population, a definitive territory, a functioning government, and an ability to conduct relations with other states" (Wunder xi). This second formulation encompasses protectorates or conquered nations (states under some form of military control of another state), thus challenging the first definition. Then we might consider the important fact that the United States, a modern, militarily dominant nation-state, regularly employs the term sovereignty to describe the status of tribal peoples within its borders. This would be another seemingly contradictory turn, for even in contexts in which the U.S. Congress is exercising its unilateral legislative authority (plenary power) over tribes, tribal sovereignty still exists. In fact, in *Menominee Tribe of Indians v. United States* (1968) the Supreme Court held that the tribe's termination meant only the loss of federal support services, not the legal abolition of the tribe; the language of the court confirms that "tribes, *even those terminated*, retained sovereignty" (Wunder xii; emphasis added). Finally, if we add to this list alternate formulations, such as Vine Deloria, Jr.'s, that sovereignty is "the aspect of continuing cultural and communal integrity," or if we consider the way that many Indian tribes today vigorously assert their government-to-government relations with the United States while simultaneously needing to lobby for federal legislation to address pressing issues on their lands, it becomes quite clear that this language is anything but straightforward.

While sovereignty is a uniquely complicated signifier in Indian country, there is no question that it remains a vitally important one. This viewpoint is regularly reinforced, both implicitly and explicitly, in the fields of American Indian law *and* American Indian literature. As will be clear to readers, *Imagining Sovereignty* was conceived as an interdisciplinary Native American studies project, one that should be put in dialogue with many peer studies in the field. To situate this book in relation to contemporary conversations in indigenous political theory, one might consider the critical debate between Glen Coulthard and Dale Turner. In *Red Skin, Black Masks* Coulthard notes that over the last forty years the self-determination efforts of indigenous people in Canada have been framed in the language of "recognition" (1). This has led to the emergence of a degree of acceptance of indigenous rights within the legal and political framework of the Canadian state, most notably the acknowledgment of "existing aboriginal and treaty rights" under the Constitution Act of 1982 (2). Coulthard challenges this "politics of recognition," however, which he sees as inextricably tied to liberal models of political pluralism. In his view, efforts to reconcile indigenous claims to nationhood with settler-state sovereignty are compromised from the start. Coulthard argues that "the politics of recognition in its contemporary liberal form promises to reproduce the very configurations of colonialist, racist, patriarchal state power that indigenous peoples' demands for recognition have historically sought to transcend" (3). In other words, indigenous-state relations only *look* less colonialist in the present framework. Since settler colonialism is based on the dispossession of indigenous people from their lands, any solution that falls short of redressing this problem is unsatisfactory. Building on the work of Frantz Fanon, then, Coulthard rejects what he calls "a Hegelian or liberal politics of recognition" as lacking emancipatory potential (23). Instead he calls for a *"resurgent* politics of recognition" that involves indigenous peoples "empowering themselves through cultural practices of individual and collective self-fashioning that seek to prefigure *radical* alternatives to the structural and subjective dimensions of colonial power" (18; italics added).

Coulthard positions himself in direct opposition to Turner, whom he sees as exceedingly conciliatory toward the settler-colonial state. In *This Is Not a Peace Pipe* Turner also focuses on the evolution of the theorization and pursuit of aboriginal rights in Canada in the wake of the Constitution Act of 1982.

In doing so, though, he stresses the importance of pragmatically acknowledging the fact that those rights are currently positioned as existing and having legitimacy only within the framework of the Canadian state (Turner 4).² Turner recognizes, of course, the ongoing fundamental disagreement between aboriginal nationalists like Coulthard, stressing that they own their lands to this day, and Canadian sovereigntists, who continue to assert and enforce claims to sovereignty over aboriginal lands (5). In contrast with Coulthard, though, Turner argues that in pursuing their goals aboriginal peoples "will have to engage with the Canadian State's legal and political discourses in more effective ways" (5).

Imagining Sovereignty might be located in dialogue with (and somewhere in between) these two critical positions. As one can see, Turner and Coulthard are directly opposed in their senses of whether engagement with the colonial state (and the legal and political discourses that frame indigenous sovereignty in specific ways) is a fundamentally useful activity. Coulthard tends to see the liberal state as relatively impervious to change through engagement. In contrast, Turner argues that a "critical indigenous philosophy," which I would take to be a form of praxis that links legal and political theory with substantive action, can be advanced by "word warriors," mediator figures who "reconcile the forms of knowledge rooted in indigenous communities with the legal and political discourses of the state" (7). I incline a bit more toward Turner's views in this respect. But I also share Coulthard's sense that mere recognition through cross-cultural mediation (without a corresponding transformation of colonial systems) is not a sufficiently robust decolonizing strategy. In the end I think both Coulthard *and* Turner may underestimate the potential for word warriors to pursue dialectical change in the colonial order by working through the threshold concept of sovereignty. My work has affinities, in this respect, with Kevin Bruyneel's *The Third Space of Sovereignty;* both of us consider Vine Deloria's work as exemplary in this regard. The examples I will consider in this study, including Deloria, suggest that a fully formed *discourse* of sovereignty has the potential to drive a decolonizing praxis that is more radically engaged. It is certainly true that in an American context a number of indigenous writers and activists have pursued their projects with a sense that this might be so.

In the field of literary criticism some examples of recent studies related to mine include David Moore's *That Dream Shall Have a Name* and Padraig Kirwan's *Sovereign Stories*. Moore's book uses sovereignty somewhat like I do, as a heuristic to read and assess the work of a number of contemporary American Indian writers. He employs a fairly broad definition of the term in doing so, however, and he uses sovereignty as one of five interpretive lenses for reading literary works. Kirwan's book, which I regrettably encountered only when I was concluding my own work on this study, engages in some questions similar to mine. *Sovereign Stories* and *Imagining Sovereignty* are complementary studies, both containing discussions of Craig Womack and Elizabeth Cook-Lynn, in fact. And even if our work is not entirely congruent (his critical methodology is directly informed by Choctaw writer LeAnne Howe's theories of "tribalography"), Kirwan and I share an interest in highlighting commonalities between writers often opposed to one another in contemporary literary critical discourse.

Two other important works that cover terrain related to that explored here are Mark Rifkin's *When Did Indians Become Straight* and Scott Lyons's *X-Marks*. Rifkin's study relates to my own in a manner somewhat analogous to how Coulthard's relates to Turner's. His position likely deviates from mine regarding the degree to which the liberal state (and the language of sovereignty itself) can be engaged as part of the work of decolonization. Nevertheless, I think Rifkin would see in some of the discussions in this study a resemblance to his own examples of the process of queering sovereignty. For example, we share an interest in indigenous redefinitions of peoplehood. On the other hand, Lyons's focus on how Indian tribal communities have been able to continue to offer a qualified "yes" to modernity strikes me as analogous to my own interest in the ways that tribal sovereignty discourse aims to interact with the Western legal tradition. Lyons rejects theories of nationalism (like Ernest Gellner's) that are based on the idea of a total rupture between industrial modernity and antecedent structural forms, recognizing that the teleological elements of those theories implicitly define tribal nationalism as a form of assimilation. In contrast, he argues that tribal nationalism is the modernization of the Indian "ethnie" (that is, a population's sense of cohesion around myths of common ancestry, historical memory, shared cultural elements, and a specific homeland) in the context of an emerging mass public culture (writing and print) and legal engagement (treaty negotiations) (S. Lyons, *X-Marks* 120). Lyons's sophisticated integration of literary and political theory in tracing this type of process is a model that I hope to emulate here.

Having situated *Imagining Sovereignty* generally in relation to other contemporary work in the field, it may also be useful to make a few points about methodology. As my subtitle suggests, my work is deeply influenced by the field of law and literature. To the extent that I can set my own work apart from that of many of my Native American studies (NAS) colleagues, those distinctions may emerge in my approach to theorizing the relationship between the realms of literary production and criticism and the real-world institutions and systems of law. In the field of law and literature there are multiple ways in which the relationship between those two spheres has been understood. One of these is looking at ways that literary works disseminate or contest ideological structures related to legal norms and institutions. This was a central theme of my first book, *Sovereign Selves*, which examined the rhetorical strategies employed by Indian autobiographers to engage with specific legal models of subjectivity during the removal and allotment eras. While I didn't use the term then, in the present study I might describe those engagements (by William Apess and Charles Eastman in particular) as attempts to advance the cause of legal sovereignty, albeit in a highly constrained colonial context. In many ways, then, the present book can be read as a continuation or companion to my earlier work in its consideration of ideological connections between law and literature. But there is an additional issue driving my thinking here. Law and literature scholarship has also begun to explore the issue of hermeneutic processes, and I am deeply interested in this inquiry in *Imagining Sovereignty*. I argue that the particular techniques of interpretation that emerge from readers' encounters with texts can be mutually informing in both literary and legal contexts. In taking up the idea of an emerging discourse of sovereignty, then, I aim to produce a complex exploration of the law-literature relationship that combines mimetic, ideological, and hermeneutic elements. This is a much richer story than I was able to tell a decade ago, and it is my hope that this richness will complement much of the other excellent Native American studies work being done in relation to the topic of sovereignty.

In another methodological vein, I should also note that I adopt an essentially tribalcentric perspective throughout this study (heavily privileging Indian-authored sources and viewpoints). While I do so, it seems to me imperative to acknowledge that the central position of the concept of sovereignty in American Indian writing today has something to do with its function as a mediating term. Legal engagement between Indian and Western perspectives remains an important concern for me, as it was in *Sovereign Selves*. It is my view that one of the reasons for the ubiquity of the language of sovereignty today is that it functions as a kind of metaphorical middle ground, or a threshold concept, somewhat in the mode that Audra Simpson discusses it in *Mohawk Interruptus*.[3] Sovereignty maintains its importance, in other words, partly because it represents a vital, evolving point of contact between the colonizer and the colonized. Pragmatically, in a settler-colonial context like that of the United States, where the tribal population remains a small minority of the overall population of the nation-state, the existence of this kind of contact point remains absolutely vital. Grasping the nature of sovereignty as a threshold concept, though, requires us to trace distinct etymologies of the term (one based on Western legal historical sources and one indigenous). This will be a major focus of the first three chapters, where I consider some of the ways that sovereignty serves as a marker allowing both the colonizing power of the United States and the resisting powers of various American Indian nations to organize themselves and their claims to authority.

Finally, an explanation of my use of the term "dialectical" in this study is in order as well, as some readers may be thrown off because of its strong materialist (Marxist) connotations. *Imagining Sovereignty* engages with dialectics in more of a traditionally Hegelian sense. I employ a dialectical critical methodology, myself, and I also use the term to describe what I see as the core critical praxis emerging in the discourse of tribal sovereignty developed by several of the figures considered in this book. Dialectical thinking is an extremely useful tool to bring to bear in analyzing sovereignty because that term has never been entirely stable. Sovereignty transforms over time by being brought into relation with new ideas (like the "nation") or by being deployed in new contexts (like settler colonialism). In *Dance of the Dialectic* Bertell Ollman notes that dialectics, historically, has been an attempt to develop a method to study complex organisms or systems whose parts interrelate and change over time. The subject of dialectics is not "things," in other words (conceived of as independent, stable entities defined at the beginning of an analysis), but "relations" (a term that denotes the idea that the various terms of any analysis make each other meaningful in evolving ways). The two central relations that occupy me here are those of identity/difference (where one considers how seemingly opposed things can be comprehended by deeper unities) and of interpenetration (where one considers how the meaning and function of an object or idea is contingent upon its context or upon the perspective from which it is viewed). If I can risk a bit of generalization here, I would say that my own dialectical analysis of legal and literary history focuses more on the relation of identity/difference. An example of this is my consideration of how nationalist and cosmopolitan approaches to self-determination might be unified by grasping their discursive commonality. The praxis of the indigenous thinkers within the study tends to be dialectical more in the sense of exploring relations of interpenetration (where the introduction of new elements into a discursive situation shifts the meanings of other key terms). Vine Deloria's redefinition of "peoplehood," in the context of constitutional reform, in order to change the meaning of "sovereignty," would be an example here. For ease of reading I will not use this technical, philosophical vocabulary throughout this study; however, I hope it will be clear to readers as they proceed how these underlying methodologies structure the book as a whole.

Finally, a word about "discourse," a term that refers, in its post-structuralist sense (via Foucault), to the conjunction of institutional systems, epistemes, and modes of representation in powerful ways that produce real-world effects. In the second part of *Imagining Sovereignty* I analyze some of the ways that contemporary American Indian writers and critics have internalized the dialectical spirit I describe above and have begun to fuse literary practices and legal structures into a fully formed discourse of sovereignty. The legal-historical discussion of part I will have brought into focus several of the key elements of this process, but these will be amplified, diversified, and further complicated throughout the literary chapters. Presented in no particular order here, the various elements I consider in mapping sovereignty discourse in the work of Craig Womack, Elizabeth Cook-Lynn, and Gerald Vizenor include the following: (1) the emergence of critical practices that blend a concern with the formal and performative aspects of texts; (2) the development of specific textual practices—both inventive and critical—designed to position the reader as a particular type of interpretive actor and thus a particular type of political subject; (3) an emphasis on the roles of legal and literary texts in the constitution of a collective people interpellated through its vox populi; (4) an emphasis on the connection between particular interpretive practices and subject positions and the specific legal mechanisms called technai (singular, techne) by which sovereignty can be expressed; and (5) the attempt to dialectically transform and indigenize elements of the Western-rooted language of sovereignty to better advance the cause of decolonization. In exploring these ideas, my goal throughout part II is to offer a series of parallel acts of criticism that can bring out the complexity of the fusion of law and literature we are beginning to see in contemporary Native American writing. I also suggest that grappling with that complexity is essential if we are to continue to move the discourse forward and to respond to criticisms that some scholars, such as Cook-Lynn, have directed at NAS scholarship, both generally and specifically in its literary forms.

In chapter 1 I provide the first half of a history of the concept of sovereignty. Registering my agreement with many Native American studies scholars, I recognize that sovereignty has distinctively Western roots, rendering it a complicated concept around which to build decolonizing projects. At the same time, though, I suggest that the failure to remember the full complexity of those roots contributes to theoretical confusion in some of the polemical writing that questions the utility of sovereignty as a threshold concept. Chapter 2 shifts the focus from Western intellectual history to indigenous perspectives, tracing the development of the concept of sovereignty as self-determination in Indian country during the twentieth century. The work of a major Indian intellectual and public figure—D'Arcy McNickle—grounds this discussion. McNickle emerges as a major contributor in his ability to demonstrate how Indian political thought could be both strategically deterritorialized and also dialectically reinvented in the face of the termination threat. Beyond this, his involvement in the 1961 Chicago Conference and its famous *Declaration of Indian Purpose* highlights his important role in the articulation of a new kind of oppositional vision centered on the capacity of a collective of Indian people to mobilize on behalf of self-determination. This awareness of the need to constitute peoplehood through a vox populi that is disseminated in Indian print culture links McNickle to Cahuilla historian Rupert Costo. The chapter concludes with a consideration of Costo's newspaper, *Wassaja*, and its suggestive fusion of the idea of self-determination with the symbolization of Indian political subjectivity. Costo's and McNickle's works, in these respects, foreshadow many of the key ideas explored later in the book. In them, we begin to see the tighter fusion of ideological and textual concerns necessary for the emergence of a fully formed literary discourse of sovereignty.

Chapter 3 focuses largely on the work of Vine Deloria, Jr., whose thinking about sovereignty I present as an attempt to develop an even more sophisticated and diversified dialectical reinvention of the concept. The chapter is largely focused on the essay, "Self-Determination and the Concept of Sovereignty," and the monograph, *We Talk, You Listen*. There we can see Deloria developing a complex vision of how the Western concept of sovereignty might, in fact, be indigenized. In discussing Deloria's writings I suggest that he deploys a broad concept of popular sovereignty (arguably brought into the forefront of Indian thinking through the Chicago Conference) in order to produce an alternative vision of how to organize the government of the state. His version of the discourse of sovereignty as self-determination also employs a model of group-centered political subjectivity to generate new possibilities for the constructive transformations of political institutions. Deloria also hints at how those political ideas foreground specific textual concerns and shifts in hermeneutic practices that many might think of as literary.

Chapter 4 begins my examination of the literary discourse of sovereignty by closely examining the influential critical project of Craig Womack, particularly as it is developed in his groundbreaking book *Red on Red*. In my reading, Womack represents a key figure in the drive to create a full-fledged discourse of sovereignty, one that links literary and legal concerns and practices in a pragmatic project designed to serve tribal communities. In exploring the core problematics of *Red on Red* I highlight how, in both its successes and its limitations, that work lays out key theoretical foundations for understanding sovereignty discourse. Recognizing this allows us to see deeper affinities between Womack's (and Robert Warrior's) work and that of writers who are often opposed to them, for instance Gerald Vizenor.

Chapters 5 and 6 deal with the critical and creative works of Elizabeth Cook-Lynn and Gerald Vizenor. Cook-Lynn's work ambitiously aims to synthesize several of the threads discussed in the preceding chapters into a tightly focused Dakotah discourse of sovereignty.[4] She develops an innovative approach to what Womack refers to as "sovereignty reading," built around her understanding of the centrality of the treaty as the legal techne most relevant for Dakotah assertions of sovereignty. As her critical engagements with cosmopolitanism suggest, however, Cook-Lynn's focus on the treaty form leads her into a struggle to engage with specific hermeneutic problems, a struggle involving the tension between assertions of separatist autonomy and the need for recognition. I present some of her solutions to those problems (rooted in her deployment of the concept of intent and her use of genre theory) while also pointing out the unintended irony that some of her critiques of the field of Native American studies tend to undercut those solutions.

Vizenor's work as a literary theorist, a prolific writer of fiction and poetry, and as the principle drafter of the recently adopted Constitution of the White Earth Nation makes him perhaps the most important figure in this study. In chapter 6 I focus on his critical theorization of "trickster hermeneutics" and the concept of the "postindian." I present these concepts as having considerable relevance as bridges between the realms of law and literature. Through them Vizenor is able to address the crucial issues of political subjectivity, interpretive practice, and the indigenization of Western legal concepts and forms, which are central to the production of a discourse of sovereignty. Having laid out these ideas in terms of Vizenor's criticism, I offer a reading of the White Earth Constitution itself, which I see as deploying the same types of textual practices that Vizenor employs in his literary work. I then turn that relationship around, focusing on how our reading of the constitutional text informs a literary work. The chapter concludes with a sustained discussion of Vizenor's novel *Shrouds of White Earth*, building on his concept of "imagic moments." In that reading I highlight how Vizenor's literary symbolizations of subjectivity support the approach to reciprocity and recognition encoded in the White Earth Constitution.

The tight fit between literary and legal practice in Vizenor's case makes him a logical culminating figure for this study. I am, however, keen to avoid conveying the impression that his work represents *the* solution to the linkage between literary and real-world concerns needed in a discourse of sovereignty. Since a part of my argument throughout the book will be to stress the need for varied approaches to the pursuit of sovereignty (through legal, political, and textual means), I conclude with a final chapter focused on archival materials from California. The particular colonial history of California produces a very different context from the ones in which Womack, Cook-Lynn, and Vizenor are working. These differences do not mean that the development of a discourse of sovereignty in California is impossible, of course, but they do suggest that the forms we find in studying those other writers would need to be adapted and inflected in new ways when situated in new localities. Through a detailed reading of the mid-twentieth-century Cahuilla leader Francisco Patencio's work *Stories and Legends of the Palm Springs Indians*, I offer some suggestions about how a California-centered sovereignty discourse might develop, in the immediate future at least.

In the end my consideration of the elements of sovereignty discourse that we can locate in the Cahuilla storyway is intended to foreground the need for Native American studies scholars to do more to appreciate and elucidate the value of divergent strategies for decolonization. I would argue that we need to develop critical models that describe, rather than prescribe, the various strains of sovereignty discourse available to, and employed by, American Indian people today. Discrete approaches that develop into effective decolonizing strategies for particular tribal communities may not, in the end, be serviceable as the centerpiece of a generalized indigenous politics or theory. In noting this I am hopeful that the work I have done here will also contribute to a direction signaled in Jace Weaver's recent contribution to Alan Velie and A. Robert Lee's edited collection, *The Native American Renaissance*. In his essay "Turning West: Cosmopolitanism and American Indian Literary Nationalism," Weaver both offers a useful survey of several recent trends in American Indian literary studies and calls for an end to what Kenneth Lincoln designated an "academic civil war" between nationalist an nonnationalist critics. Weaver points out that "the work of younger scholars [such as Lisa Brooks, Daniel Heath Justice, Sean Teuton, and many others] illustrates clearly that there is no unbridgeable gulf . . . between cosmopolitans and nationalists" ("Turning West" 32–33). I agree with that view, and I think that my discussion of the discourses of self-determination here will add further illustrations and support to Weaver's claim. As an allied critic I aim to align myself with any writers who, as Weaver puts it, "assert the reality and validity of indigenous sovereignty and through [their] work, seek to support it" (34). It seems clear to me that the field is ready to move past the schismatic criticism of recent years and focus more intensely on turning over and cultivating common ground. And it is fitting that sovereignty can provide an intellectual space for that to happen.

Part 1

Grounding Sovereignty Discourse

CHAPTER 1

COLONIAL CONTEXTS

*Tribal Sovereignty in Western
and U.S. Indian Law*

On Wednesday, June 24, 2009, *Indian Country Today* ran a lead editorial titled "Renew Sovereignty Lessons for a New Generation." The same editorial had run one decade earlier with the title "Let's Learn about Sovereignty." What had clearly not changed over the course of ten years was the editorial board's view that the concept of sovereignty stands at the heart of the political and legal future of Indian tribes in the United States. The editorial notes that a proper understanding of not just Indian tribal sovereignty, but sovereignty in general, is lacking in most of the American public; even among Native peoples there is a wide range of definitions. In the editors' view, Indian print culture has a vital role to play in addressing this problem; they point out that *Indian Country Today* has aimed to encourage a broad conversation regarding the definition and significance of sovereignty in Indian people's lives. A key pragmatic goal underlying their journalism, then, has been to address the following question: What are the bases of Indian arguments for tribal sovereignty considering the realities of living in a modern North American society? In the editors' view every Native student should know the main pillars of Indian sovereignty in legal-historical terms. Developing such an awareness of the arguments that buttress sovereignty claims, they suggest, serves both an aspirational imperative (allowing tribal members to reflect on what ought to be in terms of fundamental justice and to imagine decolonized futures) and a realistic one (helping them to develop effective, pragmatic strategies to confront present conditions and to cope with the diverse challenges confronting them). The editors conclude by noting that within the frameworks of both American democracy and international law the correlation between sovereignty and the concept of self-government is clear. The challenge for American Indian peoples today, then, is to employ every available strategy both to vigorously maintain and to exercise the right of self-determination while also coping with the reality that small nations must depend on larger ones to keep covenants and respect their autonomy.

The primary goal of this chapter is to lay out the complexity of the pillars of sovereignty and to begin to address the question of the utility of the term as a threshold concept. It is probably necessary to begin that inquiry with some kind of general gloss of the basic term. The following working definition, taken from a 1977 report on Indian sovereignty prepared by the Institute for the Development of Indian Law, strikes me as a reasonable starting point. Sovereignty is "the supreme power from which all specific political powers are derived" (Wunder 1). Taking up this idea of "supreme power" in an American Indian context, of course, requires a breadth of perspective and close attention to context. As the writers of the report note, sovereignty is an abstraction that cannot be seen in a direct sense. Rather, we recognize sovereignty by perceiving it being exercised. And the history of contact between settler colonizers and Native Americans can certainly be viewed as a long struggle, on one side, to limit the exercise of power on the part of indigenous peoples, and on the other, to resist those limitations or to reassert powers that have been taken away.

With this idea of struggle in mind, it is clear that developing a sense of how the language of sovereignty informs contemporary American Indian writing requires us to trace competing understandings of the term. Chapters 2 and 3 will focus on tribal engagements with that language. To understand how and why many Indian people employ the idea of sovereignty in the context of decolonization, though, it strikes me as important to first develop a clear sense of how the concept has been employed in the U.S. legal system. This is a nod toward the term's centrality as a threshold concept. As understood from a Western/colonial perspective, sovereignty has been employed, albeit unevenly and inconsistently, as a tool for domination and for the limitation of Indian authority and autonomy. Not surprisingly, this has led some contemporary Indian writers to legitimately question whether it can be employed at all as a vehicle for self-determination. When looked at closely, however, it seems to me that sovereignty reveals itself to be a more complicated and potentially flexible idea than it might first appear.

Among both its strongest American Indian advocates and critics, it is generally acknowledged that the term sovereignty derives from Western European political history and legal tradition.[1] In his often-cited essay "Self-Determination and the Concept of Sovereignty," Vine Deloria, Jr., notes that while sovereignty was an ancient idea, and originally a theological term, it was appropriated by European political thinkers after the Reformation to characterize the person of the king as head of state.[2] In Deloria's formulation, by the seventeenth and eighteenth centuries a dominant meaning of sovereignty emerged whereby the term referred to "the absolute power of a nation to determine its own course of action with respect to other nations" ("Self-Determination" 118). This is broadly accurate, but Deloria leaves out some key elements of the intellectual history. Most significantly, he passes over the ways in which some thinkers have located sovereignty within a natural-law framework.

It is important to recall that the idea of sovereignty developed out of the practices of European politics and not in an abstract or purely theoretical context. This has important implications for understanding the diversity of meanings that are associated with the term today. Sovereignty has always been a fluid concept, capable of dialectical transformation, whose definitions and applications have been shaped by real-world political interests and power struggles. It is particularly interesting to note, in this regard, that sovereignty has some of its roots in acts of resistance; this oppositional pedigree also offers initial hints regarding the appeal of the concept as a tool for decolonization. As political theorist Robert Jackson has noted, the term sovereignty emerged, in part, as an expedient worked out in the early modern period by kings and their agents to challenge and repudiate the overarching authority of the pope. The assertion of sovereignty was originally an act of secession from the "respublica Christiana" (or Christian commonwealth) linking Europe together through the Catholic Church and the papacy. The respublica was the only uniform political and legal institution spanning Europe in the Middle Ages, which was otherwise made up of a bewildering array of overlapping and sometimes conflicting polities and systems of dependence (Jackson xi). As rival authorities both engaged in the act of asserting sovereignty (claiming to represent an alternative to the papacy for the legitimate exercise of political and legal power) and entered into relations with each other over jurisdiction, this led to the early formulation of what is now international law and, eventually, to the emergence of the nation-state system that remains dominant today.

Recognizing the connections between sovereignty and the emergence of international law can remind us of something else often forgotten in contemporary usage—the importance of natural law as part of the concept's DNA. In his still-classic study of the history of international law, J. L. Brierly illuminates these early links. The first explicit theorization of sovereignty, Brierly reminds us, was in Jean Bodin's 1576 work, *De Republica*, a book that emerged against the background of violent factionalism and civil war in France and the slow emergence of unified states in Europe. Bodin believed that a strong central authority was needed to address problems confronting the French polity, and thus he concluded that the essence of statehood was the unity of its government. But Bodin's specific understanding of the government of the state will likely look a bit odd to modern readers. A state, Bodin argued, may be defined as "a multitude of families and the possessions that they have in common ruled by a supreme power *and by reason*" (Brierly 8; emphasis added). The inclusion of reason as a coequal ruling element in the state represents a key contrast to the positivist understanding of sovereignty that would come to dominate Western legal discourse by the nineteenth century. For by invoking reason in this way, Bodin connects the concept of sovereignty with a tradition of natural law that (theoretically, at least) provided significant limiting checks on the ruling power of human lawgivers. Bodin's formulation of sovereignty mediates between the medieval respublica and the modern state in this respect.

Like many subsequent thinkers, Bodin understood the essential manifestation of sovereignty to be the power to make laws. Since the sovereign (Bodin would have been thinking primarily of the monarch here) makes the laws, though, he cannot truly be subordinated to the laws he makes. Nevertheless, Bodin's sovereign is not the unfettered authority of later positivist political theory. For in his view, the sovereign *is* bound by something—specifically by the divine law, or the law of nature or reason (which is common to all nations), as well as by what he calls the particular laws of the government. The latter would include the rules that decide in whom sovereign power is vested and determine the nature of succession. We would call such things today constitutional laws. In placing the law of nature in such a prominent role here, Bodin aligns himself with key elements of medieval political thought—specifically with the notion that legitimate power could never be purely arbitrary and secular. The natural law both constrains and legitimizes the ruler. Bodin's theorization of sovereignty posits a strong moral foundation and framework for sovereign power, which exists as a check on absolutism. And his work implies that a theory of sovereignty incorporating natural-law concepts would also buttress a stronger sense of legal obligation than we often find in contemporary contexts (where sovereignty is more typically associated with the mere possession by some entity of the positive power to impose its will on another).

Notwithstanding these early links to a tradition of natural law, it is true that the trajectory of sovereignty theory has taken it in another direction—the absolutist one noted by Deloria. Over time, sovereignty came to be identified with a power that exists above (or prior to) the law. In addition, the sovereign power that was originally seen as an attribute of a personal ruler inside of the state has come to be seen as an attribute of the state itself. The latter conjunction emerged gradually during the sixteenth and seventeenth centuries, and as a result of this historical process the general concept of sovereignty is now synonymous with "state sovereignty" for most Western legal and political theorists. The natural-law roots are largely ignored. As Jackson rightly points out, as a foundational idea in *modern* Western politics and law, sovereignty typically connotes (1) the idea that supreme legislative and political authority is located in the nation-state and (2) the idea that these nation-states are legally independent, formally autonomous, and geographically separate and are thus entitled to be free from interference by other states in their internal governance (Jackson x). In this respect, for most Western thinkers today sovereignty simultaneously encompasses the constitutional idea that national governments have legitimate and clearly delineated powers (and duties) vis-á-vis their citizens and the international idea that nation-states represented by these governments relate to one another as autonomous entities.[3] As such, "when the government of a state is said to be sovereign, it holds supreme authority domestically and independent authority internationally, at one and the same time" (6). If it does not hold that supreme authority, the collective (even if it designates itself a state or nation) is not sovereign.

Under this definition, of course, American Indian nations within the borders of the United States would not be seen as sovereign *states*.[4] However, the United States has also never formally designated them as colonies (even during the long period before colonialism was made illegal under international law, when it would have been technically possible to do so).[5] Instead, under U.S. Indian law, the term sovereignty has regularly been associated with Indian tribal nations, but in an alternate sense to full state sovereignty. Right from the start, then, we can see that tribal sovereignty represents an interesting historical and structural anomaly. This is a crucial element to consider, I would argue, in considering sovereignty's potential as a threshold concept in a U.S. context. The somewhat surprising presence of the idea of tribal sovereignty in U.S. Indian law certainly suggests something about its potential as a fluid and evolving signifier. Assessing this potential requires a closer consideration of that American tradition.

The foundations of U.S. Indian law in relation to the concept of tribal sovereignty were laid in the late eighteenth and early nineteenth centuries during the period of the founding and the early decades of the new American Republic. The larger context for understanding this history, however, especially for the purposes of the present discussion, is the transatlantic development of the political theory of the sovereign state and of empire. By the end of the eighteenth century the concept of (state) sovereignty in Europe had evolved to contain a series of basic elements.[6] Europe was seen to be composed of a collective of sovereign nation-states, each of which was deemed to have existed, constitutionally, prior to any treaties or international organizations they might arrange between themselves. In other words, by this point the historical origins of the modern state system, which had arguably been created though a relatively recent series of wars and legal innovations, had been mythologized and naturalized into a set of universally accepted legal fictions. At the same time, European sovereign states were seen as entitled to mutual recognition, enjoying legal rights (expressed in the positive law of nations or international law) and possessing legitimate interests (addressed and acknowledged through diplomacy). These state sovereigns were expected to use their own military and economic power responsibly, but the vitally important states (which would eventually be termed the "great powers") were deemed to play particularly important roles, employing military, economic, and political power to preserve the system. Internally, states were understood as having the legitimate right to create almost any kind of political/legal systems of governance, all of which would be viewed as legitimate expressions of state sovereignty. Significantly, though, in external terms, clear distinctions were made between Western/European contexts, where imperial relations between states were largely delegitimized, and conditions outside of Europe, where they were further elaborated.

It would not be until the mid-twentieth century, with the creation of the United Nations, that a post-Westphalian system of state sovereignty would be universalized into a global system. Today, as Jackson reminds us, there is no terrestrial territory that is *formally* deemed outside of the authority/jurisdiction of a sovereign nation-state.[7] However, in the eighteenth and nineteenth centuries in the Americas (and elsewhere) European powers were really only beginning this process of incorporation. During the era of discovery and colonization, European nation-states extended their own sovereign authority over other territories and populations, justifying this through ethnocentric claims that non-European peoples had not evolved politically and socially to the point of exercising sovereignty, and further, that they would not be capable of doing so for the foreseeable future. Ironically, of course, in the New World the European conquest of indigenous peoples had initially been sanctioned under the authority of the respublica Christiana. The papal bull, *Inter Caetera*, issued by Pope Alexander VI in May 1493, and the 1494 Treaty of Tordesillas, which divided New World territories between Spain and Portugal, are generally cited as key inaugural legal documents in this context. With the decline of papal authority and the emergence of the new system of European state sovereignty, though, the legal logic of imperialism shifted in important ways.

A central pillar of imperialism was the evolution of the concept of territorial sovereignty. By the late eighteenth century states were clearly viewed as geographically specific organizations that were defined, in part, by their bounded territory. At the same time, title to territory in international law had come to resemble the right of ownership in private law, which created a theoretical basis for some states to *extend* their sovereignty beyond their natural geographic boundaries under certain conditions.[8] These developments are best understood in light of the significant role that the imperial law of Rome played in the emergence of European international law and the gradual transformation of its natural-law elements. International law, as Brierly notes, developed out of a foundation in the law of nature, but one particularly tied to a Roman way of thinking. Imperial Roman law blended together two strains: (1) the *jus civile*, the original law peculiar to Rome as a city-state, and (2) the *jus gentium*, the law believed to be of universal application, based on simple and reasonable principles and thus capable of being used in expansion of the empire. In time the jus gentium would be reinforced by the philosophical conception of *jus naturale*, developed by Stoics in Greece and later taken up in Rome. Jus naturale referred to sum of those principles that should govern human contact because they are founded in the nature of man as a rational and social being. In time, jus gentium and jus naturale became synonymous, and medieval writers would further develop the tradition and the fusion into what would later become the foundations of modern natural-law discourse. Thomas Aquinas, for example, would teach that the law of nature was that part of the law of God discoverable by human reason.

This law of nature, as we have seen with Bodin, was initially put forward as a check on the absolutist elements of the emergent theory of sovereignty, denying in some sense the full legal independence of states from one another. The more fully the Roman elements became incorporated into the emerging international law, though, the more these checks and balances were compromised. In sixteenth-century Europe, Roman law was widely regarded as *ratio scripta* (written reason), which filled the need for a text of natural law, the absence of which proved so troubling for many medieval thinkers (Brierly 19). But this Roman text included a number of elements that furthered the imperialist tendencies and appetites of the European system, its states, and its rulers. As Brierly reminds us, the founders of international law turned to Roman law for rules of their system "whenever the relations between ruling princes seemed to them to be analogous to those of private persons" (20). The rights over territory would thus come to closely resemble the rights of private individuals over property. Indeed, "the international rules relating to territory are still in their essentials the Roman rules of property" (20).

The legal status of indigenous peoples shifted in important ways as a result of these developments.⁹ Initially, European rulers had been uncertain of their ability to impose their political will on Indians, and there had been a willingness to recognize the sovereignty of non-Western rulers in accordance with natural-law doctrines. In that context, Indian tribes came to be understood in European terms as nations with sovereign authority and title over specific territories, even if that authority was limited in specific ways through the application of the Law of Discovery.¹⁰ Over time, though, the natural law came to be displaced by a new, positive law of colonialism. Racial and cultural distinctions were imposed to limit the exercise of sovereignty by indigenous peoples, and a new category of "imperial sovereignty" was created.

Essentially, imperial sovereignty represents a deterritorialization of domestic sovereign authority and its extension as something analogous to property rights into other geographic spaces. The process of articulating these legal principles of modern empire arguably began in the 1700s, but it was complete by the mid-to-late nineteenth century. "When a government exercises supreme and exclusive authority over a foreign territory and its population," the thinking went, "that government [could] be said to possess imperial sovereignty" over that territory and people (Jackson 77). As a variety of mechanisms for legitimizing the extension of imperial sovereignty over non-European territory were developed (the right of occupation of terra nullius under the Law of Discovery, cession by treaty, and claims of possession through war and conquest), the previous formal designation of indigenous people as territorial sovereigns, and thus as owners of their real estate who could thereby alienate it, created an efficient means for European expansion. As Jackson puts it, "Sovereignty was conveniently available as an institution for taking legal possession of foreign territory in an orderly fashion" (Jackson 73). The legal mechanisms employed in this "orderly" colonialism included the negotiation of unequal treaties and the imposition of ideas of trusteeship. Through them, the territorial sovereignty of indigenous people was created and validated strategically in Western law, only to be subsequently constrained, limited, or usurped by imperial fiat.

The imperialist background and related adaptation of territorial sovereignty that I have been presenting here are important for understanding the foundations of Indian sovereignty in U.S. Indian law as well as the contested nature of sovereignty as a concept among Indian thinkers themselves. Paradoxically, the struggle for decolonization in Indian country often necessarily involves not just the rejection of these legal structures of empire, but also their partial modification. For example, it is now a commonplace in Native American studies discourse to point out that the specific concepts of territorial ownership imported into an American context by European colonialists represented gross distortions of Indian ideas about their own relationship to land. When contemporary Native American thinkers and writers insist on the precontact or extraconstitutional sovereignty of Indian tribes or attempt to revise our understanding of the meaning of specific treaties, they are often trying to decouple the concept of a right of self-government from the concept of national rights of property ownership in the European sense. At the same time, the realities of the colonial experience (involving, in many cases, dislocation and diaspora) have sometimes forced tribal nations to engage with the notion of deterritorialization as part of their own process of political and cultural self-preservation. For many Indian tribes have needed to reconstitute themselves as nonimperial, sovereign polities in new geographical spaces.

To add another key dimension to our reading of this tradition, we should also take into account an additional background element from this colonial period—the rise of the idea of popular sovereignty so important to the American founding. It is at this point where theories of nationalism begin to intersect with our understanding of sovereignty. Popular sovereignty, broadly defined, is "the notion that authority . . . resides in the political will or consent of the people of an independent state" (Jackson 78). It is one of the central pillars of modern liberal political thought, and it has been expressed in a variety of different forms (parliamentary, democratic, and even totalitarian) in the modern era. The idea of the need for popular consent to legitimize the exercise of governmental power, of course, was one of the central forces that drove the American Revolution. In the wake of the Revolutionary War, sovereignty, in its fullest sense, was increasingly understood in the United States to be a manifestation of the will and consent of the people, represented through the democratic institutions of a modern nation-state. But it is important for us to realize that "the people" is an abstraction that also developed in the context of an emergent global colonial order. This fact also has important implications for the discourse of Indian sovereignty in the United States.

Influential theorists of nationalism—Ernest Gellner, Eric Hobsbawm, and Benedict Anderson—have pointed out that the ideologies of popular sovereignty and nationalism developed simultaneously in Europe and America, coincident with the rise of industrial modernity. The age of revolution and the nineteenth century produced the imaginary idea of the nation—a body of citizens whose collective sovereignty constitutes the state that expresses them politically (Hobsbawm 18–19). Anderson's major contribution to our understanding of this process was to stress the importance of the rise of the mass culture and symbolizing systems of print capitalism (though Hobsbawm's work moves in similar directions). But he also highlighted how the project of European colonialism (where imperial polities struggled to conquer and absorb others) was another key driver. This should remind us that, in formal terms, "the people" does not equal "the population." In the case of the United States in the eighteenth and nineteenth centuries it is hardly necessary to remind readers that an enormous portion of the population—slaves, women, American Indians—were not truly part of the represented people. One of the primary mechanisms employed during this time to manage the contradictions between popular sovereignty and settler colonialism in the case of American Indians, of course, was an increasingly racialized discourse, distinguishing savage outsiders from the civilized people.[11] A key historical hurdle confronted by Indian people in an American context, then, has been the basic problem of political erasure. It is in this respect that Indian leaders' gestures smacking of assimilationist capitulation in the nineteenth and early twentieth centuries—such as the push to be granted U.S. citizenship—actually make sense as legitimate acts of resistance. The colonial situation in which those actions were taken renders them meaningful in a way that criticism from the vantage point of a later time might not acknowledge.

The rise of popular sovereignty discourse represented more than just an exclusionary barrier to be confronted by Indian people, however. The basic shift achieved in the late eighteenth century toward the idea of government by the people also involved the emergence of what we might describe as a new form of political subjectivity, an imaginative model of corporate selfhood toward which an individual feels some degree of imaginative identification. As Jackson puts it, "The people do not exist as such. They are formed, and sometimes they are forged.... The people themselves cannot constitute the state and govern the state. They cannot speak for themselves or by themselves. That is because they are not an entity or agent and they cannot exist or act on their own. The voice of the people—*vox populi*—must be invoked" (80–81). To the extent that Indian people have elected (or been forced) to engage with American political structures, doing so has often involved accommodating themselves to this new form in innovative ways—re-creating themselves as political subjects as part of a mass society. Scott Lyons treats this process as a central theme in *X-Marks* in his discussion of the emergence of the tribal nationalism during the nineteenth century, highlighting Indian agency in the process. Popular sovereignty always rests on a fundamental fiction, but as a fiction the concept of "the people" is capable of transformation and manipulation outside of the ends of the state. Gellner also reminds us that nationalism often functions as a source of conflict and separation rather than assimilation and unification. This is a significant point when we reflect on the contours of a fully formed discourse of tribal sovereignty in American Indian writing.

To claim sovereignty in the present moment (in a mass culture), Indian people have engaged with and adapted new forms of mass culture and symbolization. Edmund Morgan, in his germinal book on the role of the concept of popular sovereignty in the American Revolution, has described this essential aspect of the emergence of the modern democratic sovereign state as "inventing the people." The process that Morgan traces has been characterized by Anderson and Hobsbawm, in somewhat different terms, as the beginning of the production (through print culture and mass media) of a model of political subjectivity that mediates between individual identity and collective expressions of power. In those moments when individual persons (discrete, particular, and nonabstract) respond to the interpellative "hail" that comes from the state or those who embody its power (think of the U.S. Constitution's "we the people" or an elected official's rhetorical use of the phrases "my fellow Americans" and "the American people"), he or she legitimizes and actualizes the sovereign power of the state by beginning to function, in some sense, as a different kind of self. When we respond to efforts to *call* us as a constitutive element of the people, in other words, we no longer function in those moments as differentiated individuals but rather as a uniform citizenry, and we make sovereign power real and active.[12]

What is being (implicitly) asked of us in these interpellative moments (which are manifold in a modern, technological society) is our consent to, and legitimization of, the formal structures and mechanisms through which the modern sovereign state exercises power. That consent is what is performed by the so-called vox populi (voice of the people), the national fiction whose function is to subsume individual difference into a kind of idealized and abstract totality, a model of political subjectivity needed to legitimize a democratic sovereign state and make it function. Individuals accept the fiction that the voice of the people represents them through different mechanisms—passively through the simple fact of living under a democratic constitution or more actively by choosing to participate in democratic elections, referenda, or plebiscites. But the key point here is that when popular sovereignty becomes a key constitutive element of state sovereignty, the existence of institutional mechanisms and cultural processes by which models of collective subjectivity can be presented to individuals for their assent becomes crucially important. To commit to a fully formed discourse of sovereignty in that context, then, involves a willingness to both create and submit to that kind of symbolization of one's political subjectivity.

One of the key functions of American Indian print culture, since the early nineteenth century at least, has been to facilitate this emergence of Indian political subjectivity as a manifestation of popular sovereignty. I will say more about contemporary instances of this phenomenon in chapters 2 and 3. At this point, though, we might briefly remind ourselves of some of the considerable body of recent scholarship on nineteenth-century and early twentieth-century

Indian writing that highlights this phenomenon. My own earlier monograph, *Sovereign Selves*, is very much about the process by which Indian writers (particularly William Apess and Charles Eastman) reimagined and represented their own individual experiences through the print medium of autobiography as a way of embodying models of legal and political subjectivity that could serve as the basis for acts of resistance—for specific claims made before and against the colonial state. While not always foregrounding the *legal* context of print representation in the precise way that I do, there has also been a wide range of other quite distinguished work on Indian writing and print that offers related insights. Maureen Konkle's *Writing Indian Nations,* Jean O'Brien's *Firsting and Lasting,* and Bernd Peyer's *The Thinking Indian* are some examples. Philip Round's 2010 book, *Removable Type,* is perhaps the most comprehensive study on this topic, certainly in terms of late eighteenth- and nineteenth-century Indian print culture. Round convincingly demonstrates how both the circulation of books and manuscripts and the development of tribal newspapers and Indian-controlled presses went hand-in-hand with a revolution in Native polities across Indian country and the creation of new forms of "Indian publics" (97). Round uses somewhat different terminology than I do here, but his study also draws attention to the emergence and development of specific forms of political subjectivity as integral to this process. In early phases of alphabetic literacy, he notes, Native intellectuals (like Joseph Johnson and Samson Occom) wielded that literacy from positions of "ministerial character," and it was their "Christian persona" (functioning as a form of political subjectivity) that authorized their entry into public debate and enabled them to constitute an early form of Native public sphere (98). By the late eighteenth and early nineteenth centuries, though, Native diplomats and intellectuals had available to them a much greater variety of what Round calls rhetorical poses, and they were thus better positioned to assert their own intellectual sovereignty, to use Robert Warrior's term.[13] Through its dissemination and cultivation of these symbolizing poses, then, Indian print and book culture helped to engender the kind of imaginary public (and public sphere) that Michael Warner and Jurgen Habermas have also demonstrated to be central to the emergence of the modern, liberal nation-state. Indian print, in other words, has been central to the invention of the "Indian people," and thus to the development of Indian sovereignty discourse, for a least two hundred years.[14]

It has only been in the past twenty years or so that literary and cultural historians working in Native American studies have effectively unearthed and reconstituted this history. Viewed in relation to the idea of popular sovereignty, however, the fact that Indian print culture emerged during precisely the same period that the democratic American settler-state was most vigorously engaged in efforts to assimilate or eliminate tribal populations should not be particularly surprising to us. One of the central difficulties inherent in producing workable abstractions of the people is a heterogeneous polity, and this has been a central theme in the history of the modern (popular) sovereign state. One way to express the underlying problem would be to recall that while the basic definition of the modern state posits the need for fixed borders and a defined population, it does not necessarily require a single people (Jackson 98). The ideals of popular sovereignty, however, have often tended to generate such an imperative. The ideology of ethno-nationalism, of course, emerged out of this context in the nineteenth century. Ethno-nationalism, at its most basic level, is the move to argue that every sovereign state, in fact, should contain only one nation or people defined in a specific ethnic sense. Political subjectivity, in this context, typically becomes symbolized in homogenous and normative ways. Multiethnic states that have aimed (explicitly or implicitly) to define themselves according to the one-state/one-nation model, then, have often ended up committing themselves to policies of cultural assimilation, partition, relocation, or even genocide directed toward ethnic minorities to ensure that the vox populi becomes and remains an essentially monovocal one. One can see all of these policies on display in the history of the United States vis-á-vis the American Indian population living within its borders, particularly during the nineteenth century. To the extent that Indian people have not fit into the dominant model of political subjectivity and its image of the people, they have often been removed.[15]

Having said something about the broad meaning of sovereignty in the United States in the early stages of the nation's founding and gestured toward some of the implications of those meanings for Indian people, it is appropriate now to turn to a more specific consideration of how Indian tribal sovereignty has been formulated in the framework of American colonialism through the mechanism of what we call federal Indian law. This history of tribal sovereignty in U.S. Indian law is decidedly mixed. One can make reasonable cases both for its existence/extension and for its constraint/limitation, drawing on precedents from American legislation and court cases. The scope of legislative interference in Indian affairs is one of the first things that will strike any observer, as Indian people have been the subject of more federal legislation than any other single group in the United States. Between 1790 (when the first Indian Trade and Intercourse Act was passed) and the mid-1970s, more than four thousand treaties, agreements, and statutes relating to Indian affairs moved their way through Congress (Wunder 16). In the context of a consideration of sovereignty, of course, it is important to note that Indian people were largely unrepresented in this legislative context before 1924 (when the Indian Citizenship Act was passed, unilaterally granting

United States citizenship to all American Indians), and that even since 1924 one can argue that, *as collective entities,* tribal nations remain unrepresented.[16] The operative model of legal and political subjectivity in American liberal democracy is that of the autonomous "possessive individual" who stands at the heart of the fictions of social contract theory. American Indians who vote in American elections, then, function as individual American citizens, and in this context their political subjectivity registers in the system no differently than that of any other individual American. The recognition of this fact has led some Indian commentators in the present moment to advocate for nonparticipation in U.S. elections, seeing such participation as undermining their alternative, tribal political commitments.

In this unrepresented (or underrepresented, or misrepresented) context, Congress has passed many major pieces of legislation impacting tribal life. These would begin with the six Indian Trade and Intercourse Acts (of 1790, 1793, 1796, 1799, 1802, and 1834), which in the process of regulating trade between Indian tribes and non-Indians affirmed the role of the federal government as the sole power able to alienate Indian lands while also extending federal criminal jurisdiction over non-Indians in Indian country to allow enforcement of its provisions. The Indian Removal Act of 1830 was the legislative mechanism, employing coercive treaty negotiations, to dislocate large populations of eastern Indians and move them west of the Mississippi. When deemed expedient to advance United States policy interests, Congress has also engaged in the unilateral amendment or abrogation of treaties, even though international law recognizes only a few instances where such alterations would be legitimate. Congress has often made such alterations indirectly, through the use of riders attached to other, unrelated bills. The most notorious example is the 1871 appropriations bill rider that aimed to end the treaty relationship with Indian tribes. The Major Crimes Act of 1885, which extended federal jurisdiction over Indian people on tribal lands in the case of several categories of crime, was also an appropriations rider. The last major late nineteenth-century initiative to break up tribal social structures and divide the Indian land base to foster assimilation, the General Allotment Act of 1877 (commonly known as the Dawes Act), was a strikingly egregious example of congressional interference with self-government, as was Public Law 280 (1953), part of the so-called termination policy, which I will take up in more detail later. And even in those cases of "benevolent" legislation, passed with the intent of buttressing tribal society or reversing nakedly colonialist policies, such as the Indian Reorganization Act of 1934 or the Indian Civil Rights Act of 1968, we must recognize the fact that legislation enacted on behalf of tribal peoples has often not originated from them, been passed in full consultation with them, or reflected their own political values and traditions.

The U.S. judicial system has also regularly limited the rights of self-government of Indian people. American courts have generally supported congressional interference with Indian self-government on the basis on three rationales: (1) the political question doctrine, which asserts that power of Congress over Indian affairs should typically not be reviewed by federal courts because of the political nature of the relationship between Indian nations and the United States; (2) the guardian-ward relation and federal trust responsibility, which allows Congress to take extraordinary measures to protect weaker or dependent Indian nations; and (3) plenary power, which holds that in the end, Congress possesses supreme authority over Indian affairs within the borders of the United States. And yet, even as the courts have generally upheld congressional powers over tribes, they have also often continued to recognize some form of inherent sovereignty residing in Indian nations. There are, in this context, a number of significant Supreme Court decisions that remain foundational in considerations of the question of Indian tribal sovereignty. The Marshall Court's decisions surrounding Cherokee removal remain key touchstones, for example.[17] In *Cherokee Nation v. Georgia* (1831) the court offered the first significant codification of a concept of limited sovereignty for tribal nations; there Marshall developed his famous legal fiction of "domestic dependent nations," a concept that designated a type of semi-sovereignty. One year later, in *Worcester v. Georgia* (1832), the Marshall Court refined the terms of the discussion, explicitly recognizing Indian nations as distinct political communities, with territorial boundaries within which their authority is exclusive. This sovereignty, Marshall noted, was recognized by the federal government through its treaties, and the presumption of the court, therefore, would be that unless a tribe explicitly agreed to cede its internal authority over specific matters, the United States was obliged to respect its sovereign right to regulate its own internal affairs.

The Marshall decisions highlight one of the deep sources of frustration in Indian country, the fact that definitions of tribal sovereignty remain remarkably unstable in U.S. Indian law.[18] A good subsequent example of this can be found in the series of court cases and legislative actions in the 1880s that extended federal criminal authority over Indian people living on reservations. In *Ex Parte Crow Dog* (an 1883 case involving the attempt of the United States government to prosecute one Brulé Lakota leader, Crow Dog, for the murder of another, Spotted Tail, on the Rosebud Reservation), the Supreme Court found, in a manner broadly consistent with *Worcester*, that only an Indian government could punish an Indian for committing a crime against another Indian. The court pointed out that under the 1834 Indian Trade and Intercourse Act, tribal nations retained sovereign authority over domestic affairs unless that sovereign power had been surrendered. In the wake of public outrage, this court decision was followed by the passage of the Major Crimes Act by Congress in 1885, which expressly restricted tribal sovereignty by unilaterally transferring criminal jurisdiction in the case of seven major crimes (murder, manslaughter, rape, assault with intent to murder, arson, burglary, and larceny) into federal hands. This law, not surprisingly, also ended up before the Supreme Court in *United States v. Kagama* (1886). But here, the court found the Major Crimes Act to be constitutionally valid. Relying on the concept of a guardian-ward relationship between the United States and Indian people as justification, the court now held that Indian nations were dependent on the United States for political rights, in this respect denying their sovereignty. The federal judiciary continued on this trajectory into the early decades of the twentieth century, as in *Lone Wolf v. Hitchcock* (1903), where the Supreme Court again dismissed the idea of the sovereignty of Indian nations and upheld the plenary power of Congress to exercise full legislative authority over them.

To sum up the previous discussion, then, it is fair to say that the meaning of Indian tribal sovereignty within the framework of U.S. Indian law and the American legal system is ambiguous. The United States has been at best inconsistent and at worst cynically manipulative in its use of the concept as a means of regulating its relations with tribal peoples and its management of Indian affairs. And even in the most generous interpretations, tribal sovereignty has been held, under American law, to be something inferior to state sovereignty. It is with good reason, then, that many American Indians today fear that any assertion and exercise of sovereignty on their part remains precarious within what has been historically an unstable settler-colonial framework. We should remember, in this regard, that sovereignty is truly meaningful in its *use* and not as a mere formal category or abstract concept. Not surprisingly then, there are powerful voices in the scholarly community of Native American studies, and in Indian country more broadly, who look at the present realities and see sovereignty as a phantom concept that needs to be abandoned. I would like to briefly consider some of the arguments made by two of these critics.

One of the most aggressive and damning critiques of the Indian use of sovereignty as a concept in an American context comes from Russel Lawrence Barsh (Mikmaq), in his 1993 essay, "The Challenge of Indigenous Self-Determination."[19] Writing from the perspective of global indigenous studies, Barsh presents the language of sovereignty as a kind of destructive opiate that is inevitably undermining Indian communities in the United States. Making only a few exceptions, he chastises the majority of Indian people in the United States for being isolationist and failing to engage in global indigenous struggles. "How can American Indian tribal leaders pretend to have achieved any measure of 'sovereignty,'" Barsh wonders, "when plainly they are either powerless or unwilling to respond to the murder of so many Indians, just a few hundred miles south of the Rio Grande [in Guatemala]?" (283). Barsh links what he sees as U.S. Indian isolationism directly to their focus on narrowly asserting sovereignty in their own particular American legal and political contexts. In addition, in his assessment political isolationism is also a function of the continued vulnerability of American tribal institutions to federal government retaliation (to their ongoing colonial status, in other words); most tribes, he maintains, are heavily dependent on discretionary aid administered through the federal bureaucracy. Barsh's piece predates the economic advances made in the wake of legalized tribal gaming in the late 1900s, but even in that context his basic point about the economic vulnerability of many tribal communities remains germane. Whatever its diverse causes, though, U.S. Indian isolationism seems to him to have engendered a loss of confidence in the possibility of genuine self-governance (286). As such, American Indians content themselves with asserting whatever limited authority is granted to them, masking those limitations under a seemingly powerful, but misapplied, term: sovereignty. "Isolated within the borders of the United States," Barsh argues, "American Indian leaders can perpetuate the illusions of 'sovereignty' and self-determination among themselves, without risk of challenge by indigenous peoples who come from other, less damaging experiences. It is no wonder, then, that they avoid participating in international political activities, and it is equally clear why the next generation of American Indians must begin their political education far away from North America. Without a comparative perspective, today's anesthetic illusions can persist indefinitely" (286).

As the preceding comments suggest, Barsh's critique of the concept of sovereignty is built largely on a view that assertions of tribal sovereignty within an American context and commitments to indigenous liberation within a global framework are (or at least have tended to be) antithetical. (This accusation regarding a lack of participation in international politics is, to be fair, somewhat overstated.) In this respect, Barsh wonders whether American Indians have any substantive contribution to make to the liberation and development of other indigenous peoples, beyond, perhaps, acting as United States citizens to restrain American imperialism. Employing the terms I used earlier in this chapter, it may be fair to say that Barsh is worried that American Indians have become committed in compromising ways to the model of political subjectivity favored by their oppressors. He notes that struggles for decolonization are often preoccupied with the process of wresting the mechanisms of power away from the colonizer and thus fail to give enough thought to what to do with those mechanisms and that power afterward. If American Indians are to truly become decolonized, Barsh insists, we must see something different from whatever developments in self-government have occurred in the decades since the passage of the Indian Reorganization Act. He argues that more traditional values and beliefs must actually inform tribal government and that a reliance on sovereignty as a threshold concept is impeding that process. Barsh maintains that there must be a greater incorporation of a global indigenous perspective in American Indian politics instead of the judicial construction that is tribal sovereignty (304). Lacking that, he insists, we have a situation of co-option of tribal governments into capitalist systems, where tribal people see themselves as engaged in good capitalism and good governance, but do so in a way that conflicts with tribal traditions and leads, in the end, to assimilation and self-destruction. In the end Barsh doubts that Indian people can transform a Western-rooted sovereignty tradition in a way that will make it work meaningfully for them.

A similar but more widely cited critique of the place of sovereignty in contemporary Native American studies comes from political theorist and activist Taiaiake Alfred (Mohawk). Alfred's consistent and fundamental concern has also been that the core ideas associated with sovereignty—particularly the focus on defining some kind of supreme political authority—are irredeemably at odds with the core values that he argues define traditional indigenous political practices, notions of "freedom, respect, and autonomy" ("Sovereignty" 33). In addition, Alfred worries (with considerable historical justification, as we have seen) that the use of the term sovereignty by the colonizing powers of Europe and the United States has actually served to mask the reality of the erasure of Native self-determination. As the preceding discussion has suggested, European sovereign states in North America, and later in the United States, did indeed legitimize their territorial claims, in part through treaty relationships with indigenous peoples who were deemed, for this purpose, in some sense sovereign. The acknowledgment of the independent nationhood of indigenous people has thus been part of a larger colonial strategy.[20] And yet, as Alfred rightly points out, little of this history is reflected in the current official histories of settler-colonial states or in the way that actors in those states talk about Indian sovereignty today. Sovereignty, in this respect, often has functioned as another tool for historical erasure, with its continuing formal use obscuring many of the shifting realities underlying the extension of colonial authority over tribal peoples. When approached from this perspective, the process of decolonization, as Alfred frames it, seems unlikely to ultimately succeed if tribal peoples continue to employ sovereignty as a central concept.

If Alfred's earlier work, particularly *Peace, Power, and Righteousness* (originally published in 1999), is exceedingly strident in rejecting the concept of sovereignty, in later writings he offers a slightly more meliorated viewpoint. In his 2005 essay, "Sovereignty," Alfred acknowledges that "using the sovereignty paradigm, indigenous peoples have made significant legal and political gains toward reconstructing the autonomous aspects of their individual, collective, and social identities. The positive effect of the sovereignty movement on terms of mental, physical, and emotional health cannot be denied or understated" (39). While he concedes some tactical utility in the pursuit of sovereignty, though, Alfred goes on to register a longer-term strategic concern that these positive effects "[do] not seem to be enough" (39). As such, he argues, "the next phase of scholarship and activism, then, will need to transcend the mentality that supports the colonization of indigenous nations, beginning with the rejection of the term and notion of indigenous 'sovereignty'" (41). This is also the central argument of *Peace, Power, and Righteousness*, in which Alfred insists that decolonization cannot succeed without a broad-based return to traditional cultural and political practices. Using the Iroquois ritual of condolence as his central illustrative model (he calls it a metaphorical framework), Alfred argues that for Indians to act as a "self-determining people," looking forward will mean turning away from the values of the mainstream of North American society (*Peace* xi). Decolonization, he maintains, will have been for nothing if indigenous government has "no meaningful indigenous character" (xiv). And in practical terms, this means that "the state's power, including such European concepts as 'taxation,' 'citizenship,' 'executive authority,' and 'sovereignty,' must be eradicated from politics in Native communities. In a very real sense, to remain Native—to reflect the essence of indigenous North Americans—our politics must shift to give primacy to concepts grounded in our own cultures" (xiv).

In their own ways, both Barsh and Alfred present an important critique of the Western model of sovereignty. I would note that I sympathize with Alfred's fundamental goal of developing practically effective models of criticism. I would suggest, though, that there is a problematic tendency in his thinking to fail to acknowledge the same potential for productive and legitimate change in this admittedly Western-rooted concept of sovereignty as he sees in indigenous ones. Alfred rightly registers an awareness of the dangers involved in uncritically investing in Western models of sovereignty (especially as they inform U.S. Indian law) as a vehicle for liberation. Nevertheless, he frequently underestimates the ability of sovereignty, as a threshold concept, to function dialectically. I find it suspect to argue that sovereignty cannot be transformed through its intersections with indigenous thought and experience or that sovereignty cannot play a vital role in the "next phase of scholarship and activism" (Alfred, "Sovereignty" 41). The balance of this book will offer sustained examples from tribal political theory and literature to support my view. Indeed, despite his own resistance to using the term, I would argue that there is a significant strain of sovereignty thinking running through even Alfred's own project. He insists, for example, that despite great diversity among indigenous peoples, "we share a common bond that makes it possible to speak of a 'Native American' political tradition" (Alfred, *Peace* xvi). Such a move shows, in part, the influence on Alfred's thought of the modern political discourse of popular sovereignty. Indeed, an awareness of the importance of the legacy of popular sovereignty can help us to better understand how and why abstractions like "Native American" and "indigenous" have come to be so meaningful to a variety of Indian people regardless of specific tribal origins. In Alfred's particular case, we can see him in his writing offering up for his readers' consent an indigenous vox populi. Alfred performatively creates and deploys an abstraction called "the indigenous people" as a model of political subjectivity. He then qualifies the traditionalist thrust of this abstraction by highlighting its adaptability, making the entirely justified point that, even when "working within a traditional framework, we must acknowledge the fact that cultures change, and that any particular notion of what constitutes 'tradition' will be contested" (xvii). All of this sets up what seems to be Alfred's central theoretical project—embracing a form of internationalist, indigenous Indian political subjectivity (partly modern and partly traditional) rooted in notions of *popular* sovereignty as a vehicle for challenging *state* sovereignty. His assumes that the decoupling of those two aspects of the tradition will be achievable.[21]

What I see Alfred engaged in, then, is not a total repudiation of the system of sovereignty but rather an attempt to transform at least part of it. Alfred worries that in the long run Indian people will be incapable of changing the core meaning of sovereignty or adapting that meaning in needed ways. But such a fear seems to be based on a presumption that it is structurally impossible to ever separate sovereignty from the liberal nation-state. We should not be so sure that this is the case, however, especially when we recognize that the fusion of the two was itself a historical development and not originally inherent in the concept. And we should not reject the possibility that innovative Indian thinkers and writers might come up with novel ways to approach, utilize, and transform the concept. Vine Deloria's nuanced (and quite open-eyed) use of the concept of sovereignty provides one example that challenges the presumptions underlying Alfred's claims here. The discursive approaches to the pursuit of sovereignty we find in literary figures like Craig Womack, Elizabeth Cook-Lynn, and Gerald Vizenor offer others.

In the end, of course, I would concede that Barsh and Alfred are right to ask that we think about areas of incompatibility between U.S. formulations of tribal sovereignty and indigenous views of self-determination. But the power of sovereignty as a threshold concept is that it represents a space where those potential contradictions can be first exposed and then worked though pragmatically. What I see when I survey the deployment of the language of sovereignty in the present moment is a creative and dialectical process of developing engagement. We should assess that process with a full awareness of the ideological power of colonial legal forms and structures, to be sure. But we should also recognize the revolutionary force of the indigenous thought that has developed in contact with those forms and structures—taking in, rejecting, and altering them to achieve specific goals.

CHAPTER 2

The Indian Vox Populi

To fully appreciate the significance of the concept of sovereignty in contemporary American Indian writing and thought, one must move beyond a sense that the term is wholly compromised by its connections to a Western, and admittedly colonial, heritage. In Indian hands, sovereignty has proven an evolving and multivalenced signifier, one that is deployed today in a wide range of contexts—both political and literary. My aim in this chapter is to offer an overview of the core indigenous inflections of the concept (in a U.S. context) and also to suggest how specific developments in Indian political thought and print culture helped lay the foundation for the emergence of a literary discourse of sovereignty. The rise of the language and ideology of self-determination during the termination era and the subsequent development of a national model of Indian peoplehood are my particular concerns here. I will trace these developments through a consideration of some of the work of a well-known writer and activist, D'Arcy McNickle, and a lesser-known contemporary, Cahuilla historian and publisher Rupert Costo.

While many of the basic ideas suggested by the phrase "tribal sovereignty" (the need to exercise self-governance, the importance of the recognition of inherent rights confirmed in treaties, etc.) have been part of American Indian thought for a long time, the specific term only came into prominence in the wake of World War II. As Joanne Barker has noted, sovereignty truly emerged "not as a new, but as a particularly valued term within indigenous discourses to signify a multiplicity of legal and social rights to political, economic, and cultural self-determination" in the 1950s and 1960s (1). In much the same way that state sovereignty developed out of early modern European political theory as a tool of political opposition, the language of modern tribal sovereignty was also born out of the pragmatics of political struggle. The initial rise of the term is best read in light of the effort to develop a coherent response to the postwar shift in U.S. Indian policy toward termination. In the longer term, the emergence of sovereignty talk has been tied to the fluidity of its central signifying term and to the ability of this one word to advance and underpin a wide range of decolonizing tactics. As Barker rightly puts it, sovereignty "has come to mark the complexities of global indigenous efforts to reverse ongoing experiences of colonialism" (1).

There are multiple senses in which the term sovereignty is employed in print today by American Indian people in the United States. Several of these have been in play for decades, but others are of more recent origin. In her useful schema of the major dialects of sovereignty talk being spoken in the 1970s, Emma Gross identifies four main forms. First, we have "political sovereignty," which would probably be called "tribal nationalism" in today's terminology. It generally designates a focus on asserting and achieving some form of independent nation status, and it has been associated with some of the more militant Indian political movements. The political rhetoric and tactics used since the late 1960s by members of the American Indian Movement (AIM) and by United Native Americans might be seen as earlier representatives of this strain of sovereignty talk. Second, we have "legal sovereignty," which refers to the strategies employed by individuals or groups who accept the need to work within the basic parameters of Indian sovereignty as defined by U.S. Indian law. Advocates of legal sovereignty stress several points: cultivating political relationships in Washington, developing viable litigation strategies to advance Indian interests, pressing for the honoring of treaty terms and the preservation of the existing land base, and maintaining the trust relationship between tribes and the federal government in the most advantageous terms possible. Legal sovereignty is a language spoken largely by lawyers, legal professionals (both Indian and non-Indian) and many tribal officials who advocate for Indian interests primarily within the framework of U.S. legal-political system.[1] It is one of the main dialects commonly found spoken in major national Indian news outlets, such as *Indian Country Today* or *This Week from Indian Country Today*.

Gross's third and fourth strains of sovereignty talk are "self-determination" and "self-governance." I would argue that the former term is also generally used to refer to the elements she lists under the latter. The evolving understanding of sovereignty as self-determination, which I see as grounding the emerging discourse of sovereignty, will be my primary focus in this chapter. From the U.S. government's perspective, it is fair to say, self-determination means a focus on maximizing Indian participation in the decision-making process and contracting administered through the Bureau of Indian Affairs (BIA). From an Indian perspective, what Gross calls self-governance is really a combination of that idea with more aggressive assertions of all possible aspects of internal tribal autonomy advanced through an evolving range of domestic and international legal structures and institutions. The passage and implementation of the Indian Self-Determination and Education Assistance Act of 1975 would be an example of an important site of collision between those two views.

While political sovereignty, legal sovereignty, and self-determination represent discrete strains of American Indian sovereignty discourse dating back forty years, I would also stress that these concepts often blend together in actual usage. Also, they do not represent an absolute limit on the ways in which sovereignty is spoken of in the present moment. A relatively unscientific analysis of the use of the term in *Indian Country Today* and its successor *This Week from Indian Country Today* during a four-year period (2008–2012) reveals a fairly wide range of usages. Regular columnist Steven Newcomb's writings include a combination of the political sovereignty, legal sovereignty, and self-determination strains. As codirector of the Indigenous Law Institute, Newcomb's primary focus has been challenging the legitimacy of the Euro-American Law of Discovery through international legal structures with the hope of eventually purging it from U.S. Indian law. Accomplishing this, he maintains, would lay the foundation for the full reassertion of treaty rights, the recovery of ancestral lands, and the ability of tribal communities to begin to function again as autonomous nations. Other editorials and pieces by regular columnists feature different emphases. One finds editorials focused on self-determination in the U.S. government policy sense, feature articles situating tribal sovereignty in the broader international context of the UN Declaration on the Rights of Indigenous Peoples, opinion pieces suggesting that Indian people should assert their sovereignty by opting out of U.S. politics and refusing to vote in American elections, and articles offering rather technical arguments about legal and political strategies to fix problem spots in U.S. Indian law. In addition, a wide range of pieces emphasizes what we might call cultural sovereignty or intellectual sovereignty (the ability to preserve one's way of life, modes of thought, and expressive traditions). These aspects of sovereignty talk are not always entirely encompassed under the categories of domestic law and governance, but they are increasingly a part of the international indigenous movement that links sovereignty with human rights. Duane Champagne's regular education columns in *This Week*, as well as the features focused on literature, the arts, and what we might call academic theory, are representative examples here.

This brief survey should highlight one of the challenges confronting contemporary writers who employ the language of sovereignty and readers/critics who try to engage with them. The ascendance of sovereignty as a signifier has been a political phenomenon, driven by the need to create new models of indigenous political subjectivity and new forms of decolonizing praxis, and it has progressed in a nonlinear, but generally oppositional, manner. As a result, many different visions of Indian polities and politics have been articulated through the term, with sovereignty functioning as a vehicle for the creation of varied models of both resisting and self-governing Indian people. Not surprisingly, as Barsh's previously cited critique indicates, significant fissures have also appeared as part of this process. Tensions emerge where members of Indian communities (academics, political leaders, individual tribal members) have been confronted with calls to coalesce around demands for sovereignty that have different inflections and involve different legal and political strategies. The academic and political debate between tribal nationalists and adherents of a more cosmopolitan form of indigenism offers one example of this.[2] The tensions that tribal members may feel between national Indian perspectives (or international indigenous ones) and the nuances of their own particular local situations provide another. Finally, every form of sovereignty talk entails some corresponding legal techne (by which I mean a praxis-driven commitment to a particular facet of the craft or technique of law).[3] Those who speak the language of sovereignty, then, benefit from an awareness of the ways in which their specific usages intersect with specific ideological structures and legal mechanisms.

If part of the appeal of sovereignty has been its ability to encompass varied meanings and connotations, then we need to consider how this very breadth can complicate its function as a means of generating a concrete decolonizing praxis. One way to do this is to trace some of its etymologies in Indian country. My focus from here on will be doing so, with a particular concern for the increasingly central idea of sovereignty as self-determination. Barker finds an originating moment in the work of Vine Deloria, Jr., particularly his influential 1979 essay "Self-Determination and the Concept of Sovereignty." While she is correct in noting that Deloria was the most prominent, and one of the earliest, postwar writers to draw a specific and consistent linkage between those central concepts, in developing my own narrative I want to suggest the importance of his near contemporary D'Arcy McNickle. For in laying the foundations for the rise of a rich discourse of sovereignty tied to the idea of self-determination, McNickle also played a key role in the emergence of the mass-symbolization of Indian peoplehood required for a discourse of sovereignty to develop.

McNickle is a bit of a bridge figure in twentieth-century Indian thought. In *Tribal Secrets* Robert Warrior locates him as a member of the "free agent" generation that came to prominence between the demise of the Society of American Indians (known for its advocacy of assimilation and American citizenship for Indian people) and the emergence of the National Congress of the American Indian (instrumental in the development of postwar policies of self-determination).[4] When viewed primarily through the lens of his early career—as a supporter of John Collier's reforms during his time at the BIA in the 1930s and 1940s and the creator of his best-known fiction, *The Surrounded* (1934) and *Wind from an Enemy Sky* (first published in 1978 but written during the 1930s)—McNickle fits alongside John Joseph Mathews and Mourning Dove in Warrior's canon of writers who "portrayed realities Indian people had faced in the years following allotment" (Warrior, *Tribal* 22).[5] But McNickle also played a key role in facilitating the American Indian Chicago Conference of 1961 and in drafting its influential *Declaration of Indian Purpose*. He was also the author of numerous nonfiction works about American Indian history and policy from the 1950s through the 1970s that made important contributions to the articulation of Indian self-determination. That is the McNickle of primary interest to me here.

McNickle's first contribution to the rise of the modern discourse of Indian sovereignty was his ability to demonstrate broadly how Indian political subjectivity could be effectively redefined and reasserted even in the absence of some of the key structural elements of the nation-state. While this may strike some as a rather modest contribution, when viewed in light of the experiences of the preceding generation of American Indian leaders (whose encounters with the pulverizing engine of allotment and the demoralizing massacre at Wounded Knee made the individual acquisition of U.S. citizenship seem like a worthwhile prize) McNickle's importance in laying the foundations for a new form of oppositional consciousness of tribal sovereignty in the modern United States should not be underestimated. An obituary published by his friend, Tewa anthropologist Alfonso Ortiz, in the January/February 1978 issue of Rupert Costo's influential newspaper, *Wassaja*, attests to his contemporaries' sense of this contribution. Ortiz presents McNickle as a figure who opened up new ways of conceptualizing how one might advocate for Indian autonomy in a settler-colonial context. He comments on McNickle's ability to deterritorialize his own political subjectivity—finding ways to maintain a sense of Indian identity and autonomy without being permanently grounded in his traditional land base. Commenting on McNickle's decision as a young man to sell his allotment lands on the Flathead Reservation and head off to Oxford University to pursue his education, Ortiz suggests that in doing so he "gave himself over to history, and from this time on he did not have the sense that his Indianness was rooted in a place to return to" (12). Nevertheless, Ortiz maintains, "Of D'Arcy's ultimate and enduring Indianness there can never be any doubt." The move that Ortiz valorizes here—McNickle's insistence that a diminishment of, or separation from, a national homeland does not preclude one's assertions of separateness from the colonial American polity—is a vitally important one for many contemporary Indian tribal people engaged in the work of decolonization.

Due to the realities of U.S. settler colonialism, not every claim of sovereignty can be rooted in the ongoing possession of ancestral or self-sustaining territorial autonomy—the prerequisites for many nationalist claims of political sovereignty. Many tribal groups occupy significantly diminished land bases—spaces far too small to constitute entirely self-sustaining nations in today's terms. Other tribes' land bases are not, in fact, their traditional ones (owing to historical policies of removal and relocation). And we should also remember that there are more urban Indians in the United States today—Indians who still maintain a tribal affiliation despite living in an immersive, pluralist city environment—than there are Indian people living on any type of reservation. Amplifying these points, Ortiz lays out his understanding of the central theme in McNickle's writing during the final four decades of his life. McNickle, he argues, "observed that despite what seemed on the surface to be massive and rapid breakdown in Indian cultures across the continent, *an essential core of cultural integrity* was being maintained" (Ortiz 13; my emphasis). Affirming his own support for that view, Ortiz notes, "Whatever calamities may have been suffered by Indian people during D'Arcy's witness—from mass inductions into the armed forces of the United States, to equally mass relocations into the cities—the people affected have always reconstituted themselves about a cultural core that was still Indian; different, yes, but still integrally Indian" (13). In Ortiz's account McNickle emerges as a figure who took the historical realities, first of allotment, then of termination and relocation, and worked through them to articulate an oppositional vision that would soon be refined into one of the first major forms of a full-fledged discourse of Indian sovereignty—one centered on the capacity for self-determination that could be activated by a popularly symbolized form of Indian political subjectivity and then mobilized in diverse ways by tribal communities of widely varying sizes and land bases. In this respect McNickle's role as both a scholar and a political figure, at least from the mid-1940s forward, reminds us that sovereignty has tended to develop pragmatically in specific legal and political contexts.

When we look at McNickle's nonfiction writing in the postwar period, we can see clear confirmation of Ortiz's characterization of McNickle's major theme and get a better sense of how some of the elements of a new form of sovereignty talk were coalescing in his thought in the crucible of termination. McNickle does not use the specific word "sovereignty" in his 1973 monograph, *Native American Tribalism* (a revised and expanded version of his 1962 book, *The Indian Tribes of the United States*), but the critical project in which he engages is clearly related to the concept. The central focus of *Native American Tribalism* is to offer evidence of what Gerald Vizenor would later call "survivance." While acknowledging and documenting many of the horrors and injustices of colonial history (epidemics, the genocidal hunting of California Indians, etc.), McNickle's primary topic is the remarkable endurance of traditional cultural and political structures in Indian communities, even where those communities have experienced diaspora and dislocation from their ancestral land bases. He first cites three broad indices of survival: population recovery, language preservation/use, and enduring traditional kinship systems. He also offers a common-sense observation that the ongoing existence of Indian communities is proven by the fact that in many areas of the United States they have manifestly not merged with the rural (and one might add urban) poor around them. The book includes an eclectic selection of ethnographic photographs from various tribal contexts to reinforce and symbolize this point about recognizable cultural distinctiveness and persistence. In the end, then, "the generalized picture today is of *a people* that has survived in numbers, in social organization, in custom and outlook, in retention of physical resources, and it its position before the law. This situation might be described as a survival of fragments.... The function of culture has always been to reconstitute the fragments into an operational system" (McNickle, *Tribalism* 15; emphasis added).

Considered by itself, of course, this kind of narrative of collective survival might not necessarily seem to constitute a new form of sovereignty talk. It is important, however, to recognize how McNickle positions this narrative in relation to postwar U.S. Indian history and shifts in policy. His central interest was in crafting a foundational political strategy that would allow tribal communities first to sidestep the loss of much of their territorial sovereignty (and their capacity for full nation-statehood in the eyes of the colonizer) and second to tactically reassert and reconstitute themselves at both a local and a national level with an eye toward the future. After laying a foundation by noting the lingering traces of recognition of Indian sovereignty within colonial legal history (he covers papal law, treaty negotiations, and key decision of the Marshall Court), McNickle devotes considerable attention in *Native American Tribalism* to documenting the reemergence and expansion of those traces in the modern period, beginning with the Indian Reorganization Act (IRA) in the 1930s. As he frames it, the work in which he was engaged as a BIA employee under John Collier represented only an initial step toward a reassertion of the inherent sovereignty of tribal peoples in the form of what would come to be called in the 1950s and 1960s self-determination.

The main positive impact of the 1934 IRA legislation, McNickle notes, was that it "made explicit in statutory law the principle concerning the residual right of tribes to govern themselves" (*Tribalism* 94). "In this respect," he argues, "the 1934 act was an integral segment of the humanistic tradition started by Spain, advanced by England, and incorporated into the early laws and court decisions of the American republic" (94). The humanistic tradition to which he alludes is, in part, the residual presence of natural law discourse in the conception of sovereignty as a check on imperialism—a presence that he was working to recover. At the same time, though, McNickle was prepared to recognize the limitations of the IRA and the relatively faint imprint of that tradition in the present. The degree of claimable sovereignty under the IRA provisions fell well short of the autonomy desired by many Indian people. McNickle conceded that "the tribes that made the most effective use of their political powers became, in effect, *operating municipalities*—managing property, raising revenue for public purposes, administering law and order, contracting for services of attorneys and other professional advisers, and promoting the general welfare of the people" (95; my emphasis). Additionally, the IRA was an initiative created from outside of Indian country and was either brought to them or, some would argue, imposed on them, by non-Indian authorities. Political problems appearing in the wake of the IRA, then, such as those on the Pine Ridge Reservation in the 1970s, were often derived from the failure of that legislation to sufficiently revive self-determination. "Indians had not asked for the Indian Reorganization Act," McNickle notes. "The Pine Ridge Sioux had not asked for a written constitution and an elected council" (xii). Even as one who supported the IRA as a step forward in the 1930s and 1940s, McNickle was interested in moving beyond it toward a new phase of Indian self-assertion.

We can find clues about McNickle's understanding of the dynamics of that new phase not only in his characterization of the postwar period in *Native American Tribalism* but also in his contributions to a key political text from that era, the Chicago Conference's *Declaration of Indian Purpose*. In *Tribalism* McNickle describes how the significant transformations of Indian politics from the 1950s forward were driven initially by the need to respond to the clear threat of the new federal termination policy. The philosophy behind termination, of course, was fundamentally the same as that of the allotment policy of 1887–1924, that Indian people would be better off if assimilated into American society as individuals. What differed was the mechanism for achieving this end. Termination was a process by which the federal government proposed to unilaterally end its recognition of tribes as distinct governing groups, thereby removing all trust protections over Indian lands, ending any federal aid programs directed at tribes, rendering individual Indian tribal members fully subject to all state and federal laws (including taxation on lands), and eventually eliminating the BIA. Termination was to be implemented on a tribe-by-tribe basis, with the first key legislative measures passed by Congress in 1953.[6] House Concurrent Resolution 108 authorized the secretary of the interior to review existing laws and treaties and to recommend amendments or nullifications needed to release the United States from its obligations. It also called for the immediate termination of the Flathead, Klamath, Menominee, Potawatomi, and Turtle Mountain Chippewa Nations as well as all tribes in the states of California, New York, Florida, and Texas. Public Law 280, also passed in 1953, gave individual states the right to assume legal jurisdiction over Indian reservations and granted states immediate criminal and civil jurisdiction over the Indian populations in California, Nebraska, Minnesota, Oregon, and Wisconsin. Congress then worked on passing termination bills directed at specific tribes. In 1954 it began the move to terminate the Menominees of Wisconsin and the Klamaths of Oregon as well as several smaller groups. All told, from 1953 through 1964 a total 109 tribes were terminated, and even when the policy had officially ended, the BIA continued to follow the termination philosophy for a time, with its bureaucracy slow to respond to change at upper levels of leadership.

While termination was supported by some tribal leaders during this time (often based on misunderstandings of what it would entail), McNickle rightly points out that its major effect was to engender new and innovative forms of Indian political consciousness, institutions, and practices. Tribes contested the policy and its implementation in the court system, of course, but equally important activities took place among Indian peoples themselves. McNickle notes that Indian resistance to termination was not based on a love of dependency. Rather, it was rooted in the idea that the protection of Indian trust lands and the right of Indian communities to control their affairs was a "contractual relationship not terminable by unilateral decision" (McNickle, *Tribalism* 113). The new, aggressive defense of these principles in a collective manner (through a newly constituted national Indian polity) is what McNickle calls "tribalism." The central strategies of tribalism were the reassertion of treaty rights and the creation of a national Indian polity that could push effectively for that goal. Far from a retreat into dependency, this move represents an important element of the emergence of the contemporary language of sovereignty.

As McNickle describes it, 1961 served as a watershed year in the rise of tribalism. At that time Stewart Udall, who was somewhat sympathetic to Indian views regarding termination, became the secretary of the interior. Of greater importance, though, was the inaugural American Indian Chicago Conference in that year, a gathering that drew almost five hundred Indians from all over the United States plus observers from Mexico and Canada.[7] McNickle clearly frames the Chicago Conference as marking an innovation in Indian political consciousness—the emergence of a new and potent Indian vox populi. He argues that, with some brief exceptions (the Pueblo Revolt of 1680 and the confederacies led by Pontiac and Tecumseh), "inter-tribal alliances have not characterized Indian political experience. The autonomous tribe, or band, or village, which seems best to describe the political constituency, is a projection of the autonomous individual. No Indian individual, even within his own family, speaks for another individual. No tribe presumes to speak for another tribe. To act otherwise is to act discourteously, if not indecently" (McNickle, *Tribalism* 116). In 1961, though, McNickle was a key player in facilitating the emergence of an Indian voice that did speak for, and indeed created, a national polity. The creation of this voice underpinned a new vision of Indian political subjectivity, fully engaged with the concept of popular sovereignty, which would change the dynamics of the political situation for tribal communities going forward.

Organized by University of Chicago anthropologist Sol Tax, the Chicago Conference was envisioned as an update to the 1928 Merriam Report on Indian Affairs. It aimed to take a broad look at Indian issues in the United States and to foster the kind of intertribal alliances to which McNickle refers.[8] The Chicago Conference was conceived as a way to broaden and nationalize the political focus of Indian country, directly engaging eastern tribes and spawning the creation of other important new national organizations (such as the National Indian Youth Council led by Clyde Warrior). As Lawrence Hauptman and Jack Campisi have noted, Tax's move to ensure a focus at the conference on eastern issues placed the federal recognition of tribes at the forefront of the national conversation (317).[9] McNickle's role in facilitating this process was significant; as a key leader of the National Congress of the American Indian (NCAI) he facilitated that body's endorsement of the national vision of the conference, as well as its focus on the recognition and reinforcement of tribal governments.[10] The effect of this, apparent in the *Declaration of Indian Purpose*, which McNickle helped to draft, was to engender a conversation about sovereignty issues that was framed in a manner broad enough to encompass the concerns of Indian communities ranging from those with large land bases and functioning post-IRA governments to those lacking such resources. It was, in many respects, an unprecedented effort to generate an Indian vox populi in the United States, one that could buttress a broad reconceptualization of the terms of Indian autonomy and self-governance and open up the imaginative landscape through which Indian people might reframe the struggle for sovereignty.

The *Declaration* is quite explicit regarding its underlying goal of creating a national "Indian people." The subtitle of the *Declaration*, perhaps not surprisingly, is *The Voice of the American Indian*, and its introduction credits Tax with recognizing that "this was the appropriate time for Indians on a national scale to voice their opinions and desires" (3). That introduction also notes that the role of the committees at the conference was to "assemble Indian thinking," producing a generally accepted narrative of present circumstances and a set of policy recommendations galvanizing future action (3). The fictive author of the *Declaration*, as a result, was the "Indians of North America," and the positions and recommendations of the conference became the centerpiece of a new model of Indian political subjectivity going forward. Who were the "Indians of North America" as political subjects, and how did their beliefs and claims relate to an emerging discourse of sovereignty as self-determination? The statement of purpose and creed of the *Declaration* present this quite clearly. Claiming legitimacy, in part, through the fact that 460 Indians representing 90 tribes and bands attended the conference to constitute its voice, the document notes that "in order to give recognition to certain basic philosophies by which the Indian people live, We, the Indian people, must be governed by principles in a democratic manner with a right to choose our way of life" (4).[11] Explicitly rejecting the pressures of complete assimilation, the "Indian people" embrace the language of popular sovereignty to assert their inherent right to self-determination—to direct control over their way of life. They also initiate a process of reinjecting an awareness of natural law back into the dominant discourse of sovereignty in the United States, documenting their belief "in the inherent right of all people to retain spiritual and cultural values" as part of the "normal development of any people" (5). The balanced emphasis on retention and development here clearly indicates a sense of the inevitability and desirability of change in tribal societies. The "Indians of North America" are not ethnostalgics, and neither are they radical separatists advocating for some form of nationalist secession from the United States. "Only when the public understands these conditions [the history of duress produced by U.S. Indian policy] and is moved to take action toward the formulation and adoption of sound and consistent policies and programs will these destroying factors be removed *and the Indian resume his normal growth and make his maximum contribution to modern society*" (5; emphasis added). As political subjects, the "Indians of North America" advocate what we might call a form of measured separatism and nonassimilative inclusion in the broader American polity. And they also demonstrate a conviction that their own political aspirations and reimagination of sovereignty have the potential, dialectically, to impact the broader American polity. "WE BELIEVE in the future of a greater America, an America which we were first to love, where life liberty and the pursuit of happiness will be a reality. In such a future, with Indians and all other Americans cooperating, a cultural climate will be created in which the Indian people will grow and develop as members of a free society" (5).

Embracing the model of political subjectivity embodied in the opening pages of the *Declaration* leads to a specific, and influential vision of the nature of tribal sovereignty. The *Declaration* embraces some of the conclusions of the Merriam Report (that the primary problem confronting Indian people is poverty and that the primary role of Indian policy should be educational) as well as some of the principles of the Indian Reorganization Act (its recognition of the "inherent powers of Indian Tribes") (*Declaration* 5). Speaking through the *Declaration*, the "Indians of North America" insist on a reversal of the termination policy and a return to the principles that (1) the United States has treaty obligations toward tribal peoples that require governmental support of programs that benefit Indian people and (2) Indian people must play a central role in developing and administering these programs, relying on governmental assistance only when it is asked for. These points are the central pillars of what would become the federal policy of self-determination, which would be embraced by the Nixon administration in 1970. The *Declaration* also expressly rejects the general trajectory of U.S. Indian policy from the late nineteenth century through the 1950s. As Frederick Hoxie notes, "the document's concluding section ignored the language of assimilation and Indian uplift and offered instead a vision of tribal nationhood that had been absent in national policy discussions for nearly a century," since the end of treaty-making relationships with tribes in 1871 (348). Instead, the Chicago *Declaration* "suggested that technical assistance and federal aid should be viewed from the perspective of 'a small nation' rather than as a charity designed to bring American Indians into the national mainstream" (348–49). This position redefines the trust relationship between the United States and tribal governments as one rooted in treaty relationships that index sovereign autonomy as opposed to one built around the guardian-ward language that dominated U.S. policy during the allotment era. In doing so, it aims to take into equal account the realities of settler colonialism, the present condition of tribal communities, and the persistence of (inherent) tribal sovereignty. "The right of self-government," we are reminded, "a right which Indians possessed before the coming of the white man, has never been extinguished; indeed it has been repeatedly sustained by the courts of the United States" (*Declaration* 16). The ability to exercise that right in various ways (owing to the different needs of urban Indians, tribes moved from their traditional homelands to reservations elsewhere, tribes with an inadequate reservation base, etc.) becomes a centerpiece of this definition of modern tribal sovereignty as self-determination. Fidelity to treaty obligations on the part of the federal government to buttress a flexible, local, Indian-controlled self-governance will enable the Indians of North America to "regain . . . some measure of the adjustment they enjoyed as the original possessors of their native land" (20).

As McNickle claims, in its ability to articulate a new national model of Indian political subjectivity, and in its clear articulation of new vision for advancing tribal autonomy, the *Declaration* indeed marked a watershed moment. The Chicago Conference saw the beginning of truly effective national Indian resistance to termination, and while that battle would be fought for more than a decade, the work done by the conference delegates, the *Declaration* drafters, and the members of organizations spawned by the conference (like the National Indian Youth Council) ushered in a new era in federal Indian policy—the so-called era of self-determination (in which we still remain). One can argue, of course, about whether the specific formulation of sovereignty as self-determination that emerged from the Chicago Conference sufficiently advanced decolonization. Some prominent voices in Native American studies (like Elizabeth Cook-Lynn) remain skeptical about whether the measured autonomy envisioned in the *Declaration* took tribal communities far enough. At the same time, a significant number of contemporary tribal governments (and members) do embrace the basic vision of sovereignty and model of political subjectivity that is articulated in the *Declaration*. And there is no reason to assume that the vision of self-determination emerging at this point in time represents an end point for the evolution of sovereignty talk.

In concluding this discussion of the emergence of the language of sovereignty as self-determination, it useful also to recognize the importance of the development of a national Indian print culture in advancing work done by McNickle and the participants of the Chicago Conference. Rupert Costo's *Wassaja* newspaper offers an interesting example of this phenomenon; in many respects, this paper exemplifies the increasing importance of print culture (as Benedict Anderson might have predicted) for the overall development of sovereignty discourse and tribal national consciousness. While there has been a relatively long history of tribal Indian newspapers in the United States (starting with the *Cherokee Phoenix*), *Wassaja*, which ran from 1973 until 1979, represents the first major effort to create a central organ for a national Indian print culture whose primary constituency/readership is the Indian polity, broadly defined. Significantly, it did so with the very express goal of also supporting the idea of sovereignty as self-determination.

Wassaja worked on a number of levels to facilitate the rise of a specific form of Indian political subjectivity supporting self-determination. First, the paper's name was chosen precisely because of its particular symbolizing power. Wassaja was both the Apache name of Carlos Montezuma (meaning "The Signal" or "Signaling") and the title of the political newsletter he published from his home in Chicago from 1916 to 1922.[12] Montezuma's leadership in the Society of American Indians in the early twentieth century and his subsequent activism after leaving that organization (he was a strong opponent of BIA control over Indian life) clearly resonated for Costo and his editorial staff. But there is something equally important about the conjunction of personal identity and broader subjectivity being mobilized in their adoption of *Wassaja* as the name of their periodical. The metonymic link "Wassaja" created between the print outlet and the representative person aimed to mobilize Indian peoplehood in precisely the manner needed in the early stages of the creation of a national self-determination movement. "Wassaja" *represents* an Indian body politic composed of different kinds of tribal subjects, and in this respect, the paper that ventriloquizes Montezuma's legacy through his name facilitates the emergence of a new vox populi. The editors of *Wassaja* also carefully positioned their print project as both a continuation and an extension of a tribal past in support of this new theorization of sovereignty. The masthead for Montezuma's newsletter had designated it as *Freedom's Signal for the Indian* (with a subtitle *Let My People Go*). This text is supplemented with an image of a somewhat modernized, and yet typical, Plains Indian (wearing a collared work shirt, but also with suggestively long braided hair.) This Indian man is being crushed by a log of federal bureaucracy (with "BIA" written on it), an image that also invokes the plundering of tribal lands by the timber industry in the late nineteenth and early twentieth centuries. Costo's *Wassaja* adapts the earlier phrases (and Montezuma's personal name) into a slogan reading "The Indian's Signal for Self-Determination" and "Let My People Know." And it changes the iconography into something a bit more militant *and collective*, offering us a group of three Plains Indian warriors, armed and seated on horseback. Suggestively, these warriors are facing away from the viewer in the picture, representing both a rejection of the present state of U.S. Indian relations and a sense of forward-looking aspiration or desire to advance the struggle for decolonization. Through this conjunction of text and picture, Costo initiates a rather fascinating process of political identification. He reinterprets Carlos Montezuma's image to create a symbolic representation of the basic model of political subjectivity and ideology that had come out of the Chicago Conference (with its emphasis on selective modernization, education, and self-determination) and offers this up as a representative Indian vox populi for popular consent.

In the inaugural January 1973 issue of the paper Costo comments directly on his adaptation of Montezuma's legacy, noting that while the issues the earlier leader confronted were different than those of 1970s, his spirit of political resistance (invoked through iconic Plains Indian warriors on the new masthead), acceptance of change and new knowledge, and dedication to his people should remain exemplary and representative ("Wassaja—The Name" 2). While invoking a sense of modernizing Indian identity linked to the past, Costo also clearly aims to constitute a present-day Indian polity and mobilize them in favor of self-determination (in a manner reminiscent of Scott Lyons's "x-marking"). The editorial comment in that same inaugural issue notes that self-determination is the central "strategic need of our people" (2). All other areas—education, economic development, health and welfare, and leadership—are tied to this. And "self-determination means the active use of Indian leadership, and the direct participation of the people. Indian leadership means decision by recognized Native authority" (2). This, of course, is a key element of the new sovereignty-talk emerging in the 1960s.

Costo made this link clearer by July of 1973, when he began employing the term "sovereignty" explicitly. In his Speaking Freely column of that month, on the topic of sovereignty, Costo notes that there was, by that time, a great deal of talk about tribal sovereignty in Indian country, especially since the occupations of Alcatraz and the confrontation between AIM activists, tribal authorities, and the federal government at Wounded Knee. Costo also acknowledges that the term already had many connotations. Oglala tribal chairman Dick Wilson was claiming (wrongly, Costo notes) that the actions of his government (and his paramilitary "goon squads") against the AIM protesters and other activists and traditionalists on the Pine Ridge Reservation were intended to protect the sovereignty of the Sioux tribes, as expressed in its constitution and bylaws and as permitted under the IRA. In contrast (and implicitly rejecting much of the language of legal sovereignty), Costo argues,

> Tribal sovereignty is not only adherence to a set of rules or laws, which have been, in truth, inflicted on a people. Tribal sovereignty, in its relationships with those outside the tribe, is the right to decide the goals and the needs of the people independently of pressures as well as unjustly inflicted laws. In its relationships within the tribe, tribal sovereignty means the right of the people to decide for themselves what their lives will be, what decisions to make, on every level of government and on every level of life. ("Sovereignty" 3)

Tribal sovereignty in this formulation entails the concepts of both popular sovereignty and representative government (within the tribe) and of self-determination (in terms of tribal–federal government relations).

Costo would maintain this basic political emphasis throughout the publication run of his paper, and in doing so, he highlights his understanding of the need for Indian writing to actively intervene in the usage of the language of sovereignty, to discipline that language in some respect. This sense of a relationship between ideology and print culture forms one of the foundations of the subsequently developing discourse of sovereignty. A representative example appears in a May 1975 editorial titled "One Axe to Grind." There Costo and his staff write,

> It would be foolish and inaccurate to claim that *Wassaja* does not have a policy, a philosophy, a position on Indian affairs. This policy and position is represented and expressed either in editorials, or in signed articles. It is, quite simply, self-government for the Indian people, a chance to live decently, a chance to make our own decisions and even our own mistakes, an end to bureaucratic controls, and a beginning of faithful, dedicated, trustworthy leadership. (2)

The paper's specific "axe to grind" in this context is the poor dissemination of this ideology on a national scale—in other words, the need for a national print culture to better constitute the Indian vox populi needed for sovereignty discourse to flower. "For more than a hundred years, our people have been without information," the editorial notes. "Communications has been a dismal failure." This leads to a distrust of information and to inaction, as the non-Indian mass media doesn't present Indian issues in a meaningful or accurate way. "On a national basis, therefore, *Wassaja* is the only newspaper with this aim in view, this effort dominating our policy." Today, organs like *This Week from Indian Country Today* aspire to fulfill that role.

What we can see clearly with Costo's paper, then, is the beginning of the tighter fusion of ideological and textual concerns necessary for the emergence of a fully formed discourse of sovereignty, a theme which will become my central focus in the later chapters of this book.[13] In this context, though, it is worth turning back, in conclusion, to McNickle, whose literary career represents a bit of anomaly in this respect. We do not see in McNickle's writing the same kind of close fusion between the legal-political dimensions of sovereignty and issues of literary production, interpretation, and reading practices that we will find in subsequent figures such as Craig Womack, Elizabeth Cook-Lynn, and Gerald Vizenor. There is clearly a tension between his political work, his nonfiction prose, and his fiction, both in content and tone. As David Moore notes, McNickle's novels and short fiction tend to dramatize "the drastic erosion of tribal sovereignty" (77). This emphasis on eroding autonomy is not reflected in later work like *Native American Tribalism*, however, which Moore rightly notes "expresses McNickle's sense of possibility for renewed sovereignty" (82). This contrast may well reflect the professional literary climate of his time, where non-Indian readers and editors evinced little appetite for stories that fundamentally challenged their mythologies about tribal cultures and experience. Moore reminds us that "in manuscript, [McNickle's] fiction tended toward brighter prospects, which his non-fiction eventually articulated" (175).[14] This certainly highlights the need for the robust development of a more *autonomous* Indian print culture for the emergence of sovereignty discourse. That culture was largely nonexistent in the 1930s when McNickle was pursuing his career as a novelist.

If McNickle was unable to effect a full fusion of his literary and political pursuit of sovereignty, though, it seems clear to me that some underlying sense of the requirements of a fully emergent literary discourse of sovereignty still had an impact on his creative writing. In this respect he anticipates some of the literary figures I will take up later. In its own limited ways, Mc-Nickle's fiction tries to participate (as Costo's newspaper did) in the process of mass symbolization of Indian political subjectivity that is demanded by a self-determination movement linked to invocations of popular sovereignty. McNickle understood sovereignty to be manifested largely in personal relationships of reciprocity and mutual respect. In his recent effort to translate the concept of sovereignty into a useful literary heuristic, David Moore follows that line of reasoning when he speaks of "the complexity of reciprocal relations that is tribal sovereignty" (37). It is fair to say, then, that for a writer like McNickle, in its legal and political sense, sovereignty is the manifestation of this ethos of respect and recognition, an ethos that can also be represented at the personal level. With such an understanding, we can see how his fictional narratives also functioned as gestures toward legal and political symbolization.[15] As Moore puts it, "McNickle forges a link between individual bodies and the body politic" (78). In the context of the present discussion, I might phrase this a bit differently, while maintaining a similar emphasis. Despite a thematic emphasis on the tragedy of cultural collision that would seem quite removed from sovereignty discourse, in novels like *The Surrounded* and *Wind from an Enemy Sky*, McNickle allegorizes many of the issues raised in the political struggles he would write about elsewhere. His characters provide personal, yet representative, manifestations of the broader story that Moore describes as that of "the people's power" (79). Moore's recent examination of both the allegorical dimensions of *The Surrounded* and the instantiation of a concept of reciprocal sovereign relationships in *Wind from an Enemy Sky* strike me as illuminating in this regard.[16] I would agree with his contention that McNickle's acts of storytelling represent attempts to instantiate the kind of political subjects that might constitute a modern American Indian body politic. In this respect they display their connections, albeit oblique, with other seemingly disparate kinds of texts like the Chicago Conference *Declaration* or *Native American Tribalism*.

If McNickle was unable to fully work out a fictional poetics that would bridge the gap between the legal and literary pursuit of tribal self-determination, he nevertheless remains an important figure in the development of sovereignty discourse. On the literary side, McNickle shows an inchoate grasp of the importance of working through a variety of textual and symbolic forms to "invent" the kind of Indian people who might claim sovereignty in newly defined ways. On the political and legal side, though, he was in the forefront of that process of redefinition. In turning next to Vine Deloria I will illustrate another stage in this interdisciplinary flowering of tribal sovereignty discourse. Deloria's work, as we will see, represents a more sophisticated dialectical reinvention of the concept of sovereignty, suggesting how this Western concept can indeed be indigenized. At the same time, Deloria gives us additional, suggestive hints about the ways that seemingly literary concerns have also become central to the project of decolonization.

CHAPTER 3

COLLECTIVE POLITICS AND LEGAL INTERPRETATION

VINE DELORIA AND THE TRANSFORMATION OF SOVEREIGNTY

Although we can trace roots of modern tribal sovereignty back to the work of D'Arcy McNickle, Joanne Barker is correct in noting that Vine Deloria, Jr., was instrumental in bringing the term into general usage and fully transforming it. With Deloria we also begin to see other important developments that anticipate the emergence of a fully formed discourse of sovereignty. Deloria refines and complicates the language of self-determination, demonstrating how a dialectical process of engagement with the Western legal tradition can lead to its indigenization. He introduces new cultural dimensions into the discussion of sovereignty. His work represents a leap forward in its conceptualization of the relationship between the symbolization of Indian political subjectivity and legal hermeneutics as well as in its recognition of the need for a dimension of praxis to be part of any discussion of sovereignty. Deloria's germinal work, including his 1970 essay "Self-Determination and the Concept of Sovereignty" and his influential books from the late 1960s and 1970s will be my primary focus here, not only because they disseminated important terms but also because they reveal Deloria as the first modern American Indian thinker to suggest, in its true complexity, what a fully developed sovereignty discourse might achieve.

In "Self-Determination and the Concept of Sovereignty" Deloria's primary concern is testing out the possibilities of several of the valences of those key terms. He begins with a familiar observation that the experience of colonial contact reveals a muddled and inconsistent legal history regarding the sovereignty of Indian people. In doing so, he clearly establishes the need to both engage with and move beyond the received framework of U.S. Indian law in developing an Indian approach to asserting sovereignty.[1] A passive reliance on received models of legal sovereignty is not enough, Deloria suggests, and Indian people must display a willingness to probe colonial law and discern its weaknesses and to experiment with new ranges of possibilities for confronting it. The pursuit of tribal sovereignty, he recognizes, will involve change, adaptation, and engagement.

At the time of American founding, Deloria notes, political and military expediency dictated a degree of recognition of Indian autonomy on the part of European powers, and in that respect there are foundations for a tribal sovereignty discourse even in the historical record of the colonizing powers. In context of eighteenth-century colonial wars in North America, Indian communities were acknowledged as having a European version of sovereignty "as long as they held sufficient territory and military strength to be an important factor in determining the outcome of the colonial conflicts" (Deloria, "Self-Determination" 118). In Deloria's view, a related form of expediency led American colonists to adopt a similar stance during the Revolution. The American revolutionaries were, in the view of many, "outside the law of civilized societies in their revolt," and so one reason for adopting "the most respectable posture toward the Indians possible" was to obtain international recognition and demonstrate their own ability to act in traditional political terms (118–19). In this context we might recall that two of the first treaties made by the Continental Congress (with the Delawares and Cherokees) actually made provisions for the appointment of Indian delegates to the Congress if those nations desired such representation.[2] As long as the new republic remained weak and vulnerable (roughly up to the point of the end of the War of 1812), "Indian treaties carefully distinguished the respective political rights of the two contracting parties, and passports, provisions for civil and criminal jurisdiction, and extradition indicated the belief that Indian governments were fully capable of dealing with both internal and external affairs" (119).

Locating the beginning of the recognition of Indian sovereignty in legal history, before the Marshall Court's key decisions, gestures toward an important shift in Indian political thought in the late 1960s—a move to emphasize the preconstitutional existence of Indian nations as recognizable "states," *some* of which might be fully capable of exercising all of the powers of self-determination associated with state sovereignty. Deloria does not often pursue an aggressively nationalist line of thinking in his own work, but he does open the door for this thinking in some contexts, particularly through his critical comments on shifts in U.S. policy toward tribal nations. In his subsequent treatment of the Marshall trilogy, Deloria points out inconsistencies and alternative interpretations in the court's opinion, ones that might buttress arguments in favor of political sovereignty. He stresses that even in incorporating the Doctrine of Discovery into American law in *Worcester v. Georgia*, Marshall recognized that the doctrine was a hard one to defend. Of equal interest, Deloria also cites Justice John McLean's concurring opinion in *Cherokee Nation v. Georgia*, which drew an analogy between the Cherokees and the Israelites (a common nineteenth-century trope). McLean, he reminds us, presented both groups as ones who are sovereign, in the sense of having the right of personal self-government, without that sovereignty being linked in an uninterrupted way to a specific homeland. Here we see Deloria probing through the legal archive in order to open up multiple lines of attack in sovereignty discourse, for citing McLean's reconciliation of removal and sovereignty cuts in two directions. It can be read, of course, as a biting observation regarding the legal contortions American jurists have frequently made to justify colonial policy. But it is also a suggestion that there might be ways for contemporary tribal peoples who have been dislocated to reassert sovereignty in spite of this diaspora. That view underpins the efforts of many nations to gain federal recognition in recent decades as an *initial* step toward reclaiming territory (through the trust mechanism).[3] It resonates in interesting ways with McNickle's notion that sovereignty, in the short term at least, might be deterritorialized. But it clearly moves in a different direction from the emphasis on political sovereignty toward which some of Deloria's earlier comments gestured.

Deloria takes great pains to highlight those places in American law that deal favorably with the question of tribal autonomy. He does so, however, as a vehicle for exploring the possibilities of the emergent thinking about self-determination and for further opening up the potential approaches to claiming sovereignty. In *Worcester*, Deloria reminds us, while Marshall's "domestic dependent nations" description limited the external (international) sovereignty of Indian people, in internal terms, that definition meant that Indian people could only lose autonomy by "voluntarily surrendering the remaining attributes of sovereignty or by becoming so shattered by the passage of events as to be incapable of exercising any social or political powers whatsoever" ("Self-Determination" 120). Building on this point in surveying twentieth-century legal history, Deloria highlights several moments that have the potential to reinforce a sense of the persistence of residual tribal sovereignty. In the twentieth century, he argues, we see a gradual shift toward a definition of Indian sovereignty as a reservoir of political powers that can be revived by Indian governments, if only they are willing to attempt to exercise them. In *Talton v. Mayes* (1904), Deloria observes, the Supreme Court distinguished those political powers inhibited by Congress from those that flowed from the natural rights of a distinct people, which could not be curtailed. In *Buster and Jones v. Wright* (1905), a federal appeals court spoke in related ways of the concept of residual sovereignty. Even the termination policy was scrutinized by the Supreme Court (in the Menominee case) in a way that also upheld the concept of inherent sovereignty. Building on this alternative legal history, Deloria recasts the new federal policy of self-determination, not as a unilateral granting of power from the colonizer to the colonized, but as a moment when sovereign Indian nations, understood as dependent states of some type, chose to reassert sovereign powers that they have always had *in reserve*. Self-determination, then, becomes the moment when tribal nations remind themselves and the broader society that they have always been here as nations.

With these broad foundations established, Deloria is then able to introduce his first key conceptual innovations. He attempts to redefine what many see as an exclusively Western concept in indigenous terms, and he simultaneously refines self-determination through the introduction of a specifically cultural dimension into the Indian approach for claiming sovereignty. Shrewdly, Deloria does this by starting precisely from the Western viewpoint, particularly the nationalist and popular vision of state-sovereignty, which becomes dominant from the period of the American founding into the nineteenth century. "Numerous references to sovereignty," Deloria notes, "cite the notion of a distinct people, separate from others, as the chief characteristic of Indian sovereignty, *indicating that so long as the cultural identity of Indians remains intact no specific political act undertaken by the United States government can permanently extinguish Indian peoples as sovereign entities*" ("Self-Determination" 121–22; emphasis added). In highlighting the broad concept of cultural identity as a key marker of Indian peoplehood here, Deloria follows to a degree in McNickle's footsteps in aiming to demonstrate how the concept of sovereignty might be employed and redefined in a deterritorialized fashion to serve the purposes of decolonization. "Although sovereignty originated as a means of locating the seat of political power in European nations," Deloria argues, "it has assumed the aspect of continuing cultural and communal integrity when transferred to the North American setting" (122). Such a claim, it seems to me, is in part an acknowledgment of the political realities facing tribal nations located within the United States as a settler-colonial state (many of which are too small to realistically push for full separation). But it is also, we should note, the beginning of a process dialectical redefinition of self-determination, potentially deterritorialized and mediated through the structures of popular sovereignty. Deloria is able to make an innovative claim that "[tribal] sovereignty . . . can be said to consist more of continued cultural integrity than of political powers, and to the degree that a nation loses its sense of cultural integrity, to that degree it suffers a loss of sovereignty" (123).

We should be careful here, of course, not to assume that Deloria is arguing that political powers or the possession of territory are insignificant in the broader context of struggles for sovereignty. He would hardly advocate that Indian people be satisfied with political dependency or land loss as long as they can function as a culturally distinct ethnic group. His emphasis on the vital importance of land for indigenous communities in a work like *God Is Red* is clear evidence of this. But Deloria was also heavily engaged in a strategic reorientation of the stages of the struggle as well as an attempt to shift the emphasis of Western sovereignty theory toward a more indigenous conception of political subjectivity. In Deloria's view, the Western understanding of sovereignty has typically placed too much emphasis on the sources of power (on the form of legal and political structures) rather than on the proper exercise of power (or on the communal ethos that acts through those forms). Put another way, Western sovereignty discourse obsesses over the question of who or what can exercise power over others, with the assumption that the proper definition of that machinery of power will automatically lead to relatively desirable results (in terms of the just applications of that power and the desirable form of the overall polity). Deloria argues that adopting such a view distorts indigenous communities in fundamentally damaging ways. An alternative to be pursued in an Indian discourse of sovereignty, then, would be to tactically adopt the Western view of the sovereign state as a source of authority legitimized by an integrated people but to then employ culturally specific definitions of that people to fundamentally alter the way that the state is understood to function.[4] In Deloria's writing, then, a broad concept of popular sovereignty (arguably brought into the forefront of Indian thinking through the Chicago Conference) is deployed in order to produce an alternative vision of how to organize the government of the state. His version of the language of sovereignty as self-determination employs the lens of culture to generate new possibilities for the constructive transformations of political institutions. "Cultural integrity," as a locus of tribal identity, "involves a commitment to a central and easily understood purpose that motivates a group of people, enables them to form efficient, albeit informal social institutions, and provides for them a clear identity which cannot be eroded by the passage of events. Sovereignty then revolves about the manner in which traditions are developed, sustained, and transformed to confront new conditions" (Deloria, "Self-Determination" 123).

One way to understand what Deloria is offering here is to recognize in his work an early form of an indigenous human rights talk, which mobilizes the internationalist strain of sovereignty discourse represented today by something like UNDRIP (the United Nations Declaration on the Rights of Indigenous Peoples). Deloria offers up a tactical alternative to the pursuit of complete political autonomy. The language of Indian sovereignty, as he formulates it, becomes a means to preserve what Kevin Bruyneel calls a "third space" from which tribal communities can adapt to present conditions and preserve what is essential about themselves while also exerting transformative influence on the purportedly dominant Western culture. As Deloria puts it, "A self-disciplined community that holds itself together and acts with a unified vision possesses *sufficient* sovereignty to confront and resolve any difficulty" ("Self-Determination" 123; my emphasis). With the threat of termination fended off, the central difficulty confronting Indian communities in the context of self-determination would be to avoid having the implementation of that policy involve the American government employing tribal peoples as its agents in advancing strategies of development unconnected to their underlying values (in other words, avoiding the scenarios that Alfred and Barsh fear). "An urgent need exists to return to traditional ways of participating in social and cultural functions of the community," Deloria argues, and "this need is presently articulated under the general theme of self-determination and is expressed politically in support of Indian sovereignty" (123). Deloria seeks to use the concept of cultural sovereignty, in other words, as a means to recast self-determination as a broader policy of decolonization. He concludes,

> "Sovereignty" is a useful word to describe the process of growth and awareness that characterizes a group of people working together and achieving maturity. If it is restricted to a legal-political context [by which I think Deloria is referring to what we have described earlier as a myopic commitment to legal sovereignty], then it becomes a limiting concept, which serves to prevent solutions. The legal-political context is structured in an adversary situation, which precludes both understanding and satisfactory resolution of difficulties and should be considered as a last resort, not as a first instance in which human problems and relationships are to be seen. (124)

Deloria's advocacy for sovereignty aims to achieve precisely that which Alfred expressed such skepticism about—to shift the concept out of an exclusively Western legal and political register and to reform it in an indigenous manner. With Deloria, then, we see clear evidence of the emergence of a dialectical approach to sovereignty in Indian political thought and print culture.

If "Self-Determination and the Concept of Sovereignty" offers a theoretical articulation of the possibilities of a decolonizing discourse of Indian sovereignty, the other key innovation in Deloria's thinking at this time is his insistence that such theoretical formulations must involve a specific political praxis connecting broader acts of textual production/interpretation and political symbolization. The centrality of praxis to the contemporary discourse of Indian sovereignty in literary contexts is an issue that I will stress in subsequent chapters of this book. I would argue here that Deloria is a foundational figure/writer in that tradition. The most focused and interesting illustration of this appears in his 1970 monograph, *We Talk, You Listen*. There Deloria synthesizes his own political experience and understanding of indigenous issues and cultural practice with the media criticism of Marshall McLuhan to argue that modern America (both Native and "colonial") is entering a period of "retribalization." Deloria echoes McLuhan's claim that we now live in an era of "concept inundation," which replicates and expands the alienation effects produced by colonial contact. In American society in the late 1960s, he maintains, all of the people were overwhelmed by electronic media in a manner analogous to how a native of Ghana (his example) would have experienced the introduction of a print literacy that fractured his links to a precontact tribal world. One clear effect of this media-driven concept inundation has been the breakdown of traditional mythologies, which have lost their potency as much for the colonizer as for the colonized. In this respect, Deloria diagnoses a broad breakdown in the symbolizing systems that underpin the kind of corporate political subjectivity and imagined community needed for popular sovereignty to function. Deloria's examples of the collapse of these mythologies in mainstream America center on the loss of faith in concepts like American exceptionalism and manifest destiny, both of which began to be challenged in serious ways in the 1960s. Lacking the foundation provided by these mythologies, he suggests, the settler-colonial culture begins to find itself coming unmoored in a manner that opens up opportunities for the colonized. Deloria observes with some irony, "Like the tribesmen who were our ancestors, we have become objects of a universe we do not understand and not subjects with a universe to exploit" (*We Talk* 30).

The new tribalism Deloria sees emerging is not unlike what some academics today would refer to as the postmodern condition. His pragmatic approach to confronting it, however, is quite different from that of the typical postmodern theorist. Faced with the dissolution of the master narratives of colonial society, Deloria proposes as a cure for the ills of both Native and non-Native America his redefined concept of sovereignty as self-determination, refocused into specific forms of political action and tied to new ways of imagining political subjectivity. "If the nature of our electronic world is that it retribalizes," he argues, "then we must begin to create a new mythology and symbols to explain that world" (Deloria, *We Talk* 30). That new mythology and symbolism can be provided by reimagining sovereignty in terms of collective/group political subjectivity and cultural values. "If young people and minority groups are to survive the repression that we see today," Deloria claims, "the harmless group feeling must be translated into the demand for recognition of the sovereignty of their groups. This can only come through political action as a defensive weapon of protection" (31). The template both for group-centered sovereignty and for group-based political action comes from modern Native American tribes who, in the wake of termination, began to formulate an alternative model of political subjectivity rooted in traditional cultural values and focused on the model of the tribal collective, as opposed to the liberal individual. As Deloria puts it, "Any future coalition of groups for change must adopt Indian formats. The desire to have spectacular demonstrations and disruptions must give way to a determination to maintain the community at all costs. This can only be possible by the creation of new mythologies internal to each group in a manner similar to contemporary tribal understandings of the history of the people" (31). The result of this creative process, it would seem, would be the beginning of a larger revolution whereby alternative polities within the larger framework of the United States might carve out new spaces for autonomy and self-determination.[5] "We have a chance to build a cosmopolitan society within the older American society," Deloria notes. "But it must be done by an affirmation of the component groups that have composed American society" (31).

Deloria's optimistic appraisal of the possibility of radical political and cultural change in the United States may strike modern readers as a classic expression of late-1960s idealism. Clearly the predictions he makes in *We Talk, You Listen* about the imminent proliferation of communes and other countercultural forms were not born out in the decades that followed. Nevertheless, I would argue that *We Talk, You Listen* represents an exemplary methodological moment in the dialectical development of the concept of tribal sovereignty. Deloria pragmatically draws attention to what I have referred to as the technai of sovereignty, making the point that it is essential to link whatever operative, theoretical definition of sovereignty one embraces to some specific legal or political instruments. He also recognizes that transformations in political subjectivity and interpretive practice go hand-in-hand with truly revolutionary use of those technai. The former transformations, in other words, are essential to ensuring that in adopting and employing specific technai of sovereignty, tribal peoples do not find themselves unwittingly assimilated into the structures of colonial society. This, then, is Deloria's anticipation of the type of critique of Indian sovereignty discourse offered by Alfred and Barsh. And this, I would argue, represents his uncanny anticipation of the literary projects of writers as diverse as Craig Womack, Elizabeth Cook-Lynn, and Gerald Vizenor.

So how does this all fit together in terms of the development of a specific praxis? In *We Talk, You Listen* Deloria's basic definition of sovereignty is essentially an earlier version of the formulation he would later offer in "Sovereignty and the Problem of Self-Determination." Taking into account the realities of the contemporary situation, he emphasizes the need for discrete groups within the American nation-state to maintain their own cultural integrity and develop varied strategies to confront the challenges of a changing world. The mechanisms through which this model of sovereignty can be pursued, he argues, include the United States Constitution, treaties, and the "corporation," but the meaning and function of each of these structures is transformed when approached from the perspective of the group. The model of political subjectivity in the discourse of Indian sovereignty, Deloria insists, is a collective one, and when one reads/interprets and mobilizes specific technai from that point of view, one has the potential to effect significant change. Consider, in this regard, what Deloria has to say about the importance of the Constitution. Confronted by the fragmentation of modern society, we should recall, Deloria sees it as both imperative and increasingly possible for groups to maintain and develop their own myths, symbols, and traditions (their cultural autonomy) as the locus of their sovereignty. "There must be a drive within each group to understand its own uniqueness," he notes (Deloria, *We Talk* 42). Significantly, Deloria sees this as achievable within a constitutional framework: "What has been important and continues to be important is the Constitution of the United States and its continual adaptation to contemporary situations. With the Constitution as a framework and a reference point, it would appear that a number of conflicting interpretations of the experience of America could be validly given" (43). We should note here that Deloria is seeing unrealized potential in the Constitution; he is not arguing that the text has been typically used or read in that manner. Yet he sees the possibility of reading the Constitution differently to be a very real one. "We can survive as a society if we reject the conquest-oriented interpretation of the Constitution," Deloria writes. "While some Indian nationalists want the whole country back, a guarantee or adequate protection for existing treaty rights would provide a meaningful compromise. The Constitution should provide a sense of balance between groups as it has between conflicting desires of individuals" (43).

The idea that Deloria is grappling with here is that one must develop an ability to read the Constitution in a way that ensures the recognition of group rights as opposed to merely individual ones.[6] We should note, of course, that as part of the overall argument in *We Talk, You Listen*, he offers an extended critical analysis of the ways that mainstream American culture has commonly marginalized "others" and rejected difference as a meaningful political and experiential category. He maintains, in this context, that it is imperative to reject the melting-pot ideology that impedes needed redefinition of the concept of "the people" in an American context. "American society has never recognized that groups exist," Deloria argues. "But they always have. We must recognize the integrity of groups, the need for negotiations between groups. We must create situations where decisions affecting certain groups are made by people of those groups" (*We Talk* 106). If our sense of the basic political unit of the state (its central form of political subjectivity) shifts so that we view the national people as composed of many sovereign peoples (as opposed to a multitude of sovereign selves), the Constitution can be reread (or, if needed, amended) in significant ways. Deloria sees the greatest significance of the black power/black nationalist movement of the 1960s to lie in its recognition of this need to foster solidarity in minority groups. But again, the best model for this type of thinking, in his view, is the traditional Indian tribe: "If groups work out their own mode of political expression *internal to their group*, then as a group they can relate to the Constitutional framework and the national political scheme will not be irrelevant to each group.... The present system is built upon individual expression and has no place for group expression—with the exception again of Indian tribes" (112). Adopting the new model of political subjectivity that is being generated by the tribal discourse of sovereignty, then, would have both a political and what we might call a hermeneutic effect—changing both the ways that groups function and the way that the law is read. As Deloria puts it,

> With the continual threat of co-optation facing minority groups as they are presently constituted, it is imperative that the basic sovereignty of the minority group be recognized. This would have the immediate effect of placing racial minorities in a negotiating position as a group and would nullify co-optation. While there would be the constant desire to co-opt, the chances of such behavior would be lessened and a balance of power could be achieved through political alliances. *Recognition of new interpretations of the Constitution based on the concept of the group would be the vital step in this process.* (113; emphasis added)

What Deloria is calling for in *We Talk, You Listen* is a sort of new constitution, brought into being by the practical activity and innovative reading practices of political collectives modeled on Indian tribes—a *constitutional criticism*, if you will. In making this call, it is worth noticing, he also introduces a second key techne—the treaty as a vehicle for asserting sovereignty. Deloria's particular formulation of collective political subjectivity also allows for an innovative reading practice that reformulates the significance and function of the treaty as a form. From the colonial legal perspective, we should recall that the termination of treaty relations with tribal peoples in the nineteenth century was rooted in conventional understandings of state sovereignty. To be a party to a treaty, in that context, it is necessary to be an autonomous, territorially discrete, nation-state. Deloria's reformulation of sovereignty discourse, however, places the group, as opposed to the nation-state, at the focal point. Demonstrating his remarkable ability to turn colonial discourse against itself, Deloria is clear about the potential for a deterritorialized form of sovereignty to function as tool for decolonization. He notes that, ironically, the history of discrimination and colonization confirms the autonomous existence of the oppressed as peoples who merit recognition. Discrimination against blacks, Indians, and Mexicans, he argues, has historically been built on a tacit recognition of the "groupness" of these communities, and this produces further dialectical effects. Because discrimination has been based on group identity, it is through group action that progress has been made in changing the political structure. "In order to validate the persecution of the group, the persecutors must in effect recognize the right of that group to be different," and it is only a matter of time before those minority groups coalesce around their difference and define an alternative political subjectivity (Deloria, *We Talk* 117). What has been missing, in an American context, has been a move on the part of those groups to make full and innovative use of the political concepts employed against them. "Implicit in the sufferings of each group," Deloria notes, "is the acknowledgment of the sovereignty of the group. [But] it is this aspect—sovereignty—which has never been adequately used by minority groups to their own advantage. Perhaps they cannot conceive of sovereignty outside of a territory within which they can exercise their own will" (117–18). Deloria clearly *can* conceive of sovereignty as something that can be asserted outside of autonomously controlled territory—outside of conventional forms of nationalism and state sovereignty. And precisely because he can do so, he is able to insist, like many other Indian leaders and thinkers of his time (and since), that treaty rights can be claimed by sovereign groups even if those groups are not able to (or do not wish to) function as sovereign nation-states as understood by conventional Western political theory.[7]

Deloria reimagines the political subjects of treaties to include not primarily state sovereigns but rather group (tribal) sovereigns, and in doing so he alters the very meaning of the treaty form (in a way, in line with indigenous worldviews). Treaties, then, are dialectically transformed through Deloria's approach to tribal sovereignty. He reclaims the Indian treaty from the law of contract and the positivist law of nations, where imperialism had relocated it and where the subjects of the discourse are imagined as discrete individuals or, perhaps, corporate individuals. Instead, according to Deloria's thinking, "when groups of people are thrust into a political relationship, it is impossible to use a contract basis" to define that relationship (*We Talk* 148). Rather, the situation calls for a treaty to be understood as a covenant relationship: "The treaty-covenant relationship defines the spirit in which groups or nations will relate to one another. Little has to be spelled out in specific items because what is important is the pledge of faith between groups and the promise of each group to police itself on a moral basis" (148).[8] Read this way, a treaty becomes a guarantee of the perpetual right of groups to continue to exist as discrete entities, regardless of any specific exchanges of goods, territories, or the like between them. "Contracts have specific items that are severable, that is to say, can be fulfilled by themselves," Deloria notes. But when a treaty is no longer viewed as a contract, the door is opened for reemploying treaties as a central mechanism for decolonization. "Breaking a contract alters the relationship between [individual] men but [doing so] cannot ultimately affect the relationships between groups of men" (148).

If Deloria's approach to transforming the concept of sovereignty sets up a fundamental shift in the way that treaties are read and made meaningful, it is fair to say that the same is also potentially true for other central technai of sovereignty (like the Constitution) and for other key American institutions. Not a rigid originalist in his thinking in *We Talk, You Listen*, Deloria acknowledges that the U.S. Constitution was drafted by property owners, with the protection of property a central focus, and consequently with a range of specific ideological features tied to the political subjectivity of the possessive individual. "The Constitution is built upon a theory of radical idealism of the individual," he notes. "It defines everything in terms of the solitary person willingly assuming his responsibilities as a citizen and participating in the forms of government on the basis of his understanding of absolute and abstract justice. Unfortunately, the world has never been composed of this kind of individual" (Deloria, *We Talk* 143). Significantly, though, Deloria sees great potential for the Constitution to be radically transformed when reread through the lens of group, as opposed to individual, subjectivity. Again, the position of Indian people (as well as of black and Mexican American citizens) within the Constitutional framework—having been given the voting franchise *as a group* long after ratification—positions them to lead the way. Out of the dialectics of colonial conflict again emerges the potential for innovation: "Entering the Constitutional framework as groups, Indians ... have had to have legislative adjustments on their behalf every time they had a problem" (146). But if the American legal order, in this respect, has recognized Indian political subjectivity as collective since its inception, from this fact springs the potential for radical change. "What is needed is not the rewriting of the Constitution," Deloria argues, "but the recognition by society as a whole that there is a place within the Constitutional framework for group aspirations considered without reference to individualism" (147). Such recognition, he notes, is authorized by the preamble itself, so long as that preamble is reread in light of the Indian version of popular sovereignty—where the national vox populi is a composed of a chorus of sovereign groups. Deloria advocates centering the Constitution on its preamble and reinterpreting its "we the people" in a new context, not on a Lockean basis where the people is a gathering of individuals concerned primarily with the protection of property, but on a tribal basis where the focus is on group cultural difference. As he puts it, "The contemporary interpretation of 'we the people' in reality means 'we the peoples,' we the definable groups, and thus admits minority groups into Constitutional protection which they should have received a century ago" (152). Significantly, Deloria argues that American society has unconsciously been moving the way he predicts for some time. In his view, "it remains for American society only to recognize group rights . . . to provide a thorough-going ideological revision of Constitutional theory to encompass modern problems" (152).

Out of a dialectical encounter with the colonizing power of the United States, and focused on the concept of Indian sovereignty and its reorientation of political subjectivity, Deloria is able to theorize a new, transformative legal hermeneutic, a new way of reading the Constitutional text and treaties. Gerald Vizenor, Elizabeth Cook-Lynn, and Craig Womack do something similar. It is not my intention, of course, to present Deloria's sovereignty-centered praxis in *We Talk, You Listen* as a fully realized model, ready for adoption. His late-1960s and early-1970s writings carry with them some of the overly optimistic, perhaps utopian, glow of the broader era (pre–Wounded Knee II, pre–Rehnquist Court, etc.). There are problematic tendencies to elide political and racial criteria for group subjectivity in his model. And elsewhere Deloria himself registers ambivalence about the approach to sovereignty he developed at that time.[9] Still, grasping the methodological complexity of Deloria's project in *We Talk, You Listen* strikes me as tremendously useful in understanding the emergence and contours of a fully formed discourse of sovereignty. Deloria shows us how it is possible for a Western political concept to be transformed into an indigenous one with the potential not only to further the process of decolonization from a tribal perspective but also to transform the colonizing culture itself. He offers a clear example of the dialectical processes through which a central legal-political concept can develop. And he highlights how the legal and literary dimensions of the pursuit of sovereignty can be brought together in powerful ways. Not surprisingly, then, in the wake of his germinal writings, we see considerable creativity and diversification within Indian print culture (in its literary forms in particular) in its approach to sovereignty.

I will not trace that diversification in the remainder of this chapter in the same detailed fashion that I have been pursuing so far. I would, however, like to highlight one additional example of the development of the discourse of sovereignty as self-determination. This is the internationalization of sovereignty and the related emergence of indigeneity as a central category of thought, which I want to track in part through the writings of Seneca activist and leader John Mohawk. This discussion usefully extends some of the themes developed in the preceding discussion of Deloria without leading us into a labyrinthine legal history. Mohawk also strikes me as an important figure to consider in the context of this study precisely because his own project is similar in striking ways to Deloria's in its foregrounding of key elements in a discourse of sovereignty.

JOHN MOHAWK'S *BASIC CALL* TO SOVEREIGNTY

The movement to internationalize the struggle for sovereignty has a fairly long history, dating back to the era of the founding of the League of Nations, though its more complete realization has taken place in the period between the mid-1970s and the present. In 1923 the Cayuga leader Deskaheh from Six Nations territory in Ohswekan, Ontario, Canada, traveled to Geneva to register a complaint before the League regarding the Canadian government's interference with traditional Haudenosaunee governance (O. Lyons 13). Two years later, in 1925, the Maori religious leader T. W. Ratana also attempted, unsuccessfully, to gain League support for the 1840 Treaty of Waitangi between England and the Maori, which in theory, recognized the Maori's original sovereignty in New Zealand and granted them the status and rights of British citizens. In 1977, quite self-consciously following in the footsteps of these earlier figures, a collection of activists representing groups from the United States, Canada, Peru, Chile, and other South American countries petitioned the United Nations (through its permanent forum for nongovernmental organizations in Geneva) to take up the issue of indigenous rights. This began a thirty-year process of negotiation that culminated on September 13, 2007, with the General Assembly adopting the United Nations Declaration on the Rights on Indigenous Peoples (UNDRIP).[10]

To get a sense of how the shift into an international law framework was originally conceived as an extension and transformation of sovereignty discourse, a useful place to turn is the *Basic Call to Consciousness*, a text originally published by the Mohawk Nation newspaper *Akwesasne Notes* in 1978 (and subsequently reissued in 2005). The *Basic Call* reproduces the report (drafted by John Mohawk) that was brought to Geneva and the nongovernmental organization (NGO) forum by the Haudenosaunees, and it offers us a powerful overview of some of the key elements of the contemporary, internationalist approach to self-determination, many of which we can also find reflected in Native print coverage of the passage and implementation of UNDRIP. Oren Lyons's 2005 preamble to the *Basic Call* makes clear that one of the initial goals of the Iroquois delegation to Geneva was to shift the focus of the debate about sovereignty out of a framework bounded by the norms of U.S. law and into an international law, natural law, and human rights law. This move was an extension of ideas that had been discussed by Mohawk and others at the international treaty council in Wakpala, South Dakota, in 1974, and it reflected concerns about relying on the domestic political and legal structures of nation-states as a vehicle for decolonization. Following this line of thinking, Lyons traces the roots of colonialism to the international Doctrine of Discovery, arguing that until this foundation is challenged and overturned, decolonization in an American context will be impossible to achieve. In Lyons's words, "The Law of Nations forever displaced indigenous peoples in our own lands. The 'doctrine of discovery' doomed us to centuries of merciless and tragic struggles that continue in the present. That's why we went to Geneva in 1977, and that's why states continue to refuse to recognize our rights to self-determination today" (O. Lyons 15). Indigenous peoples saw the United Nations as a "beacon of fairness and justice," feeling that the 1948 Declaration of Human Rights was written in a way that potentially included them. As such, Lyons maintains, the Haudenosaunee delegates did not distinguish between working with NGOs and with member states, as simply engaging with the general UN structure was the point. In ways reminiscent of Deloria's thought, the focus of their sovereignty discourse would be on the interaction of groups, not limited to the nation-state form. The key was to begin a process of undermining the Law of Discovery and finding a way to apply the norms of human and natural rights law to open up space for indigenous people to define and regulate themselves in the manner of their own choosing. The initial trip to Geneva in 1977 merely began a process that, for now, has culminated in UNDRIP.

If finding a way to claim autonomy through an assertion of human rights was a central element in the diplomatic mission of the Haudenosaunees to the United Nations, it is important to recognize that this did not automatically imply the abandonment of claims of nationhood. It did, however, involve an even more radical process to redefine nationhood (as a form of group political identity) than what we saw in Vine Deloria's work. As Mohawk writes about his own people in the *Basic Call*,

> We are nations by every definition of the term. [But] we have been unable to obtain any semblance of justice in the court systems of the United States or Canada, and we suffer horrible legal injustices that have terrible economic and social consequences for our people. Many of our legal problems involve land and sovereignty over land, and land is the basis of our economy. We are seeking our rights in those areas under international law. (117)

Mohawk makes clear here that the Haudenosaunees in 1977 approached the NGO forum as a "nation." But in asserting their nationhood in this particular international law context they were foregrounding the idea that the structures and values of the nation might be redefined in very different ways from the standard models of sovereign statehood that organize the United Nations itself. This idea has been a key pillar of the indigenization of sovereignty discourse, which has aimed to shift the definition of "nation" to allow for a much wider range of decolonization strategies to be employed by people working in their own local contexts.

The documents presented in Geneva by the Iroquois in 1977 nod toward standard Western legal discourses of statehood while dialectically redefining them. A key pillar of the assault on the Law of Discovery involved the assertion of the precontact, preconstitutional, and anti-Western nationhood of the Haudenosaunees. In a section titled "The Haudenosaunee: A Nation Since Time Immemorial," Mohawk notes that the members of the Iroquois Confederacy lack migration traditions and are the original inhabitants of their lands. These original inhabitants have an extremely long and distinct history of political development all their own and can demonstrate the presence of continuous government over time. Mohawk stresses the emergence of the distinctive Iroquois version of a confederated polity through their own history of war and conflict, brought to an end by the prophetic leadership of Deganawida. It was the innovative thought and teaching of this leader (who was called the Peacemaker) that formed the basis for what some refer to as the Iroquois constitution, their Great Law of Peace. Through the historical processes initiated by Deganawida, "the Confederate state of the Haudenosaunee became the embodiment of democratic principles that continue to guide our peoples today" (*Basic Call* 26). In this context, Mohawk notes, "we have continually been aggressive in asserting that we are a state, a government, and a people who have a right to a place in the international community" (30). To many readers, the evidence of nationhood that Mohawk presents (possession of specific territory, continuous governmental structures, representative/democratic political institutions) would seem to match up very well with standard Western political discourse about sovereign statehood.

We would do well to pause, however, before assuming that kind of nationhood that the Haudenosaunees assert is so transparent and familiar, though. In many respects, the indigenization of sovereignty discourse (of which I take the *Basic Call* to be a representative example) has involved an effort to totally redefine the nature of the state in terms of the principles of natural law and human rights. Even the latter experiences considerable transformation in the hands of Indian thinkers. The reason for this redefinition is twofold. On the one hand, the categories of natural law and human rights maintain considerable force in international law contexts, if not necessarily in the domestic legal contexts of nations like United States. Thus, to embrace them is to open up new possibilities for asserting and defending the rights of tribal peoples for self-determination. It is also, I would note, an attempt to return sovereignty discourse, in some respects, to its pre-Westphalian roots. On the other hand, the redefinition of the state in terms of "nature" also enables a more radical reassertion of traditional, local, tribally specific perspectives. These perspectives, in some ways, actually conflict with the universalizing legal discourses of human rights and natural law as they are sometimes understood from Western perspectives. This fact explains some of the emerging anxiety surrounding the ratification of UNDRIP (worries that its human rights framework is too liberal to work as a vehicle for indigenous self-determination) and the importance of the upcoming struggle to determine how to interpret and employ that text in practical ways as a vehicle for asserting indigenous rights. It highlights, in other words, the need for a fully formed *discourse* of international indigenous self-determination to complement the emergence of this new legal techne. Mohawk's writings, both in the *Basic Call* and elsewhere, illustrate some of the underlying imperatives here.

In his description of the Great Law of Peace in *Basic Call*, Mohawk glosses its key political principle, peace, in the following way: peace is the active striving of humans for the purpose of establishing universal justice, not simply the absence of strife or conflict. The purpose of government, from a Haudenosaunee perspective, is to facilitate this form of striving. The Peacemaker's teaching, in this context, is presented as a uniquely clear example of natural law—a system of political and social norms rooted in human logic/reason and observation of the natural world—that reveals "peace" to be the way the world *ought* to be organized. As Mohawk puts it elsewhere, in an essay called "The Creator's Way" (originally published in *Akwesasne Notes* in 1975), "The Creator's law is the real natural order" (Barreiro 3). Significantly, then, after demonstrating the Haudenosaunees' national existence in terms comprehensible to Western legal thought (even if not in its current dominant form), Mohawk offers a specific vision of "nature" as a corrective to modern Western political models and norms (which errantly see themselves as universal). "The majority of the world does not find its roots in Western culture or traditions," he argues. "The majority of the world finds its roots in the Natural World and the traditions of the Natural World that must prevail if we are to develop truly free and egalitarian societies" (*Basic Call* 90). Mohawk's vision of Iroquois natural law, then, is not the same as the universal natural law discourse rooted in Western thought.[11] It is a philosophy rooted in the idea that *local* knowledge and the social structures and practices that derive from that knowledge provide the basis for national self-definition and determination. Much like Deloria offers up "tribalism" as a corrective to American constitutionalism, Mohawk offers the principles embodied in the Great Law of Peace as a corrective to the historical trajectory of sovereignty discourse in Western-dominated international law.

To take another example of his appreciation for the intricate dialectical dance of contemporary international indigenous approaches to sovereignty, we might consider Mohawk's understanding of the nature of representative government among the Haudenosaunees, and his treatment of how the national institutions of the People of the Longhouse differ from modern Western models of popular sovereignty. The primary focus in the Iroquois political system, as Mohawk notes, is not popular representation for its own sake (where the central focus of politics would be to ensure that governmental power and authority are legitimized as expressions of popular will). Rather, for the Iroquois it is seen as necessary that the structure and principles of popular representation reflect the natural order of things in a world organized around principles of peace. In the Longhouse, power and authority *does* reside with the people, and it is expressed most visibly through chiefs (the members of the Longhouse as a governing body). This makes traditional Iroquois government look, superficially at least, like Euro-American style representation.[12] In the end, though, the Iroquois people are not constituted of the same collective of sovereign selves that we find in Western political theory.

Reflecting on this alternative understanding of "the people," Mohawk registers uneasiness with using the term "representative" to describe the Longhouse structure. As he notes, councils of women appoint men to their positions of leadership. This and other features of the system of government reflect ideas of natural balance, kinship, and reciprocity, as opposed to some ideal of universal voting franchise.[13] Once appointed, those men are understood to act as "conduits of the will of the people," as opposed to being "independent representatives of the people" (*Basic Call* 38). But conducting the will of the people means something different here than it would in, say, the political writings of Rousseau. Part of what Mohawk is getting at with his distinction is the idea that it is only to the extent that the Longhouse structure and the men serving in it represent and embody peace (defined in the specific sense above) that the government is considered legitimate as an expression of what the people believe and value. Haudenosaunee political theory would hold that if they fail to live up to the ethos of the Great Law, the abstraction that is the represented people would not be an accurate reflection of nature, and thus not really a people at all. As Mohawk puts in "The Creator's Way," "It is our awareness of the spirit of a common dedication to the provisions of a good life for our children and our children's children *that makes the nations real. Real nations* provide for peace within the local community and also within the community of human beings because they exist in the hearts of the people, and peace, the unity of spirit and reason, is the natural condition of society" (Barreiro 3; my emphasis). In other words, there is no theoretical space in the Iroquois approach to popular sovereignty for totalitarian sovereignty (fascism), as there is in Western theory. Indeed, in its ideal form, there is not even really a space for liberal possessive individualism in Iroquois popular sovereignty. In the end, the constitutional limitations on the use of power in Iroquois society are not primarily formal, but rather ethical. Thus, the abstraction that is "the people" in an Iroquois context *must be symbolized* in ways that involve specific ethical commitments and worldviews. And the central symbolic form for this would be the Iroquois's particular articulation of their local cultural and religious values.

This idea forms the basis of the model of political subjectivity that has come to be called "indigenous." The central elements of that political subjectivity would render it, to many Western political observers, a religious polity, though the categorical separation between religion and other aspects of culture and governance would probably not make sense to many indigenous communities. Indeed, the integration of a general cosmology/worldview into the full range of political and social practices in the traditional Iroquoian system may even make my use of the qualified term "political subjectivity" somewhat misleading here. The indigenous model of subjectivity rejects distinctions between different spheres of life and experience, being instead an integrating practice. "Spiritualism is the highest form of political consciousness," Mohawk argues, and he deems the adoption of such a form of consciousness not only central to the process of decolonization but central to one's very being as a real human person (*Basic Call* 91). This position is widely held in the contemporary indigenous discourse of sovereignty, and we see a version of it in Taiaiake Alfred's work. It is central to the emergence and basic definition, in the present period, of the model of *indigenous* peoplehood that circulates through Indian print culture. There is a reason that UNDRIP refers to the rights of indigenous "peoples" and not "persons."

A fairly representative example of the parameters of this model of indigenous subjectivity can be found, again, in Mohawk's writings. His 1975 *Akwesasne Notes* essay, "All the Children of Mother Earth," offers a clear articulation of his understanding of what is involved in living as what he calls one of the "Natural People" or "Real People of the Earth" (Barreiro 11). As Mohawk explains it, the basic principles of an indigenous cosmology hold that individual beings are simultaneously autonomous and intimately interconnected. The spirit that manifests itself in the created world is made manifest in each individual being (a category that includes human people, animals, and plants), and each of these beings thus has a real (or material) and a spiritual nature.

What renders indigenous people distinct from Western man, for Mohawk, is that the former recognize this structure in the created world and set out to live accordingly. The "Natural" or "Real People" understand that they are individually distinct yet also parts of a greater whole. They approach the rest of creation from a perspective of kinship, and live in a way that is intended to be mutually supportive of the continuity of life. This may involve individual sacrifice, of course—as the "Rabbit gives of its flesh so that the Fox may live"—but all actions are taken with a view of the totality in mind. As long as one lives according to such principles, then one constitutes a member of the body of "Real" or "Natural People." To do otherwise is to "leave their real ways," to "cease to support Life," and to "break away from the Life cycle" (Barreiro 9). The model of subjectivity foregrounded here, then, dictates that to be an indigenous people one must be part of a community that (1) understands that individual humans are simultaneously autonomous beings deserving respect and part of a greater whole (that includes both other humans and the rest of the natural world); (2) seeks to participate in the processes of life in light of that understanding; (3) ensures that such participation will be possible for subsequent generations; and (4) refuses to "participate in ways that deny people an access to the celebration of all life or that are destructive to another life species" (Barreiro 11). Indigenous political life, to be legitimate, must represent peoplehood in a manner that follows these core principles. And the international indigenous discourse of sovereignty has sought to locate or create new legal forms (technai) to facilitate decolonization and allow the development of these kinds of polities, each of which may be somewhat distinct in light of its specific local culture. But those formal mechanisms cannot function without a broader network of symbolism and storytelling to regulate and mobilize them. In an international legal context sovereignty cannot be realized without a fully formed discursive apparatus around it. Mohawk's recognition of this, of course, drives his sense of the relationship between his engagement with legal forms and his work as a writer.

I do not wish to suggest that the theorization of indigenous sovereignty has reached some sort of culmination with the internationalization of the concept of self-determination and the related effort to bolster the political agency of indigenous peoples in international forums. It is indeed true that a central facet of today's indigenous sovereignty movement, as reflected in the writing and activism emerging from tribes within the United States, involves efforts to leverage new international legal technai to create space for decolonization and the reassertion of tribally specific politics and religious/cultural practices. To be sure, this represents a fascinating and important example of the ongoing development of sovereignty talk. Precisely because of the challenges involved in producing a fully formed discourse of sovereignty at a global level, however, there remains considerable uncertainty as to whether the tools provided by UNDRIP will work (in the short term at least) in the way that the peoples desire. It is also uncertain whether even a fully functional declaration's theoretical breadth will prove enough to allow sufficient local flexibility on the part of the indigenous polities it aims to serve. UNDRIP itself likely needs further dialectical transformation.

To conclude in these preliminary chapters, then, I have aimed to make several interrelated points. First, I have tried to show that a full understanding of what contemporary Indian thinkers and writers mean when they invoke "sovereignty" requires us to develop a grasp of the complex intellectual and political history of the concept. Second, I have asserted that taking a tribal-centric approach to studying at least part of history reveals a legacy of remarkable innovation. This shows the existence of real potential to radically transform the concept of sovereignty, despite its Western roots. Finally, I have suggested that the emergence of a fully formed discourse of sovereignty involves not only the dialectical transformation of key legal concepts but also the emergence of new forms of political symbolization and a complementary focus on transformative practices of textual interpretation. This last point remains to be fully established, but it will be the focal point of the second part of this book. The legal history I have laid out here has rich implications for our understanding of the literary pursuit of sovereignty, and in the chapters that follow I will suggest that Craig Womack, Elizabeth Cook-Lynn, and Gerald Vizenor have all done compelling work in connecting law and literature. In their various approaches to that project they offer a range of possibilities regarding how literature and literary criticism can have a meaningful relationship to the broader pursuit of self-determination by Indian peoples today.

Part II

Literary Discourses of Self-Determination

CHAPTER 4

The Pragmatics of Literary Nationalism

In recent years numerous Native American literary critics (Craig Womack, Robert Warrior, Jace Weaver, Daniel Heath Justice, Lisa Brooks, and Elizabeth Cook-Lynn to name just a few) have published significant books intended to define and encourage an American Indian literary nationalist movement. Almost universally the literary projects pursued by these critics suggest specific links to real-world struggles for tribal sovereignty. In the introduction to *Our Fire Survives the Storm*, for example, Daniel Heath Justice announces an intention to "inquire into the idea of 'Cherokeeness' within the Cherokee literary tradition" in order to cultivate "indigenous nationhood" as a response to "the assimilationist directive of imperialist nation-states" (7–8). Similarly, in *Red on Red* Craig Womack asserts, "Native literature, and Native literary criticism by Native authors, is part of sovereignty," for, he maintains, the "ongoing expression of a tribal voice" is interdependent with the "political status of Native nations" (14). These kinds of claims about the interdependence of literary production, criticism, and tribal sovereignty speak to the heart of part II of this book, which aims to inquire into the specific nature of those connections and the ways that they constitute a discursive system. Toward that end, in the present chapter I would like to begin by considering some of the ways in which prominent theoretical articulations of the project of literary nationalism build on the genealogies of sovereignty traced in part I.

Womack's widely referenced 1999 work, *Red on Red*, is probably the most influential text to come out of the literary nationalist movement, and I will focus a great deal of this chapter on that work. I will begin, though, with Robert Warrior's efforts to develop the critical concept of intellectual sovereignty in *Tribal Secrets* and *The People and the Word*. In contrast with the position that Native American literary theory must develop out of a primary engagement with the question of personal identity emerging from literary texts (a common starting point in the criticism of the 1980s and early 1990s), Warrior builds his own critical project around self-determination. He is committed to the notion that Indian theoretical knowledge and political praxis in the present can be developed inductively through a deep engagement with the large, heterogeneous, and heretofore largely ignored tradition of indigenous nonfiction. Warrior also acknowledges that his thinking in this project is tactical and that his critical terminology is both evolving and historically situated. Not surprisingly, then, he also expresses great admiration for earlier writers in the Indian intellectual tradition who demonstrate similar resourcefulness and rhetorical adaptability (figures such as William Apess, John Joseph Mathews, and Vine Deloria, Jr.). "Intellectual sovereignty" is a term Warrior uses to emphasize the need for flexible and adaptive thought *that is nevertheless rooted in, and responsible to, Indian communities*. The word "sovereignty" in the phrase is inflected toward a communal/political vision.

In *Tribal Secrets* Warrior observes that the process of exercising intellectual sovereignty involves (1) understanding Indian experience in wider contexts and (2) realizing that the "struggle for sovereignty is not a struggle to be free from the influence of anything outside ourselves, but a process of asserting the power we possess as communities and individuals to make decisions that affect our lives" (124). Intellectual sovereignty as Warrior formulates it, then, is not to be defined as intellectual separatism—a refusal to acknowledge the unquestionable fact that cultures interpenetrate one another or that concepts from different intellectual traditions can interact productively.[1] Neither is intellectual sovereignty intended to be an ethnographically descriptive term, in other words, presenting a fantasy of cultural purity. Rather, it is a politically performative term, intended to generate a productive shift in the kinds of questions and methods employed by Native American studies scholars in order to lead to a more effective form of praxis.[2] As Warrior puts it, "what we need to do as intellectuals, on this reading, is to move toward our own definition of sovereignty that confronts the chaos of contemporary Indian lives" (111).

In his contribution to the volume *American Indian Literary Nationalism* (cowritten with Womack and Warrior), Jace Weaver similarly describes one of the major foci of the nationalist movement as the attempt to criticize Native American literature in a way that "serves the interests of indigenes and their communities, in particular [by supporting] Native nations and their own separate sovereignties" ("Splitting" 15). Such a characterization of the literary nationalist movement foregrounds the tendency on the part of many of its participants to build their projects upon a pragmatic foundation—addressing a perceived set of political needs and interests. As Warrior puts it, "The struggle for self-determination and sovereignty, then, is not an unrealistic attempt to live in the Romantic old days, but seeks to live out a form of humanism in a new situation" (*Tribal* 111). Literary nationalism, in this respect, is part of the larger effort to dialectically indigenize the concept of sovereignty that I traced in part I.

For myself, one of the great appeals of literary nationalist criticism as a component in the effort to constitute a fully formed discourse of sovereignty in the present moment is that its practitioners set the bar for their own (and others') critical work fairly high. It is the responsibility of other scholars and critics, inspired or provoked by the nationalists, to rise to the occasion, then, and to think carefully about how their own work might advance the cause of sovereignty. Here I would suggest that Womack, in particular, has not always been well served by his readers. Both celebrants and critics of Womack's work have displayed a tendency to interact with his thinking in limited ways— pulling a few particularly inspiring or damning quotes out of his books and building arguments around them rather than trying carefully to make sense of the totality and structure of his thought. What I want to offer in this chapter, then, is a more extended discussion of Womack's nationalist project, particularly as it develops in *Red on Red*. In doing so I think we will be able to see that Womack exposes the central challenges that must be confronted in an attempt to craft a fully formed discourse of sovereignty that bridges the realms of law and literature and that takes as its object a model of political subjectivity intended to be efficacious in today's decolonization struggles.

In the introduction to *Red on Red* Womack tells us that his work arose "out of the conviction that Native literature, and the criticism that surrounds it, needs to see more attention devoted to tribally specific concerns" (1). This statement emphasizes that what drives and legitimizes the effort to define and foreground a Creek perspective is not the naive idea that such a perspective is "pure, authoritative, and uncontaminated by European influences," but rather the fact that "non-Indians have historically controlled the discourses that analyze and represent Indian cultures" (1).[3] Essentially, Womack insists that because the very possibility of Indian perspectives has been suppressed, it is necessary and legitimate to assert them—an admittedly blunt form of pragmatic political logic. But what specific form of Indian (and specifically, in Womack's case, Creek tribal) perspective is needed? For surely such a perspective, to the extent that it can be defined, changes over time and varies according to context. To get a sense of how Womack answers that question one must turn to his treatment of the concept of sovereignty, to his articulation of Red Stick literary criticism, and to the methodologies used in *Red on Red*.

In his introduction to the book, Womack outlines a number of goals and assumptions for his project. His initial formulation of the central goal is surprisingly modest—to generate Indian dialogue about "what constitutes meaningful literary efforts" (Womack, *Red* 1).[4] As he further articulates his approach, however, it becomes clear that the stakes are much higher than simply diversifying the critical voices in Native American literary studies. The real prize that Womack is after is a political one, and the central project of *Red on Red* is to develop critical principles to define a tribally specific field of Creek literary study that advances the cause of Creek sovereignty in the modern world. Similar to Warrior, Womack maintains that, despite the deleterious impact of colonialism and the history of Euro-American contact, it is possible to discern a coherent, Native-authored, written intellectual tradition that can yield a literary praxis capable of buttressing tribal assertions of the sovereign right of self-determination in the realm of law. In this regard, one can discern some of the reasons behind his resistance to postmodern and deconstructive criticism, where the attention to textual surfaces can come at the expense of underling political imperatives. Womack argues, "There is the legal reality of tribal sovereignty that trumps postmodern concerns about representation" (5). Womack is loath to invest fully in a battle over the truth claims of postmodern discourse, however, opting instead to assert the superior *utility* of alternative discourses in the present moment. He is, in this respect, a pragmatist at heart.

When one reads *Red on Red* closely, one is struck by the many ways that pragmatic and utilitarian structures and rhetoric crop up. In the introduction, Womack takes care to strike a conciliatory note of inclusiveness as he sets up his project; he notes that his "tribalist" approach in the book does not preempt or cancel out earlier works and critical models. It is essentially an appeal to utility, then, that drives claims like the following: "In this study, I will concentrate on the idea that Native literary aesthetics *must* be politicized and that autonomy, self-determination, and sovereignty serve as *useful* concepts" (Womack, *Red* 11; emphasis added). Womack initiates a departure from earlier critical models (the "trickster theory" of the 1980s, for example), in other words, not because they are wrong, but because they do not do much of the work that needs to be done in the present context, where Native American literature (and by extension the Native America from which it emanates) remains in a largely colonized state. Womack cites several pieces of evidence to support this latter contention, noting that (1) the Modern Language Association has few, if any, ties to Indian communities; (2) Native literature faculty are often hired into ethnic literature positions; (3) there are not enough

Native professors in Native studies jobs, overall; and (4) traditional knowledge and authorities from Native communities lack recognition (7). In making these points about the present colonial situation, he aims to shift the evaluative metric employed in Native American studies toward a focus on what other writers have characterized as more "ethical" criteria.

In making this move, Womack adds his voice to those of numerous others in Native American studies during the last decade or so—such as Devon Mihesuah, Linda Tuhiwai Smith, Lisa Brooks, and Elizabeth Cook-Lynn— making similar appeals.[5] The challenge that Womack puts forward for himself in this context is precisely to find ways to make literary study useful to the Creek *people*, and to do so in a context where particular legal and political concepts, such as sovereignty, occupy a dominant position. He aims to produce, over time, a full-fledged discourse of sovereignty and to transform Native American literary studies as part of the humanities. We can find an echo of this pragmatic emphasis in Robert Warrior's own description of his critical project in *Tribal Secrets*. Warrior notes,

> The project, therefore, is several steps removed from a full-blown American Indian criticism.... Categories such as sovereignty, self-determination, tribal, and process appear without much detailed specification of how I am using them. I have tried to recognize that these words are problematic in spite of continuing to carry a certain political, emotional, and critical force. This is perhaps most true of sovereignty, a term from European theological and political discourse that finally does little to describe the vision and goals of American Indian communities that seek to retain a discrete identity. To simply abandon such terms, though, risks abandoning their abiding force and utility. (*Tribal* xxi)

So how can American Indian literature and literary criticism change their focus to facilitate the emergence of an effective discourse of self-determination? In *Red on Red* Womack offers a tentative, but instructive, example. Modeling, in a Creek context, what he thinks a tribal sovereignty–focused literary discourse might look like, Womack develops the principles of what he terms "Red Stick" criticism. The Red Sticks were a group of traditionalist Creeks, active 1813–1814, who articulated a nativist vision (influenced by the contemporary movement led by Tecumseh) to engender a form of political activism that could counter colonial encroachment. As described by historian Joel Martin, the Red Stick movement involved "the application of tradition in radical new ways with attention given to analysis, criticism, and political reflection" (Womack, *Tribal* 12). In his own characterization of the Red Sticks, Womack sees the importance of emphasizing their innovation on tradition rather than their position in the world created by contact. To be culturally Creek in the Red Stick sense, then, is not to embody some form of pure precontact cultural identity. Rather, the Red Stick model of Creekness involves having a specific connection to Creek history but showing a willingness to innovate within the terms of that traditional history in order to defend the community from outside pressures. In this respect Womack's formulation reveals much closer affinities with Deloria's deployment of the idea of cultural identity as a vehicle for reinterpreting sovereignty than to essentialist formulations of selfhood. In other words, to be Red Stick is not to be a particular kind of Creek individual, but rather to embrace a particular approach to Creek politics.

When Womack characterizes Red Stick consciousness as traditionalist, then, he is also redefining that latter term. In another suggestive nod to the pragmatics underlying his nationalism, Womack characterizes traditionalism as "anything that is *useful* to Indian peoples in retaining their values and worldviews, no matter how much it deviates from what people did one or two hundred years ago" (*Tribal* 42; my emphasis).[6] One can see some critics scratching their heads, of course, at the claim that a person can retain values and worldviews by deviating from past practice. And it is surely true that there must be some limit beyond which one cannot go and still be seen as retaining values and worldviews.[7] But his basic point—that "Creekness" can change, at least in certain ways, and still be Creek—is surely a legitimate one, especially if the central lens through which Creekness is being read is the political collective, the tribe. The continuity of nations, despite perhaps radical changes in the formal structure of government and society, is probably not something one might challenge in the same way one could challenge the continuity of individual identity. And this is a particularly important claim to make in a settler-colonial context.

Womack's choice to continue using the term "traditional" even as he redefines it in this way, though, does remain an index of the delicate, and often problematic, rhetorical balancing act involved in his project.[8] It functions, in a sense, as another type of threshold concept for him, like sovereignty itself. Womack knows he must write about Creekness in a way that allows for considerable cultural change, but he must also do so in a manner that (1) allows his Creek (and non-Creek) readers to imagine continuity as the dominant force in the life of the community and (2) allows those individual Creek readers to identify with a Red Stick political model of Creek subjectivity that can advance sovereignty. Womack is engaged in a project related to the imagined community of popular sovereignty, in other words, "inventing the people" and endeavoring to produce a vox populi along the lines imagined by critics such as Benedict Anderson. Theorizing this process while actually engaging in it is a real challenge, however. As I will suggest shortly, one of the keys to rising to that challenge is to ensure that one's tribal nationalist critical discourse carefully maintains its focus on political subjectivity while also building itself around engagement with specific technai of sovereignty (treaties, constitutions, common law, etc.).

To better appreciate the degree of critical innovation involved in realizing this kind of nationalist project, however, we need to look a bit more deeply into how Womack translates his powerful call for a literary discourse of sovereignty, rooted in the needs of Creek people, into a form a practical criticism. As he moves in the early chapters of the book to more fully define the principles of Red Stick literary criticism, Womack offers a brief account of the history of the Creek nation, which is clearly intended to suggest that significant aspects of what some would call precontact lifeways never disappeared in the face of external pressure. Not surprisingly, of course, he rejects the term "precontact" in favor of "traditional Creek life," seeing the former as too strongly connoting essentialist binaries, and the latter being more fluid and useful. Womack begins his history with a decolonizing gesture, positioning the origin/migration story of the Creeks, rooted in oral culture, as integral to the nation's political history. From the origin story (and other historical narratives, both oral and written), Womack culls several qualities that he sees as quintessentially Creek. These include (1) a spirit of cultural adaptability; (2) an ability to incorporate other groups into the framework of an existing nation; and (3) a careful balance between an ethos of disputation and direct conflict and one of reconciliation, indirection, and peace.

So why isn't this essentialist, a reader might wonder? The best answer to this would be to note that *if* Womack is claiming that Creek character on an individual level is *always* reflective of these qualities, we might indeed have a problem. But as Womack is primarily focused instead on a general ideological structure, or a set of political values or principles, revealed in collective embodiments of Creek culture (its political institutions, for example), we are on safer ground. Womack is offering up for consent a vision of the nomos of Creek society. What he is doing, then, is not so different from John Mohawk's definition of the Haudenosaunee "Real People" in the context of the structures of the Longhouse religion and Iroquois political order. Indeed, in his first chapter Womack draws particular attention to the political structure of Creek towns and town councils, with their traditional divisions into "red" and "white" (the military and peace functions, respectively). He goes on to emphasize the historical Red Sticks' ability to take this red/white structure and employ it in reinterpreting narratives from the oral tradition to give them contemporary political resonance. From these claims, then, emerges Womack's general model of a Red Stick criticism, the application of which is to underpin his project of literary nationalism.

Red Stick criticism, Womack suggests, is built around three intertwined assumptions: (1) that a coherent, collective, Creek vox populi can be articulated;

(2) that Creek acts of resistance to colonialism and assimilation, focalized around an image of Creek peoplehood, can be successful; and (3) that working from within this political perspective is a legitimate way of examining literature. These propositions are mutually constitutive, I would suggest, and they represent another example of how Womack's project is best understood in pragmatic terms. Red Stick criticism looks to abstract from Creek literature a political discourse that can be accepted as legitimately expressing a Creek nomos, through a voice of the people, capable of mobilizing the political action. What Womack is getting at, then, is not entirely different from a political scientist pointing out how the discourse of a modern political party represents an aggregate worldview with which its constituent members (despite their individual differences) can identify, and then works to channel the energy of that membership toward specific goals and actions. To make this claim is not to say that there is no variation at the level of individual consciousness or experience, which would be an essentialist position. Rather, it is to acknowledge that individual members of political communities, to the extent that they experience themselves as part of a collective entity—the Creek nation in this case—do so by identifying with some model of political subjectivity that they feel sufficiently expresses their worldview, desires, and aspirations.

Following this line of thinking, Womack further elaborates on the processes of Red Stick criticism. He notes that the Creek nationalist critic/reader would examine Creek literature (oral and written) in order to draw attention to political ideals (such as the willingness to innovate within tradition by finding new connections between the form and content of traditional oral narratives and current politics) and to identify and mobilize the symbols and mechanisms that allow the individual subject to identify with a collective polity. Reanimating the culturally pervasive symbolism and underlying ideals of the red/white division, with its balance between conciliation and resistance, would seem to serve both functions. At this stage, then, we are able to discern more clearly precisely *how* it is that Womack feels Native literary aesthetics must be politicized in a Creek context. One of the key challenges to realizing this kind of political discourse is establishing symbolic systems through which individual members of the society can identify with the collective model of political subjectivity. I have suggested elsewhere some of the ways that print culture can play a central role in that; Costo's use of "Wassaja" in the context of the movement toward self-determination would be one representative example of this. Womack's most direct version of this, which I will take up shortly, is his ventriloquization of Alexander Posey's dialect letters and characters from *The Fus Fixico Letters*. This recognition that literature is a particularly useful space through which to effect the forms of identification needed in the political sphere is one that Womack shares with the other writers I am considering in this study. In this respect—his recognition that tribal *literatures* must participate in the struggle for sovereignty if that struggle is to have a chance of succeeding in the long run—most clearly indexes the change he is helping to drive in Native American literary studies.

At this stage, though, we have reached the point where we should look more closely at how Womack is imagining the legal side of sovereignty discourse. It is when we do this, I would argue, that we can begin to identify some of the limitations of his initial formulations of his project in *Red on Red* (to discern its "problematic," in other words).[9] Womack's deployment of the concept of sovereignty in his early work is loose and fluid, to say the least. He opens *Red on Red* by claiming, "Native literature, and Native literary criticism, written by Native authors, is part of sovereignty" (14). A general definition of sovereignty as simply the right and autonomous power of (separate) self-determination looms over this sentence. Quickly, though, we introduce another term with the potential to complicate the picture: nation. "A key component of nationhood," Womack maintains, "is a people's idea of themselves, their imaginings of who they are" (14). The implication here is that, if the sovereign right/power of separate self-determination is advanced by the literature and literary criticism in and through which a people imagines itself, that process of imagining must culminate in a real, lived experience of some form of *nationhood* to be fully successful.

What precise form of nationhood does Womack have in mind here, though, and what specific mechanisms or structures of national self-assertion does he favor? Considering the subtitle of *Red on Red*—which invokes the idea of separatism—one might reasonably assume that the form of nationhood to which Womack refers would be the one most commonly tied to the modern European definition of sovereignty—the autonomous nation-state. Confirming this impression, he makes a move common to treaty-centered nationalist discourse, using the term sovereignty, again, to read backward beyond the history of European contact in order to assert the prior existence of a Creek polity that looks, as he presents it, a lot like a modern state. Womack tells us, "Sovereignty is inherent as an intellectual idea in Native cultures, a political practice, and a theme of oral traditions; and the concept, as well as the practice, predates European contact" (*Red* 51). His specific examples of this prior Creek sovereignty stress the existence of a federal-style representative political structure, rooted in Creek towns (*talwa*). This includes mechanisms of local representation centered in the towns, extensions of those mechanisms into regular regional/national assemblies, and a sense of communal tradition and distinctiveness running through the entire structure. It should probably be clear, too, how Red Stick criticism is related to this vision of national sovereignty. Womack's assertion that the "concept of ancestral memory is related to nationalism in that sovereignty is an intersection of the political, imaginary, and literary" should remind us, again, that the central goal of Red Stick criticism is to yoke the literary/imaginary to the political (26).

If one initially has a sense that Womack's Creek discourse of sovereignty might be centered on the goal of asserting a separate, federated nation-state, though, that sense of clarity becomes somewhat unsettled as he continues to use the concept in *Red on Red*. He notes later, "Sovereignty, it seems to me, like the oral tradition, is an ongoing dynamic process, rather than a fixed creed, and evolves according to the changing needs of the nation" (Womack, *Red* 59). This is somewhat awkwardly stated, but the main thrust here is to take us back to the general definition of sovereignty as the right/power of self-determination and to suggest a desire to avoid committing to a particular Western political structure or praxis toward or through which that power is to be expressed. On the one hand, this is a perfectly reasonable move to make, to avoid making problematic transhistorical claims about what Creek nationhood has and will look like in perpetuity. At the same time, though, one is confronted with the very problem of utility Womack raised earlier in the book. For if a nationalist literary criticism is to help advance the cause of sovereignty in the present moment, surely it needs to commit to some specific political forms and strategies in doing so—to specific technai of sovereignty. In addition, it probably also needs to directly and fully tackle the important debate over how, precisely, to indigenize the concept of sovereignty in deploying it.

The internal struggle over these fundamental problems, it seems to me, is one of the defining elements of the contemporary discourse of sovereignty, and the diverse approaches to resolving it is one of the primary factors that differentiate thinkers in this study. Elizabeth Cook-Lynn commits herself wholeheartedly to the treaty as a mechanism for the assertion of separate nationhood. She also advocates for a reinterpretation of the nation-state structure along traditional kinship lines—an interpretation that indigenizes sovereignty, in this respect. Gerald Vizenor immerses himself in the realm of constitutional law and focuses his energies on problems of recognition surrounding that form of self-governance. In *Red on Red* Womack is willing to embrace a basic definition of sovereignty, but he hesitates to commit to a specific techne through which to pursue it. In other words, Womack's praxis is murky at this stage. As such, we find a passage like this on the literary origin of sovereignty:

> The concept of nationhood itself is an intermingling of politics, imagination, and spirituality. Nationhood encompasses ongoing treaty relationships with

the U.S. government. Nationhood has to do with federal Indian law, and the tribes' testing of the sovereignty waters through new economic developments and other practices. Nationhood is affected by the imagination in the way that citizens of tribal nations perceive their cultural and political identity. Nationhood recognizes spiritual practices, since culture is part of what gives people an understanding of their uniqueness, their difference, from other nations of people. Literature places a vital role in this, since it is part of what constitutes the idea of nationhood; people formulate a notion of themselves as an imagined community through stories. (Womack 60)

This is a wonderfully evocative pastiche that suggests a great deal about the diverse range of understandings of sovereignty at play in the present moment (containing in it elements of the legal sovereignty, political sovereignty, cultural sovereignty, and self-determination strains). But it is easy to notice here Womack's resistance to articulating a specific vision of how sovereignty and nation are to work as mutually constitutive ideas. Underlying the passage, of course, is a tacit acknowledgment that the actual legal position of tribal peoples in the United States is a highly equivocal one. That fact that nationhood "encompasses" (an admittedly odd term here) treaty relationships, but also "has to do" with federal law, testifies to the peculiar legal status of "domestic dependent nationhood" under which American Indians live. But Womack tells us little about his own views on how best to approach this equivocal situation, and more specifically, how literary study might inform a larger struggle to address it. As such, there is an underlying limitation to the following claim: "Extending the discussion of sovereignty beyond the legal realm to include the literary realm opens up the oral tradition to be read contemporarily by tribal nations so that definitions of sovereignty, which come from the oral tradition, might be used as a model for building nations in a way that revises, modifies, or rejects, rather than accepts as a model, the European and American nation" (Womack, *Red* 60). To generate a fully formed discourse of sovereignty that connects the legal with the literary requires more clarity in addressing the nature and contours of that legal realm and in theorizing the kind of nation one aspires to build. While doing so should not necessitate boxing oneself in by adopting static, inflexible models of Creek nationhood, there is a clear need to incorporate *some* specific legal models into the literary realm for a project of literary nationalism to have the kind of utility that Womack desires. And again, it is Womack himself who has placed the bar at this level, making a compelling case that the literary critical work being done in Native American studies needs to find a way to bridge the divide between literary production and the real-world problems of tribal communities. It needs to bring law and literature together.

The problematics within *Red on Red* that create these frictions have been generative ones for Womack, of course. In his later work he begins to more directly address the value of specificity in models of sovereignty and the need to commit to particular technai. In his bibliographic essay in *Reasoning Together*, for example, Womack draws attention to a range of legislative achievements since the 1970s, creating new opportunities for self-determination. In what appears to be a nod toward the value of pursuing strategies of legal sovereignty, he comments on a range of statutory instruments (the American Indian Religious Freedom Act, the Indian Child Welfare Act, the Indians Tribal Government Tax Status Act, and the Native American Graves Protection and Repatriation Act) that have proven useful to tribal governments (Womack, *Reasoning* 5–6). Amplifying this partial endorsement of strategies of legal sovereignty, in a subsequent discussion of Cook-Lynn he notes that "sovereignty, for all its problems and contradictions, is a reality in Indian country, *embedded in the U.S. Constitution and two centuries worth of federal Indian law. In short, it is what Native people have to work with*" (74; emphasis added). And yet, we see lingering hesitation toward committing wholeheartedly to specific strategies and definitions in Womack's later work. In *Art as Performance* his focus turns again, this time away from engagement with statutes and toward more conventionally nationalist formulations: "in its most literal terms, sovereignty has to do with government-to-government relationships between tribes and the United States, *based on treaties*" (86; emphasis added). In making this pivot, Womack talks of the need to "reimagine sovereignty apart from funding and federal programs" (89) and stresses his agreement with Warrior's view that "sovereignties [plural] must be viewed as open-ended processes rather than static definitions" (86). This is, of course, a position very much in line with the one taken in the present study. All I would point out here, then, is that in his criticism Womack seems reluctant to *sustain* his focus on specific strands of sovereignty, contenting himself, rather, with laying out the general terrain and looking forward (and to others) for subsequent innovation. He ends *Art as Performance* with the comment that he "would like to see us attempt representations of sovereignty that do not exist yet, dreams of nationhood that move toward inclusion and compassion, and a vision of community that involves an expansion of human rights" (332). As I will suggest at the end of this chapter, it is probably in his fiction (rather than his criticism) that he himself comes closest to such an achievement.

At this point in the discussion, though, I want to turn to the second problematic that registers in *Red on Red*, one that reflects another, broader, debate that has begun to emerge in Native American literary studies. Womack's project (along with the projects of many of his contemporaries) is generally animated by the problem of theorizing the relationship between the realms of literature and the real world. An interesting manifestation of this debate appeared in the wake of David Treuer's publication of *Native American Fiction*, a text that stirred up a considerable amount of controversy for what many readers saw as its unnecessary attacks on the cultural authenticity of writers such as Louise Erdrich and for its advocacy of a rigid form of cultural traditionalism. Particularly telling about the Treuer kerfuffle are both the lack of agreement on the part of the participants regarding what *Native American Fiction* was actually arguing and the fact that this literary debate erupted into a broader political sphere. A series of editorial articles and letters appearing in the pages of *Indian Country Today* in August of 2007 is revealing in this context. Matthew Fletcher (Odawa), director of the Indigenous Law and Policy Center at Michigan State University, strongly criticized Treuer's book in an August 8, 2007, op-ed column titled, " 'Native American Fiction' Tough on Indian Culture." Fletcher positions Treuer as a strict traditionalist, paraphrasing the latter's main argument to be essentially that there can be no "Native American fiction" because Native Americans traditionally didn't write fiction. Fletcher reads Treuer as arguing that even good writing by American Indian authors is, at best, a kind of simulacrum—able only to invoke Indian culture as a memory. And by extension, Fletcher argues, Treuer is denying the very ongoing existence of Indian culture in a changing world. He illustrates what he sees as the danger of Treuer's position through a legal analogy, referencing the efforts by many modern tribal governments and courts to restore tribal customary law as an important piece of their legal infrastructure. This process of recovery and application is not easy, Fletcher notes, but the courts continue to press onward in the attempt, for they recognize that "Indian culture must change or it will die—just like all other nations' laws and culture." In contrast, "Treuer's Indian culture is a culture that is monolithic and unchanging" (Fletcher, " 'Native' " A3). Thus, even if Treuer's intended purpose were to prevent writers like Sherman Alexie and Louise Erdrich from claiming authenticity, Fletcher sees him as simply reserving for himself the right to decide who may contribute to the culture, and doing so in a way too narrow to allow the culture to survive.

Responding to Fletcher's argument in a letter to the editor printed on August 15, Treuer notes quite simply that he has been misunderstood. He maintains that his book isn't about what constitutes Indian cultures or the identities of specific Indian writers at all. He is willing to concede that Indian culture is different today from what it was one hundred years ago, but he denies that his primary concern is to argue that this makes today's Indians inauthentic. Instead, Treuer insists that his focus is on *what readers think a work of fiction can tell us*, on the kinds of questions and assumptions readers bring to bear when approaching an American Indian novel. "We are taught and tempted to read Indian novels as cultural repositories," he claims, "providing Indian lore and 'worldviews' and replicating, in writing, oral culture. The point of my essays is that novels don't tell us about culture as much as they map our dreams about culture" ("Treuer" A2). There is a noticeable logical flaw in this position, of course, as it is not at all clear why one should not consider an act of novelistic storytelling as a part of culture (unless one is limiting authentic acts of Indian storytelling to precontact orality). Moments like this, then, reveal why many readers suspect Treuer of engaging, essentially, in an act of what Scott Lyons in *X-Marks* calls "cultural policing." At the same time, though, Treuer *is* raising an important point, drawing our attention to a question that much Native American literary criticism has probably not addressed adequately (and which is vitally important for a sovereignty-centered literature and criticism): How do we understand the relationship between the fictional world presented in a work of art and the real world of lived experience? What Treuer is particularly worried about (probably with some justification) is that many readers of Indian literature approach the material with a naive sense of its mimetic accuracy. Indeed, this fear is what stands behind his argument that "novels are imbedded in the culture(s) of literature more so than the cultures (evolving, changing, shared, contested) that we live" (A2).

I do not wish to detour too extensively here into what Scott Lyons calls, in his own *Indian Country Today* editorial of August 15, the "Battle of the Bookworms." Nevertheless, it seems to me that the outlines of the debate I have just traced are suggestive in important ways of a critical problem that particularly troubles Womack. Treuer is certainly right in asserting the need for recognition on the part of literary critics that literature has some form of autonomy; literary works are both part of, and connected to, larger cultural contexts, to be sure, but it is important for us to think carefully about how we understand that connection. Treuer is probably also correct in noting that many readers (even highly trained professional critics) approach characters in many works of American Indian fiction as if there were examples of what real Indians are like, that they see fictional characters, in other words, as representative examples of individual identity. And it is surely instructive to notice in this context that, while he is rightly sniffing out some of Treuer's own traditionalist rigidity, Fletcher's provocative analogy between the literary and the legal realm also tends to blur the distinctions between the two. If law and literature *are* related—a claim on which Womack's literary nationalist project hangs—then what the Treuer-generated debate highlights is that the nature of that relation has not been thought about as deeply as it needs to be in a Native American studies context.

One of the insights developed in the interdisciplinary subfield of law and literature, of course, is that there are multiple ways in which the relationship between those two spheres can manifest itself. We may, of course, be dealing with a *mimetic* relationship, where a literary representation of the world imitates that world in a way that speaks relatively directly to some aspect of the political struggle for sovereignty. Native American studies needs its *Uncle Tom's Cabin*s, too, though even here it is important to attend to Treuer's point that literary characters are fictional constructs, operating in relatively autonomous ways. But there will likely be even more cases in which the relationship is more subtle or mediated. It may be that a literary work encodes or disseminates a structure of thought and a nomos that are related to political struggles for sovereignty. This was one of the central themes of my earlier book, *Sovereign Selves*, which looked at the rhetorical strategies of Indian autobiography in engaging with specific legal models of subjectivity. It may also be that the key point of connection between a literary work and the legal-political realm relates to hermeneutic processes—the particular techniques of reading and interpretation that emerge from our encounters with texts and the ways in which those encounters in literary and legal contexts can be mutually informing. And indeed, the relation in question may be a combination of all of these elements (and others I have not mentioned or considered).

If we recognize the relatively undefined nature of the relation between law and literature to be another central issue confronting Native literary nationalism, though, we are able to read the works of key thinkers like Womack and Robert Warrior more insightfully, and we are better positioned to work *with them* to move the critical discourse forward in the ways that they hope, rather than engaging in a regressive discussion that pulls all of us back into the mire of authenticity debates that often dominated the criticism of the 1980s and early 1990s. Let us first consider Warrior's approaches to the problem, which it seems to me, have been threefold. Warrior's focus on nonfiction writing in his efforts to develop critical genealogies for Native American studies seems at least in part intended to allow him to avoid some of the problems of naive mimetic reading. His approach here is not devoid of problems, however, as he tends to understate the literariness of nonfiction writing and to overstate the seamlessness of the relationship between the experience of authors and the content of texts.[10] In *The People and the Word* Warrior makes the questionable argument that nonfiction has typically allowed Native authors to speak more directly to the situation and conditions of Native people than fiction and poetry have (xx–xxi). His supporting example is a hypothetical claim that Taiaiake Alfred's call for political reform would not register in a fictional setting, poem, or standard autobiography. I find this to be unpersuasive, and indeed I think some of Warrior's own subsequent readings in his book successfully demonstrate that fictional texts are quite capable of conveying complex political ideas. A novel, a poem, or an autobiography is also a form of thinking, or if one prefers, we might describe these kinds of texts as alternate forms through which thinking can occur. The mere fact of generic difference from, say, the nonfiction essay does not preclude the possibility of critical consciousness flowing through a text. I would also note that there has been a copious amount of scholarship on autobiographical narrative during the last fifty years that demonstrates the value of approaching such texts not simply as transparent, positivist documents of objective fact, but as fictional constructions of selfhood.[11] Warrior's readings of William Apess's autobiographies in *Tribal Secrets* only partially register the impact of that scholarly work.

Warrior's second, related, attempt to resolve the problem of connecting text and the real has centered on his development of the concept of experience as a critical tool. As with many of the key terms he employs (including sovereignty), Warrior never gives his own readers a clear definition of the meaning of experience, but we can make some reasonable inferences by looking at his specific usage of the word. At the end of *Tribal Secrets*, when he first introduces the term, he does so as a way of discussing how many critics, in his view, misread the significance of the work of Vine Deloria. Earlier in the book Warrior had argued that while Deloria's arguments in *God Is Red* tend to reduce both Christianity and American Indian traditions to monoliths, "his most important analyses ... [are] in the fundamental questions that lurk, in his estimation, behind traditional theological questions" (*Tribal* 71). The great value of Deloria's work, then, is in its polemical force and in its ability to cut through reified structures of thinking to urge a reorientation of inquiry. At the end of *Tribal Secrets* Warrior amplifies this point through the concept of experience, noting that Deloria's abiding criticism of modern Christianity is its concern for interpreting experience rather than having an experience (104). According to Warrior, Deloria counters this Christian ideology through a counterexample of Indian "traditional life," where people don't seek to "escape from the influence of the lands on which they lived" through concepts like individuality or eschatology, but rather remained in the world of experience (105). In this usage, then, experience emerges as a term that refers either to contact with the real, unmediated through critical abstraction—something, at the extreme limit, akin to mysticism—or to the ability to break through externally imposed ideological structures or false-consciousness by means of knowledge that emerges organically and inductively from within a community—something synonymous with intellectual sovereignty.

In *The People and the Word* it seems to me that Warrior proposes to read Native nonfiction in a way that is connected with both of these rather distinct ways of comprehending experience. He is interested both in looking for examples and models of the experiential ability to connect to the real in the works of Native writers (he finds them in Apess, Clyde Warrior, and N. Scott

Momaday) and also in seeking to cultivate his *own* experience of intellectual sovereignty through his encounters with those texts. As Warrior puts it, "Reading experience in texts . . . is not an endpoint but a point of departure for readers to pursue further understanding of [our] historical . . . obligations" (*People* xxvi). Yet Warrior clearly senses some of the problems that arise through his use of the concept in these ways. While he insists on the utility of experience as a category in relation to the production of criticism, he also wonders whether it is possible to use the concept without a problematic embrace of identity politics. In a somewhat contradictory moment he professes general agreement with the classic essay by Joan W. Scott, "Experience."[12] In that piece Scott actually cautions against reliance on experience as a form of uncontestable evidence of historical truth. Instead she suggests focusing on processes of identity production and the "discursive nature of experience and on the politics of its construction" (Warrior xxiii). This is, of course, a fairly standard post-structuralist position, rooted in the work of Michel Foucault and a range of Marxist and feminist thinkers. But Warrior does not want to commit himself to such a position, instead sidestepping post-structuralism and simply reasserting the concept of experience.[13] "Insisting on using a critical notion of experience in developing Native criticism," he writes, "I am claiming the importance of working through the panoply of issues, some tasty, some not, that make up the complexity of Native texts. Experience, mediated in representations of it through language, is the material manifestation of the connection between Native texts and Native lives" (xxvi). Here again, it seems that the crucial issue being attacked through the concept of experience is the problem of theorizing the link between the text and the real. Warrior's formulations in this case are not fully clear, however. On the one hand, we are told that we can access experience only through imitations of it in language (a phenomenological position). On the other hand, we are told that experience itself is a material link between text and life (which would mean that language and texts are somehow being differentiated in an unexplained manner). And earlier, we should remember, Warrior acknowledged (through Scott) the need to be wary of treating experience as having an a priori existence outside of discourses that construct it. It is rather difficult to reconcile these positions into a coherent critical project. In the end, then, what we see is that experience functions in Warrior's own criticism not so much as a clarifying concept but as an index of a range of unresolved problems.

If experience proves unsatisfactory as a tool for resolving the problem of the connection between the text and the real, Warrior's work does offer a third, more promising, potential solution. This involves his discussion of the role of the reader, a discussion that in my view sees him attempting something that Womack (as well as Elizabeth Cook-Lynn and Gerald Vizenor) will take up in a more sustained way—an effort to translate the structures of orality into a written context to redirect the processes of reading and interpretation. In the preface to *The People and the Word* Warrior articulates his goals for the book by noting, "The idea of reading is crucial here. Much of what has promoted the direction I have taken in my critical practice regarding Native texts is a conviction that the act of reading and what the act reveals are crucial to the enterprise of Native intellectual development" (xiv). The subsequent discussion of the role of the reader in the critical process will sound familiar to students of Roland Barthes and of reader-response criticism, though there are some important nuanced differences. "Reading," continues Warrior, "as I use the term, moves beyond mining information from a text or merely extrapolating pertinent facts from the biography of an author. It is, in contrast, a process that highlights the production of meaning through the critical interaction that occurs between a text as a writer has written it and a text as readers read it" (xiv). In a sense, I suppose, we can see this reader-centered approach to the concept of textual meaning making as a usefully corrective complement to the concept of experience. When Warrior writes of reading experience in texts, then, we might take him to be saying that a Native reader's encounter with texts (especially Native-authored texts) is capable of yielding instances of intellectual sovereignty.

One wishes Warrior had more to say on that intersection. What is clear, however, is that he sees a reader-centered critical practice as a useful mechanism to ensure that literature does relate in significant ways to the real. And this is, indeed, a central element of the discourse of sovereignty, which I will trace in the next two chapters. In a sense, the reader-response solution reformulates the problem of what a text *means*, in terms of its mimetic relationship to the real, in favor of a consideration of what a text *does*, performatively, to help engender a critical praxis. Warrior makes a point of agreeing with critic Frederick Luis Aldama's position that "literature and the reading of it are not self-contained political actions" (*People* xxiv). Accordingly, as Aldama would put it, a "text-act" doesn't equal "being." The link between a literary work and being, then, appears in the act of interpretation (leading to action). This is what gives political significance to texts. Warrior argues in turn that "literary texts are, or it may be better to say, can be, part of larger processes of social and political engagement, and they are processes that Native people experience. Something similar is true of what has come to be known as the oral tradition" (xxix).

The invocation of the oral tradition here might seem, at first, to come out of left field, but it strikes me as an extremely interesting, suggestive hermeneutic gesture. As with Womack, there are significant parallels between Warrior's adaptation of a reader-response approach to meaning making and an understanding of the relationship between text and interpretation in an oral context. Warrior, it seems to me, is trying to build on these parallels without fully declaring his intentions in doing so and perhaps without fully working out the implications. In his chapter on William Apess in *The People and the Word* ("Eulogy on William Apess"), for example, he notes that his intention is not to produce a conventional exegetical interpretation of Apess's writings. Rather, Warrior responds to Apess's life (and writings) in a manner intended to *supplement* them to produce useful political results in the present moment. "My interest here is not so much in expositing Apess's text," Warrior tells us, "as in arguing for a particular reading of Apess and his contribution to Native intellectual history" (2). Warrior's central goal is to show how Apess's life and career speak to a contemporary Native intellectual agenda. He argues that "Apess's experientially based work provides a model for a more historically focused approach to Native life than one emphasizing static notions of culture or strict attention to texts absent the material realities, available through discourse on experience, that literature reflects" (3). The goal of reading Apess, in short, is not primarily to focus on ferreting out new nuances in his texts, but rather to draw inspiration from Apess for contemporary praxis. If Apess's life/work is "the Word," then Warrior's reading is the part of the homily that applies it. "I want to relate Apess's experiences to other Natives who spent part of their careers in New York, including myself," Warrior notes. "By doing so, we can look for synchronicity between Apess and later writers, and thus learn more about what writers like Apess, who left so little in the way of detailed archives, might have done" (6).

In many respects what Warrior is doing in reading Apess in this way is acting as if Apess's life and work is an open-ended "text"—in the sense that Dennis Tedlock uses the term in his wonderful essays on Zuni oral culture—that not only allows but requires supplementation by subsequent tellers in order to activate and apply it. What is missing in Warrior's discussion, perhaps, is a simply a sense of balance. There is actually not very much attention to the generative written text (what Apess actually wrote), in proportion to his established biography and to what Warrior admits is speculative discussion about how Apess's life *might* have ended, how that end *might* be seen to resemble Clyde Warrior's, and how those resemblances (Warrior calls this "synchronicity") offer a model of "how an experientially aware intellectual praxis leads us to critical issues" (*People* 47). In a sense, then, what we as readers encounter in our own reading of *The People and the Word* is a critic who is pushing toward the development of some new kind of form for critical inquiry and interpretive practice (what I will refer to in the next chapter as reading in the oral tradition). Reading Warrior (and Womack for that matter) suggests that a sovereignty-centered literary criticism will likely need to invent for itself new hermeneutic structures and a new "poetics." If this criticism won't necessarily look like conventional text-based literary criticism, it will need to be better contextulized and legitimized in the academy in new ways in order to move the field of Native American studies forward in its decolonizing efforts. Womack's recent work in *Art as Performance* represents a continuation of his own efforts in this direction, and Warrior's own example also highlights how the pragmatic undercurrents of literary nationalism are driving the field in new directions, even if that process of change and critical evolution is an ongoing one.

At this stage, then, as a way of further contextualizing my own efforts to contribute to that conversation and process of development, I would like to turn back to Womack and offer an examination of his own efforts to resolve the crucial problematic of the literary text and the real in *Red on Red*. This critical problematic emerges alongside the text's construction of the principles around which a Creek nationalist literary canon might be assembled. One place where we see this first manifest itself is in Womack's efforts (related in some ways to Warrior's) to articulate and justify a shift in the focus of literary study away from exegetical questions of what a literary text *means* toward performative questions of what a literary text *does*. If Womack doesn't *fully* manage to achieve this, his clear understanding of the problem and his often-innovative critical praxis puts him ahead of many of his contemporaries and critics. Womack's second and third chapters on the Creek oral tradition, which he admits to viewing as flawed, are extremely helpful in this respect. In chapter 2 ("Reading the Oral Tradition for Nationalist Themes: Beyond Ethnography") he seems to set out at first with the goal of combing the written archival record of Creek oral culture in order to cull from it evidence of the "inherent sovereignty" of the Creek people, dating back to antiquity. He also aims to demonstrate that for Creeks "literary acts, particularly metaphor, were/are an important part of Creek political society" (Womack, *Red* 53). As a bridge between these two issues, Womack is interested in finding in the oral tradition traces of the political structures of the talwa (towns) and broader nation, as well as examples of how contemporary Creeks have managed, in a Red Stick spirit, to reapply that oral tradition in order to cope with new realities. For example, he cites written transcriptions of a telling of the Creek origin story by Philip Deere as evidence of a storyteller able to "provide a political gloss to the story of Creek migration" (55). In doing so he aims to recover a sense of how the meanings of stories from the oral tradition are largely found in our understanding of how those tales are applied and performed in new and varying contexts, a process that Womack calls "unfixing the narrative." This becomes a central reading strategy for the nationalist critic, then, one that aims to counter the tendency of many non-Indian readers and compilers to depoliticize traditional narrative.[14] This, of course, is another part of the strong appeal of an emphasis on oral foundations for a nationalist literary critic. A well-executed written transcription of an oral performance solves the critical problem of defining how a text interacts with its broader culture—how the literary and the real intersect. Indeed, much of the best recent non-Native scholarship on traditional oral culture (I'm thinking of the work of Dennis Tedlock, Julie Cruikshank, and Keith Basso) beautifully illuminates what Womack characterizes as the political dimensions of oral materials that can be simultaneously rooted in tradition and also remain flexible and applicable to changing realities.

Throughout *Red on Red* Womack's inclusion of his Alexander Posey–inspired Jim Chibbo/Hotgun letters represent his own attempt to illustrate how this process can serve as a mode of critical thinking and practice. Those pieces of the text are among some of its most effective moments. In his contribution to *American Indian Literary Nationalism* Womack gives us a tantalizing clue regarding the function of the dialect letters in *Red on Red*. He notes that while he realizes that he is read by many, "I do not write for everyone. I write for Muskogee Creek People" ("Integrity" 143). A key part of what he means by this, it seems clear to me, is that his own writing is an attempt to cultivate a Creek vox populi. For Womack, the act of imagining a Creek audience is both a vehicle for testing whether he is living up to the pragmatic imperative of nationalist criticism (serving his community in meaningful ways) and part of a process of actually inventing that audience as a people (in the manner in which that process was discussed in part 1). Womack concedes that his use of the dialect letters and the characters of Jim and Hotgun "are an attempt to imagine how a Muskogee Creek audience might respond to the book *Red on Red*." Further, he notes, doing so is a kind of ethical test for himself, forcing him to "confront questions of how Creeks might react to the way they are depicted in *Red on Red*" (149). (Womack is one of the few writers I have encountered who might be said to have self-consciously interpellated himself.) Beyond this, Womack's imaginative development of these literary symbolizations of Creek readers and political actors (which is what Jim and Hotgun are) represents something analogous to Rupert Costo's deployment of "Wassaja." Womack creates and offers up a model of Creek political subjectivity and a voice of the Creek people for consent, and in doing so he reveals that one of his goals as a critic is to actively constitute not just an audience for his books, but a polity.

Posey's letters, we should recall, were not simply propaganda in support of his own specific political views. Posey's support of single-statehood for Oklahoma (as opposed to the creation of separate Indian and non-Indian states), and of allotment, was not shared by many contemporary members of the Creek nation. Most specifically, the traditionalist Snake faction led by Chitto Harjo vigorously opposed both positions, insisting instead on a battle for Creek autonomy based on prior treaty relationships. The historical Hotgun, who was ventriloquized by Posey in the letters, was one of these traditionalists. It is suggestive, in this respect, that Womack elects to reinvent Hotgun as the present-day addressee of his epistolary fictions. Womack's letters are all addressed to Hotgun by Jim Chibbo; the central characters in them are Stijaati Thlaako, Big Man, and Rabbit, with the occasional mention of his own academic alter ego, Chebon. The link to Posey through Hotgun (as an embodiment of the treaty faction) is probably the closest that Womack comes in *Red on Red* to identifying himself with a specific legal techne of sovereignty. But his more immediate goal here is to try to imagine and symbolize an image of Creekness that is diverse and adaptive, in line with his pragmatic comments about traditionalism cited earlier. We should recall in this context that the principle characters in Posey's letters (men like Hotgun) were the kind of rigid traditionalists whose views on the appropriate legal strategy in the early 1900s were directly opposed to his. Part of Posey's project in the letters, though, was to incorporate a range of Creek viewpoints into an imaginative symbolization of the polity and to urge that polity toward a pragmatic and adaptive approach to present-day political realities. Posey tried to use humor, then, as a way of sidestepping political division to reconstitute Creek peoplehood in an extremely divisive time. Whether or not we see his literary project in the *Fus Fixico Letters* as having been fully successful in this regard, Womack clearly identifies with the effort. He also shares with Posey the insight that a forward-looking discourse of sovereignty will require a blend of adaptation and traditionalism as well as a Creek literature that finds a way to directly support Creek political life.

Womack's effort to advance the preceding goals involves, in part, employing Jim and the modernized Hotgun as vehicles for unfixing his own critical discourse. This function of the letters is implicit through the entirety of the book, but it becomes quite explicit in the letter appearing on pages 103 through 105, concluding the section of *Red on Red* that deals exclusively with the oral tradition. In this letter Jim Chibbo writes to Hotgun and tells him a story about Stijaati Thlaako's visit to an Oklahoma school to "talk about old-timey Creek culture to the kids so they wouldn't forget their ways" (Womack, *Red* 103). During the visit a distraction created by a cockroach leads to Stijaati's ironic re-creation of "Turtle Sings Himself Back Together," the traditional narrative that serves as the centerpiece of Womack's preceding chapter, "In the Storyway." Reflecting on this unexpected conjuncture of "old-timey" culture and present-day experience later with his friends, Stijaati notes that the Indian students' enthusiastic reaction to his visit (and his unsuccessful efforts to crush the roach) was evidence of their efforts in "mapping out their own nation" (104). Stijaati's interpretive commentary on his own experience in effect reallegorizes the traditional story of turtle healing his broken shell through song into a reflection on the endurance (and transformation) of Creek government across the history of Creek-American contact (a central theme of Womack's nationalist discourse). "You can't understand Creek storytelling or Creek language or Creek customs without knowing something about Creek government," Stijaati notes, "and these kids are gonna be the ones making up the new stories and running the next government" (105). Their ability to do so, the text implies, is a central element of the literary facet of their engagement with and promotion of Creek sovereignty (following in the footsteps of the Red Sticks of the past).

What Womack is gesturing toward, both in his initial discussion of orality and in the development of the Jim Chibbo letters, then, is the need to develop a nationalist literary criticism that is simultaneously focused on pure formalist close reading as well as on the performative potential of texts, grasping how they can function in different contexts and produce varying effects on readers. He will offer another articulation of this kind of project in *American Indian Literary Nationalism* through his concept of "sovereignty reading" (which I will discuss in more detail in the next chapter). One of the things that *Red on Red* reveals, however, is how difficult it is for literary criticism to reorient itself in this way. As Tedlock's work on the Zunis suggests, Western readers are more prone to experience a text as something fixed, complete, and self-contained and thus have a much easier time doing a *formalist* close reading of a text than what Clifford Geertz might call a "thick contextualization" of that same material. Womack himself is engaged in a struggle to break out of that single-minded mode of reading—no easy task, indeed. This process of extrication and critical exploration explains what might strike many readers as the unevenness and methodological inconsistency on Womack's part throughout *Red on Red*. In his third chapter ("In the Storyway"), for example, Womack finds himself wrestling with a variety of competing imperatives. His stated goal is to produce a nationalist reading of the traditional story of how turtle got his cracked-looking shell. To do so, on the one hand, he tries to pull from the details of the story examples of motifs and literary rules that designate the tale as a repository of quintessentially Creek culture. Put another way, Womack wants to read the story formally, to pull from it evidence of its Creekness (in the political sense I discussed earlier). At the same time, though, Womack wants to account for the story's trajectory across historical time and through different forms (its movement "in the storyway"). It is this second imperative that mitigates, to a degree, Womack's dismay at his own limitations as a nationalist reader. For his formal analysis he relies largely on two written transcriptions of the tale recorded by white ethnographers. And his performative analysis relies on his own transcription of a contemporary telling of the tale in Creek, and then in English, which leads to a limited reading because Womack himself (by his own admission) lacks the Creek language skills to realize his own vision. When Womack asserts that the turtle story is "very much a story of Creek nationalism," then, he is only able to make a partial case of how this is so. This largely has to do with the challenges involved in fully realizing a performative nationalist criticism, in developing a methodology for what I will call, in the next chapter, reading in the oral tradition in the service of sovereignty.

In the end, I think it is the difficulty involved in developing the kind of two-pronged (formalist and performative) nationalist criticism that I have been discussing here that led Womack, in the balance of *Red on Red*, to reorient himself around what seems to be a more straightforward facet of the nationalist agenda—canon formation in the service of an image of Creek peoplehood. (This turns out to be none too simple either, however.) His critique of Alice Callahan's *Wynema* is a particularly illustrative example in this regard. One might wonder at first why Womack even bothers to write a chapter on Callahan and her novel, as he seems to loathe the book, seeing it as an act of erasure of Creek history and voices written by an assimilationist collaborator. It is unlikely that Callahan (born of Creek lineage) is included here simply because she is often recognized as one of the first Indian novelists and thus needs to be part of a "complete" history of Creek intellectual tradition. Inclusiveness is not Womack's goal in *Red on Red*, as he notes in his introduction, explaining that many Creek writers are left out. Instead, Callahan's role in the text is pretty clearly that of a kind of limit case, an example of someone whose writing has gone too far away from offering an acceptable image of Creekness to be useful in the nationalist project. But even in choosing what would seem to be the easiest example possible for such a limit case, Womack runs into difficulties. For where, exactly, can we locate the line that Callahan crosses that renders her work "un-Creek"? The literary and the real are problematically elided here.

Womack's (largely formalist) reading of *Wynema* makes a number of observations about the text in this regard. He opens his discussion by noting that, "under literary analysis that pays attention to nationalism, however, there are also the considerations mentioned earlier. In what ways does the novel record Creek history, create a sense of place on Creek land, advance Creek culture, or strengthen Creek autonomy? How deeply is it engaged in things Creek?" (Womack, *Red* 121). As evidence of the novel's lack of engagement in "things Creek," Womack notes a relative paucity of Creek characters who speak in the novel. He goes so far as to count words to make this point and seems to imply that some amount of Creek dialect would have been an appropriate inclusion. He notes the book's lack of reference to the broader historical experience of European contact among the Creeks, although interestingly he spends relatively little time contextualizing the novel in relation to its own situation of production (tied to Callahan's biography and historical situation). All of this could work to make a legitimate, pragmatic point about what is needed in performing and symbolizing the Creek vox populi, of course. But Womack doesn't stop there. Instead, he veers into a more problematic critique of Callahan's individual identity, as opposed to maintaining his focus on a discussion of the lack of utility of her fictional characters as models of political subjectivity.

Throughout the chapter Womack shifts back and forth between a disdainful view of the novel's protagonist as "brainwashed," a discussion of the novel itself as an assimilationist distortion of true Creek culture, and biographical speculation about whether Callahan was really culturally Creek even though she was biologically so (*Red* 118). Even in his attempt to offer an alternative and slightly more conciliatory reading of the text in one of his Jim Chibbo/Hotgun letters, Womack ends up in a similar muddle. He initially frames the letter as a clever allegory regarding the political limitations of Callahan's novel. Callahan herself and several of the female characters in her book are confined in the back seat of a police car driven by an abusive redneck state trooper. Suggestively impotent in this situation, they engage in a literary debate, witnessed by fellow prisoner Stijaati Thlaako, over Callahan's representation of Creek life. That debate largely replicates Womack's own critique of the novel, though. And the problematic elision of the biographical Callahan and her fictional characters continues to be instructive here. The fictionalized Callahan attempts to defend her book on the basis of its status as a fiction and as something that was not intended to be, nor should be viewed as, an accurate reflection of Creek life. This defense is jarring in light of Womack's implicit elision of the fictional and the real throughout the letter as a whole. Sitting in the police car, the (symbolic) character Wynema wonders aloud, "Did [the real] Callahan even *like* Creek people, given the revulsion expressed throughout the book at all things Creek?" (128). Continuing to personalize the debate over *Wynema* in light of its author's biography in this way unhelpfully tends to shift focus to problematic issues of identity and personal authenticity. This letter, alongside the Callahan chapter proper, then, reveals the problem of the link between art and the real to be still unresolved, at least in *Red on Red*.

Considering Womack's avowed sense that the line between criticism and story needs to be broken down in a sovereignty-related praxis, perhaps it is not surprising that his most successful effort in addressing both of the underlying problematics I've noted (the art/real divide and the commitment to a techne of sovereignty) is in his novel *Drowning in Fire*. In *When Did Indians Become Straight* Mark Rifkin highlights how Womack's novel balances the investigation of queer experience on an individual level with reflection of the settler-colonial "project of reorganizing Muscogee peoplehood" on a collective one (277). In doing so, he notes, "Womack foregrounds the relation between contesting sexual normalization and invigorating Creek sovereignty." Rifkin's reading deftly traces the dialectical project of engagement that runs throughout the book, though his focus there is on overtly religious, rather than legal, symbolism. Womack resituates a range of tropes from Christian theology—water, snakes, and fire—and redefines them in a way that "interrogates the assumptions about home and family undergirding Euroamerican-style sovereignty" (Rifkin 279). As Rifkin suggests, though, Womack also begins to invoke the treaty as a specific techne for advancing a redefined tribal sovereignty, albeit in a latent manner. The novel draws explicit parallels between its present-day protagonists and the experience of the Creek polity during the Crazy Snake uprising and their struggle against allotment at the turn of the twentieth century. And it presents a commitment to upholding the 1832 treaty with the U.S. government as crucially important in generating a modern-day Red Stick politics and defining Muscogee political subjectivity going forward. While some of the crucial connections between law and literature remain latent in the text (Rifkin's reading supplements the work in a number of interesting ways), we can nevertheless see Womack moving forward in *Drowning in Fire* in relation to the problematics of his criticism. In that sense, the next logical move for him has been to turn back from the purely fictional to a reconstituted critical practice as a means of further developing a Creek-centered sovereignty discourse. *Art as Performance* moves in that direction, to a degree. As suggested earlier in this chapter, though, Womack's retreat in that text from specificity (in relation to the strains and technai of sovereignty that might be tactically pursued in the present moment) also represents a bit of a step away from the lines of thinking being developed in *Drowning in Fire*.

What I hope has come across in this discussion is a sense of how Womack's and Warrior's critical practices usefully reveal the central issues involved in the effort to fuse law and literature into a fully realized discourse of sovereignty. The moves made by each of them to use the performative aspects of the oral tradition as a way to reimagine how we approach written texts strike me as particularly promising in this context. I will explore that promise in more detail in the next two chapters' treatment of the work of Elizabeth Cook-Lynn and Gerald Vizenor. In those chapters I will also attempt to reiterate the value of a clear focus on specific technai of sovereignty as the foundations for such a discourse. Cook-Lynn and Vizenor both seem exemplary to me in this regard. I should stress again, though, that the thinking about sovereignty discourse in which I am engaged throughout this study owes a great deal to my reading of Warrior and Womack. In this chapter I have self-consciously worked in the spirit of intellectual sovereignty as formulated by Warrior—taking up the challenge he laid down in *Tribal Secrets* to work ethically from *within* Indian intellectual traditions to facilitate the further development of those traditions. I have kept my references to other theoretical models as discrete as possible. As the preceding discussion has demonstrated, there is more than enough energy and vitality in that tradition today (compared to twenty years ago when Warrior was first writing on these issues) to push the discourse of sovereignty forward *inductively*, from within Indian country and its print culture. Finally, as my subsequent discussions of Cook-Lynn and Vizenor will suggest, I am motivated in this study by the belief that contemporary debates in Native American studies have often been too schismatic, with critics too quick to choose sides between nationalists and cosmopolitans rather than considering how engaged readings of writers and critics from different positions can reveal deeper unities.[15] There is an enormous reservoir of innovative and creating thinking on tribal sovereignty today, and realizing this should link critics together, not divide them. I hope this discussion has shown how the literary nationalist movement sets before us the pragmatic challenge of exploring those connections.

CHAPTER 5

Elizabeth Cook-Lynn and Treaty Reading

WHY I CAN READ ELIZABETH COOK-LYNN

In her effort to reshape the discipline of Native American studies (NAS), Elizabeth Cook-Lynn offers a strident and complex vision of tribal sovereignty, strongly tinged with a spirit of nationalism. Numerous articulations of this vision appear throughout her published writings, but some remarks from her 2007 essay collection, *New Indians, Old Wars*, provide an appropriate starting point. In a chapter titled "Defensive, Regulatory, and Transformative Functions of Indian Studies" Cook-Lynn argues that to effectively and ethically respond to the pragmatic calls for political relevance made by nationalist critics (such as Craig Womack), Indian Studies must organize itself around two central concepts: indigeneity and sovereignty. She provides her own basic definitions of those concepts: "In broad terms, the discipline of Indian Studies defines 'indigenous' as aboriginal, inborn, natural, or originating in and characterizing a particular region or country. It defines 'sovereignty' as the quality of independent power or authority" (Cook-Lynn, *New Indians* 128). While these general concepts can serve as organizing principles for the field, Cook-Lynn stresses that their practical application requires close attention to the particular experiences of tribal communities. Indeed, it is only in that local application that they achieve their fullest definition: "Without understanding that these terms are defined in specific geographies, which is the reason to study what is called the 'mythic experience,' it is impossible to understand the history of disinheritance and genocide suffered by Native peoples and, therefore, impossible to find solutions to past and current events" (128).

In many ways these statements sum up Cook-Lynn's career as a writer and thinker, but almost every term employed here (authority, geography, mythic experience) unfolds into a broader set of issues and writings constituting her own distinctive Dakotah vision of sovereignty. That vision includes topics such as treaty history, textual interpretation, the writer's vocation, canon formation, and the treatment of Indian women in the U.S. and tribal court systems. It also aims to synthesize several of the lines of thought regarding tribal sovereignty discussed in part 1. Appreciating the scope of Cook-Lynn's critical vision is central to assessing even her most apparently provocative and polemical pronouncements—why she says she "can't read" Wallace Stegner, for example. Assessing the totality of the work of this central writer is also important, I would argue, for understanding the ways in which law and literature are fusing into a discourse of sovereignty in Indian print culture at the present moment.

From the beginning, Cook-Lynn's oeuvre has been centered on critique. As such, perhaps the best approach to tracing the contours of her thinking about sovereignty would be to consider her criticism of NAS for failing to advance the cause of "independent power or authority." Each of Cook-Lynn's major essay collections (*Why I Can't Read Wallace Stegner*; *Anti-Indianism in Modern America*; *New Indians, Old Wars*; and *A Separate County*) contains at least one polemical piece on the field. While there has been some shifting of her positions during her two decades of writing, a few central themes are present throughout this work. Like many nationalist critics Cook-Lynn laments the lack of practical impact that scholarship has had on the lives of tribal peoples, especially in regard to their struggles for sovereignty. In her view, even those reasonable efforts within the field to define and theorize key concepts have been pursued to excess. In *New Indians, Old Wars*, for example, Cook-Lynn wonders, "Are we going to continue to ask what sovereignty is and never get around to finding ways to actually use the concept to better our lives and defend our lands? We are still asking questions that have little relevance if land reform, economics, defense of treaty agreements, and survival as nation-to-nation entities are the salient directives of the discipline" (12). The explanation for this problem (the tendency within the field to be distracted by infelicitous questions and the failure to use the concept of sovereignty effectively) can be found, she maintains, in an overly conciliatory mindset among some critics, a lack of commitment to tribal-centered nationalism on the part of too many Indian writers, the disproportionate influence of interdisciplinary thinking on NAS, and the general dominance of the scholarly discourse by English and humanities departments. For Cook-Lynn the effects of these disciplinary problems are potentially dire. She fears recent decades have brought "a steady crippling of nationalism that derives from various failed theories of failed liberation as well as a willingness on the part of [Indian] intellectuals to repeat the imperial colonial experience simply because it is easier" (Cook-Lynn, *Separate* 174). In the terms I have been using in this study, one might say Cook-Lynn has been troubled by a lack of praxis in the field, insufficiently clear commitments to specific technai of sovereignty, and a failure to craft a satisfactory understanding of the relationship between law and literature in the work of decolonization.

In its simplest form Cook-Lynn's critical challenge to Native American studies involves one foundational question: How can any field of study exist if it fails to preserve the existence of the very thing that it takes as its object? Axiomatically, Cook-Lynn would say, Native American studies is an impossibility without the persistence of politically distinct Native American *nations*. As such, the effective advocacy for those nations must be NAS's prime directive. It is for this reason that Cook-Lynn laments the institutional trajectory of NAS over the last thirty years (echoing the pragmatics of Womack and others, but in a more forceful way). Rather than developing sui generis, as an autonomous discipline with its own sovereignty-focused research paradigms, resource streams, and communal ties, Cook-Lynn believes that NAS in many university contexts has become an interdisciplinary hodgepodge, cobbled together with courses from different fields and lacking autonomy, a core sense of purpose, or institutional support. She laments, "Our faculties in Indian Studies continue to be small, weak, and without the prestige of even our local tribal politicians who have risen to power through SEATA and gambling casinos" (Cook-Lynn, *New Indians* 13). This, in her view, is a betrayal of the original promise of the field, which was rooted in the indigenous activism of the 1960s and 1970s. "Indian Studies as an academic discipline was meant to have as its constituencies the native tribal nations of America and its major purpose the defense of lands and resources and the sovereign right to nation-to-nation status," she argues (Cook-Lynn, *Anti-Indianism* 153).[1] Its secondary purpose was to "counter the related disciplines that have been in the business of colonizing the natives" (that is, history, literature, and especially anthropology), rather than being constructed out of those fields (153). What remains a core problem for Cook-Lynn is how NAS can accomplish these ends when, first, its academic programs are often constituted from selections of courses imported basically unchanged from fields such as history and literature and, second, it fails to speak in a unified voice for a "separate sovereignty" (*Separate* 166).

It should be noted, of course, that the precise meaning of the term "Native tribal nations" here is not necessarily self-evident. Much of Cook-Lynn's writing is concerned, however, with elaborating her specific vision of this nationhood. On the one hand, the term "Native" indexes her commitment to a coherent, and politically distinct, national identity built on the foundation of shared cultural norms—an approach that should be familiar to students of Vine Deloria, Jr.'s, writings. In this respect Cook-Lynn's positioning of indigeneity and sovereignty as distinct central concepts for Native American studies is a bit misleading, as they overlap considerably. In *Anti-Indianism*, for example, Cook-Lynn glosses nationalism in a cultural sense, defining it as "a concept in the arts that argues for nation-specific creativity and political unification in the development, continuation, and defense of a coherent national mythos" (35). Her commitment to indigeneity as a core concept, then, represents an effort to link the cultural dimensions of nationalism to more explicitly legal ones (dimensions picked up in the phrasing "tribal nations") in a manner that is somewhat congruent with the human rights language of contemporary international law. However, one senses that Cook-Lynn envisions a more radical and aggressive approach to tribal autonomy than what is currently possible within the framework of UNDRIP. She has consistently maintained that the geographic specificity of the mythos of a people provides the essential foundation for the possession and control of territory central to separate nationhood (political sovereignty). And she links this idea to "the indigenous view of the world—that the very origins of a people are specifically tribal (nationalistic) rooted in a specific geography (place), that mythology (soul) and geography (land) are inseparable, that even language is rooted in a specific place." (Cook-Lynn, "Fiction Writers" 85). With this in mind, it seems clear that the concept of sovereignty for Cook-Lynn always entails as a central goal the preservation (or reclamation) of an autonomously ruled tribal land base and the tribally specific knowledge embedded in it. Her evaluation of the scholarship and activism emerging from NAS focuses on the question of whether that work advances this central goal.

In this context, it is not surprising that Cook-Lynn fears that the ability to defend tribal sovereignty is compromised when NAS blends with Ethnic Studies. The primary factors that must distinguish the two fields, she argues, are political and legal. Cook-Lynn is not alone among Native writers and critics in fearing the absorption of NAS into Ethnic Studies, but she is one of the most vigorous proponents of the argument that Indian people within the borders of the United States have a history of being politically distinct entities, of being some form of *nation-states* whose sovereignty cannot, finally, be deterritorialized, even tactically. She would differ from McNickle and Deloria in this respect, I think. From that perspective, Indian people inevitably find their experiences and issues distorted or minimized by being placed into critical frameworks more appropriate for studying immigrant groups or cultural enclaves within a larger political totality.[2] Cook-Lynn's view would seem to be that if Indian people stop asserting that their land-based political autonomy and cultural distinctiveness defines them (and establishes the parameters of the academic field that is most centrally concerned with their experiences) this would be tantamount to surrendering their sovereignty and to vanishing, in essential ways, as Indians. "Indian studies is about government and politics and sovereignty for Indian nations," she notes (Cook-Lynn, *New Indians* 16). If it is not *about* those things, if it is merely *about* the experiences of Indians as one ethnic group among many, then NAS has no reason to exist.

As we have seen, of course, there are many different legal strategies by which Indian sovereignty might be asserted and defended. One of the strengths of Cook-Lynn's work is its effort to refine this situation down to a small set of applicable tools. Cook-Lynn's particular Dakotah form of nationalist thinking focuses on the treaty as the central techne of tribal sovereignty, and on this point she again finds NAS to be lacking the appropriate emphasis. In further elaborating on the desired content of NAS, she insists, "It is about rights based on the extraconstitutionality of government-to-government relationships with the U.S. federal government unlike any other in the United States" (Cook-Lynn, *New Indians* 16). "Extraconstitutionality" is the key term here, foregrounding Cook-Lynn's skepticism toward tribal constitution writing and constitutional law as viable technai for decolonization. Unlike Gerald Vizenor and (to a degree) Vine Deloria, Cook-Lynn shows little interest in current movements to revise tribal constitutions or to shift the norms of constitutional interpretation as viable mechanisms for asserting tribal sovereignty. Essentially, she views such work as complicit with a colonialist American legal order. Present-day constitutional reform, Cook-Lynn maintains, cannot transcend its roots in the compromised constitutionalism of the Indian New Deal. As she sees it, "American Indians and their nations are the most colonized people and enclaves in the United States and have been for over two hundred years *especially since the passage of the 1934 Reorganization Act*" (Cook-Lynn, *New Indians* 22; emphasis added). Because even today, within the borders of the United States, tribal constitutions function within the framework of congressional law and the administrative authority of the U.S. Department of the Interior. Cook-Lynn views the faith that constitutionalism provides a path to sovereignty as naive.[3] Rather, she insists, "the legal paradigm of nations within a nation is a fragile concept with massive possibilities for corruption of democratic ideals, especially when examined within the constant legal battle between federalists and states' rightists so characteristic of U.S. policy since the late 1800s. To cling to such colonial-based law is probably a rationalization (in self-flattering ways) that all is well in the seeking of justice" (Cook-Lynn, *Separate* 78). In the end Cook-Lynn puts her faith in treaties as the only legal form that allows for an assertion of separate nationhood: "To return to these documents, then, is to begin to understand how Native peoples organized themselves politically and culturally from the 1500s to the

1930s," the latter date representing the moment when the U.S. government began its reorganization and put in place colonizing strategies designed, in her view, to completely erode Dakotah sovereignty (189).

The case Cook-Lynn makes against the influence of postcolonialism in NAS is related, in some respects, to this skeptical critique of constitutionally based assertions of sovereignty. In this context we might note the contrast she drew, quite early in her critical career, between what she calls the work of third-world intellectuals and the critical sensibility she calls cosmopolitanism. The latter term describes what she views as a dominant strain in postcolonial criticism, especially that produced by academics who are not themselves grounded in specific third-world contexts. In her often-cited essay "The American Indian Fiction Writers: Cosmopolitanism, Nationalism, the Third World, and First Nations Sovereignty," Cook-Lynn presents that opposition in the following terms: "The Third world intellectual . . . argues that cosmopolitanism becomes the enemy of 'resistance literatures' specifically because its criteria arise from Western tastes, or, in other words, for aesthetic reasons"(79). While she doesn't use the specific term, what Cook-Lynn is articulating here is her view that postcolonial critical discourse is in the thrall of a cosmopolitan aesthetic, which causes it to distort indigenous writing and politics by framing them exclusively in terms of Western tastes. These framing strategies include (1) the privileging of novels over poetry, testimonials, plays, and other forms; (2) the privileging of writing in European languages; (3) an attraction to writing that merely "thematizes colonialism" but lacks a strong critical perspective or praxis; and (4) an attraction to writing that fits easily into the tradition of "great art" in a Western sense, thus providing first-world readers with a comfortable sense that third-world peoples are "like us."

Strategies three and four are of particular significance, for there Cook-Lynn both locates a tendency in much postcolonial scholarship to gloss over the concrete legal structures of colonialism and begins to raise the issue of interpretation as a central element in her nationalistic thought. She sees postcolonial literary critics as having often focused too much on individuals and their identity issues rather than on "the sovereign condition of institutions and systems" (Cook-Lynn, "Fiction Writers" 91). Rather than a rigorous analysis of colonialism as a system, Cook-Lynn argues, postcolonial/cosmopolitan critical approaches give us discussions of essentially romantic archetypes (the Indian as exile in his own land, the Indian as one who tragically lives in two worlds) and yield a body of scholarship that is disproportionately drawn toward consideration of novels about highly individualized protagonists experiencing sensations of hybridity. Cook-Lynn is bothered, in this context, by many successful American Indian writers (ones with a mainstream readership—like Louise Erdrich) who seem to her to have followed the same paths. Instead of crafting a discourse of sovereignty that productively connects the realms of law and literature, she suggests, those writers merely "present Indian populations as simply gatherings of exiles, emigrants, and refugees, strangers to themselves and their lands, pawns in control of white manipulators, mixed-bloods searching for an identity—giving support, finally, the idea of national/tribal cultures as a contradiction in terms" (86). In the end she argues that postcolonial theory impacts American Indian writers' artistic and political work (their "efforts toward the recovery of memory through writing") by rendering it "thwarted, selective, and narrowly interpreted within the imposed context of Western knowledge and aesthetics" (80). Further, it inoculates the readers of this work against its most significant and politically transformative textual effects.

Many of Cook-Lynn's critical comments about Native writers and postcolonial theory in this context strike me as unfair, especially since the problem may lie more in her own interpretation of their work than with the work itself.[4] Rather than engage in a debate about the critical value of Louise Erdrich's or Homi Bhabha's work, though, I want to address Cook-Lynn's articulation in the "American Indian Fiction Writers" essay of a more significant hermeneutic problem, one that comes up repeatedly in her work. In her discussion of its fourth framing strategy, Cook-Lynn suggests that critical cosmopolitanism's (or postcolonialism's) primary interpretive aim is to make Indian writing as recognizable as possible to a non-Indian audience, not to advance the cause of Native sovereignty. There is some hint in this criticism that in her view recognizability may be, if not inconsistent with sovereignty, then ambivalently related to it. Cook-Lynn is conflicted on this point (as she should be, I think) and that conflict strikes me as one key to the *aesthetic* problematic at the heart of her development of her own form of sovereignty discourse.[5] There are fundamental, unstated questions driving Cook-Lynn's decolonizing project (both in her critical and creative writing). For example, how is one to balance the imperative to resist recognizability and/or interpretability with the imperative to employ the treaty (which is an exchange of recognition) as the centerpiece of national identity and sovereign autonomy? How is one to guide or control interpretation in a way that serves the cause of treaty-nationalism and sovereignty and resists colonialism? How is one to balance the aesthetic integrity of a literary work of art with the political imperatives of a sovereignty-centered NAS?

It is no accident that interpretation stands at the heart of Cook-Lynn's most recently articulated objections to the influence of postcolonialism in NAS. Elaborating on her general critique in the "Native American Fiction Writers" essay—the idea that postcolonial scholarship employs a shallow, generalized, and universal model of colonial experience—Cook-Lynn currently offers a historical counterargument. Postcolonial theory, she argues, fails to properly contextualize not only indigenous aesthetics but also American Indian historical experience, and as such it fails in another way to effectively advance the cause of sovereignty because it leads to a chronic *misreading* of that history. Cook-Lynn maintains that employing a postcolonial critical framework to understand settler colonialism, as opposed to classic imperialism, distorts political and historical reality.[6] In her view, postcoloniality is an "elaborate and indefensible scholarly endeavor, both in academic . . . and in political life" (Cook-Lynn, *Separate* xvii). It either involves "obfuscation, denial, and discrimination," or it is "a deliberate strategy to take away the nationalistic or tribal autonomy from millions of people" (xvii). There is clearly an element of strawman caricaturing of postcolonial theory here, of course. We should note the failure on Cook-Lynn's part to appreciate that there is clearly a strain of writing typically included in the postcolonial canon that focuses on the process of liberation from settler-colonial structures, rather than on post–World War II decolonization.[7] At the same time, there may be some legitimate justification for her concerns that literary critics tend to employ the critical abstractions of postcolonial theory in a way that obscures local realities and fails to attend to legal historical particulars.[8] This is a point made by Womack in his critique of Elvira Pulitano's *Toward a Native American Critical Theory* in *American Indian Literary Nationalism*.

To be sure, in the specific American Indian context that concerns her, Cook-Lynn would be able to muster considerable evidence for her more pessimistic interpretation of the legal and political history in Indian country in the United States. Court cases such as *Oliphant v. Suquamish Indian Tribe* in 1978 (which denied tribal courts criminal jurisdiction over non-Indians on tribal lands) and the more recent *Carcieri v. Salazar* in 2009 (which limited the ability of tribes to put land into trust under the Bureau of Indian Affairs unless those tribes were formally federally recognized as of 1934) underwrite her sense of urgency. Even more direct and personal examples for her, as a Dakotah woman, would include the unresolved land claims case over the theft of the Black Hills and the 1989 criminal case she refers to as the "Big Pipe Case," which involved the unilateral extension of federal authority in unprecedented ways in Indian country by defining parental neglect (prosecuting an alcoholic mother who nursed her child while intoxicated) as "assault."[9] Throughout her career, though, Cook-Lynn has made a *particular* point of arguing that the integration of the Doctrine of Discovery into the very DNA of U.S. Indian Law at its origin most clearly marks the United States as a settler-colonial power, which it remains today. This view also informs her skepticism, mentioned earlier, regarding constitutionalism as a path toward sovereignty and drives her alignment with the internationalization and indigenization of sovereignty discourse dating from the late 1970s. Postcolonial literary theory, she insists, remains insufficiently attentive to the persistence of this and other foundational legal fictions, and thus it misinterprets the political situation it purports to address.

For a critical counterexample that shows the centrality of the problem of Discovery Law for Cook-Lynn, we might turn to her 1999 book, *The Politics of Hallowed Ground*, cowritten with Lakota attorney Mario Gonzalez. This volume has as its primary focus Gonzalez's navigation of a variety of political minefields and conflicting legal structures at the tribal and federal level in an effort to create a memorial to the victims killed at the 1890 massacre at Wounded Knee Creek. From the beginning the book makes clear its authors' view that not only the history leading up to that massacre but much of U.S. Indian policy and law ultimately derives from the Doctrine of Discovery. In his preface Gonzalez recapitulates the relevant legal history, starting with John Marshall's decision in *Johnson v. McIntosh* (1823), which put Discovery at center of U.S. Indian law, employing it there as the vehicle for asserting the exclusive federal power to extinguish title to Indian lands within the boundaries of the states and organized territories. Marshall's subsequent decision in *Cherokee Nation v. Georgia* (1831) further elaborated the subordinate position in which "savage" or aboriginal peoples are placed by Discovery Law (the notion that the first civilized nation to "discover" an empty territory, or *terra nullius*, occupied only by savage peoples, gained the preemptive right to claim those lands by conquest or negotiation). Setting up the framework of "sovereign within a sovereign" into which Indian tribes might be placed, Marshall's argument that Indian tribes represent "domestic dependent nations" defined their legal status as a form of political wardship. Whether that status has been understood in benevolent terms (through the trust doctrine) or in purely patronizing ones, it represents a diminishment of a notion of sovereign autonomy.

Gonzalez and Cook-Lynn highlight how subsequent history consistently reveals a pattern of ongoing assault on Indian sovereignty by Congress, for example in the Major Crimes Act of 1885 or Public Law 280 of 1953. Gonzales also reminds us that the federal courts have systematically diminished sovereignty through development of "federal common law," as in a case such as *Williams v. Lee* (1959), which, though advantageous in some ways for tribal governments, also precipitated further weakening of tribal civil, criminal, and taxation power (Gonzalez and Cook-Lynn xiii). Even though there has been some official acknowledgment of the notion that Sioux sovereignty predates the sovereignty of United States (a point conceded in a 1934 Interior Department Solicitor's Opinion), Congress's plenary power to extinguish that sovereignty (validated by the Supreme Court in *Lone Wolf v. Hitchcock* in 1903) is also still maintained. To be "discovered," in legal terms, then, is to be colonized, and until U.S. law is purged of the Doctrine of Discovery, Cook-Lynn argues, decolonization remains a fantasy for tribal peoples within the borders of the United States. In this context, she believes engagement with postcolonial studies and theory on the part of NAS scholars often serves to take away national or tribal autonomy by overlooking the underlying conditions that make this autonomy impossible.

There are, not surprisingly, professional and methodological implications that flow from Cook-Lynn's sense of the need to discipline the field of NAS in the specific nationalist ways I have been tracing (purging or limiting the influence of other fields, and shifting the questions, central concepts, and interpretive paradigms governing it). Her views on the desired core principles of the field have led her to be extremely critical of one of the largest explicitly NAS professional organizations of our time, the recently formed Native American and Indigenous Studies Association (NAISA), for its lack of focus and integrity. It is worth briefly considering this argument, as it gathers together several of the themes I have been discussing thus far. In *A Separate Country* Cook-Lynn takes her NAISA colleagues to task for failing to create the kind of field needed by contemporary tribal peoples. She begins her critique by disapprovingly referencing comments made by Duane Champagne, urging Indian students to major in mainstream disciplines like business and education as opposed to Indian studies, while encouraging non-Indian students to enter the field of NAS.[10] Cook-Lynn challenges what she sees as Champagne's willingness to redefine NAS as a site for cross-cultural and cross-disciplinary conversation. She finds in this gesture a spirit of capitulation that represents a failure to live up to the activist roots of the field dating back to its origins in the 1970s. NAISA's organizing philosophy (which stresses interdisciplinarity, openness to "anyone who does work in Indigenous/Native/American Indian studies," and democratic governance by this eclectic membership) represents, in this context, an extension of the same seriously flawed vision:

> This "big tent" approach has been the flavor of the week of the past decade in the field of Indian studies; it is a safe trajectory not only for students but also for faculty and Native enclaves of all types. Until recently such thinking directly influenced curricular offerings in the field toward literary studies rather than political science.... Today this curricular trend suggests that by putting forth the economic, diversity, and cross-cultural doctrines demanded by the "big tent" approach, nationalistic tendencies can be disarmed. (Cook-Lynn, *Separate* 19)

Supporting her view, Cook-Lynn mentions another critique of NAISA, made at its inaugural Minneapolis conference in May 2009 by James Riding In (the current editor at the *Wicazo Sa Review*, the tribal-nationalist journal that she founded). Also seeing the big tent approach as troubling, Riding In calls for a move away from the current interdisciplinary approach to Indian studies (dominated by history, literature, and anthropology) for an approach embracing law, politics, land, sovereignty, and specific indigenous issues. Finally, as a counterpoint to NAISA, Cook-Lynn mentions her involvement in the creation of the American Indian Studies Consortium in 2004. The stated purpose of that organization is to "to adopt a constitution for the purpose of organizing a national consortium to bring together the Native American professoriat from all sectors of Native education to codify standards for the discipline." These standards aim to reflect some of the themes discussed already in this chapter, including a much narrower focus on sovereignty and indigeneity in NAS (Cook-Lynn, *New Indians* 118).

Based on these comments, one wonders whether Cook-Lynn's concerns about the big tent of NAISA might be mitigated if she saw *different* fields as dominant within its larger structure, or at least if a critical reorientation of a field like literary studies around sovereignty issues took place. At present, though, Cook-Lynn views NAISA as divided into factions and hamstrung from the start in its political effectiveness. She blames this, in large part, on "literary studies collectives" of activist English departments and humanities enclaves that were also central to the initial development of NAS. In Cook-Lynn's view, this collective is responsible both for moving NAISA toward its big tent approach and for channeling the intellectual energy of the field in unproductive directions:

> There is no question that the ambiguity in literary studies allows for greater diversity than Indian law and federal Indian policy, thus allowing the schism to fester. An emphasis on indigenousness and sovereignty, which is the crux of Indian studies, is rarely the intent of literary studies in terms of problem solving, solutions, and research. Literary studies has mainly been effective in the study of major figures and creative works rather than politics. (Cook-Lynn, *Separate* 20)

Not surprisingly, I would suggest we look critically at Cook-Lynn's claim that there is something fundamentally and inevitably lacking in literary studies within an NAS context. It strikes me as unfair to suggest that literary scholars *cannot* advance the political agenda that Cook-Lynn sees as vital to tribal peoples as a whole, emphasizing indigenousness and sovereignty in ways that buttress treaty-centered nationalism. Indeed, I would argue that her polemical challenges to the field actually suggest that we need *more* interdisciplinarity, not less. Cook-Lynn's forcefully articulated concerns about the excessive influence of literary studies in NAS actually serve to draw our attention to the unstated, and largely *literary*, problematic driving her own work, a problematic that, if addressed by other critics, has the potential to move the field forward in productive ways.

In my view, Cook-Lynn herself has always been driving toward the elaboration of a fully formed discourse of sovereignty. Axiomatically, such a discourse demands the kind of fusion of law and literature (or legal technai and storytelling) that only interdisciplinary scholarship is able to engender effectively. Not surprisingly then, Cook-Lynn's discomfort with literature and literary studies is deeply conflicted. On the one hand she is a critic who has been willing to lavish praise on the works of many Native American writers. In her published *Notebooks* she celebrates N. Scott Momaday's *The Way to Rainy Mountain* and *House Made of Dawn* for having "used a mirror to reflect the rise of the NCAI." Momaday, "without really wanting to, wrote to protest the white supremacy and incredible genocide of public policy that had happened during those years prior to his birth. He is a genuinely brilliant artist whose classic novel is inspired by politics, like the work of Arthur Miller. . . . What is at stake in both of these works is the sense of survival of the village and the tribe" (Cook-Lynn, *Notebooks* 92). She also regularly discusses the power of the written word and encourages Indian people to pursue careers in writing. At times she is even willing to concede the political utility of literary studies as a field. Again in the *Notebooks*, Cook-Lynn argues, "The study of literature and such literary techniques as the use of irony gives clues as to how the story achieves broad meanings and influences. *The politics of irony is dangerous to the status quo. It is tricky. And it must be conceived as emancipation*" (101). Gerald Vizenor could have written those sentences.

These kinds of positive assessments are often outweighed by more troubled reflections, however, revealing that Cook-Lynn (like many of her contemporaries) has struggled to arrive at a satisfying theorization of the relationship between literary representation and the real world. One way she has attempted to address that relationship is in her thinking about canon formation. Cook-Lynn regularly stresses the need to do more to cultivate a separate literary canon of tribal peoples that can underpin the advocacy of treaty-centered nationalism. That canon, she notes, should include texts (both oral and written) that address the following: (1) the places, mythological beings, genre structures, and plots derived from the tradition of specific tribal peoples; (2) wars and war leaders; and (3) treaties and accords with other nations. This corpus would constitute for Cook-Lynn essentially the literary half of a treaty-nationalist discourse of sovereignty; in her "Fiction Writers" essay she has a long list of Dakotah/Lakota writers she would put into her own particular version of this tradition (figures who, to be fair, seldom appear in college literature classes). In the end Cook-Lynn maintains, "Reference to the body of nationalistic myths, legends, metaphors, symbols, historical persons, and events, writers and their writings *must* form the basis of the critical discourse that functions in the name of the people" ("Fiction Writers" 85). Where Native literary studies has most clearly come up short, in her view, is in its failure to systematically develop a corpus that supports this kind of critical discourse.

Cook-Lynn may have a fair point in suggesting that many literary critics have not moved with sufficient confidence and purpose in foregrounding texts and raising critical questions that speak to issues of sovereignty. Referencing Rigoberta Menchú Túm's Nobel acceptance speech as a touchstone, she has argued that Native literary criticism still often focuses too much on issues of identity and authenticity and not enough on "treaties, agreements, and other constructive accords" (Cook-Lynn, *Anti-Indianism* 36). She argues that the central scholarly questions advanced by literary critics in Native American studies (during the period from the 1970s to the 1990s) have often been things like "Who is an Indian?" or "How can Indians cope with Modernity?" These questions have often been approached not through the lenses of sovereignty or citizenship (that is, defending the right of tribes to define their own membership) but through a focus on the distracting spectacle of poseurs (like Jamake Highwater and Ward Churchill) or debates about the hybridity of Indian writers.[11] These foci serve to place nontribal members in the role of authenticity police and encourage them to claim authority over Native American writing. And they can generate a self-referential cycle of critical discourse where authors go back and forth debating such questions as whether, based on our reading of *Black Elk Speaks*, we can determine if Nicholas Black Elk was really Catholic. This is disempowering for Indian writers and critics, Cook-Lynn claims, and it also distracts our attention from more important matters, like treaties and accords, and how those are connected to *political* questions, like "Who is a tribal citizen?" and "What does that citizenship mean?" (39).[12]

What I hope we can see clearly at this point is the linked emergence of the two broader imperatives that underpin almost all of Cook-Lynn's thinking about literary discourse and criticism: the need to establish a specific legal context for NAS and the importance of employing that sense of context to drive the selection and interpretation of literary work. In many places in her published writing Cook-Lynn has argued that her own work *must* be placed in the context of treaty-nationalism for its intended meaning to emerge. Put another way, she is demanding the creation of a new literary critical paradigm, one that we might call "treaty criticism" or "treaty reading." In her *Notebooks* she provides a reading guide for her novel trilogy, *Aurelia*, that foregrounds a series of treaties and land claim cases and, in unusually blunt terms for a novelist, suggests that the work is "mostly, a story about crime, both the institutional crime of theft of tribal lands and individual crimes like murder and rape" (51).[13] Throughout *Aurelia* itself Cook-Lynn regularly offers similar commentary—authorial or character-based—that also works to foreground this desired awareness of interpretive context. In *A Separate Country* she is equally explicit: "I certainly consider my work, even my fiction, a literary reaction to law. My first published novella, *From the River's Edge*, examined the illegal flooding of hundreds of thousands of acres of treaty-protected land all up and down the Missouri River and the struggle of the Sioux Nation to survive despite the U.S. government, the law, and American justice" (69).

These types of comments represent an attempt on Cook-Lynn's part to change the dominant questions driving literary studies within the framework of NAS. In interesting ways they echo remarks by Craig Womack in his contribution to *American Indian Literary Nationalism* in which he calls for "compassionate nationalist critics" to apply a "theory of jurisdiction" to Native literature ("Integrity" 172). Shrewdly observing that Cook-Lynn has been working on writing a novel of "jurisdiction" for years (*Aurelia*), Womack argues essentially for the adoption of a specific set of historicist close-reading strategies that foreground legal issues and contexts that advance an understanding of sovereignty issues. He calls this "sovereignty reading."[14] When approaching an Indian text from such a viewpoint, he suggests asking the following kinds of questions: (1) Why did the events represented in the work occur? (2) How can you locate these events on a map? and (3) How is jurisdiction exercised in this particular space? In many respects Cook-Lynn's literary and critical work advances a similar project, one that she further specifies as a way of buttressing treaty-centered nationalism for the Dakotah people. Where she differs from Womack is in her more precise (indeed narrow) definition of one core legal techne (the treaty) to be placed at the center of this new critical paradigm.

If Cook-Lynn's critique of conventional literary studies suggests her own quest to develop what Womack would call the protocols of sovereignty reading, there is nevertheless an element of uncertainty in her thinking. Even as she advocates for the specific reading strategies needed to appreciate the separatist nationalist bent of her work, she does not seem entirely confident that this project can succeed. Despite the breadth of her own writing career (as author of multiple volumes of poetry, a short story collection, three novellas, and considerable criticism), Cook-Lynn has been unable bring herself to trust her own ability to generate a discourse that is capable of advancing the cause of treaty-based sovereignty by blending law and literature. We might recall how in an earlier quote she described her work as a "literary *reaction* to law" (Cook-Lynn, *Separate* 69; my emphasis). A reaction falls well short of the goals and ethical imperatives Cook-Lynn has set for herself and the field. "Unfortunately," she believes, "few language tactics offer a real long-term strategy to rid governance and land issues of the heavy hand of the plenary power of the U.S. Congress, which is the seat of colonialism" (7). In the end this personal, skeptical unease is part of what drives her ongoing resistance to the typical interdisciplinary conjunctions in NAS as a field, or in NAISA as an organization within that field.

Rather than simply accepting Cook-Lynn's self-critique, however, I suggest that we allow her ambivalence to direct us toward a deeper consideration of the productive tensions in her own work, in a similar manner to what I attempted in considering Craig Womack's project in the previous chapter. Her unease emerges in an almost structural sense from the way she pursues the development of a discourse of sovereignty in her own work. But when we look more deeply at the problematic of her project, I think we discover two important things. First, Cook-Lynn's form of literary nationalism does in fact *work* as a system of thinking, but it does so only under very specific interpretive conditions. In this context, the limitations she has confronted in her work have often been aesthetic ones, exacerbated by her unwillingness to recognize the value of nonrealistic modes of literary expression. This reluctance is an unanticipated consequence of the separatist elements of her own form of treaty nationalism. At the same time, Cook-Lynn's deployment of the treaty form as the centerpiece of her Dakotah discourse of sovereignty has also generated for her some significant theoretical tensions. Because of her (understandably) intense focus on the specific historical experiences and challenges confronting the Dakotah people (and the people of the Crow Creek Reservation, in particular), Cook-Lynn has developed a vision of sovereignty that is probably unworkable for many Indian constituencies. I suspect that she recognizes this on some level. But her dual chosen academic roles (as both an advocate for Dakotah-specific sovereignty issues *and* a general theorist working to shape the field of NAS as a whole) render this lack of intellectual flexibility problematic. Put in terms that resonate both with her earlier-cited remarks about NAS and with my own efforts in this book to map out some of the key strains of the discourse of sovereignty, we might say the following: Cook-Lynn's work draws our attention to how difficult it can be to blend *indigeneity* (as a universal critical category and a model of political subjectivity) with *separatist-nationalism* (as a local tactic). Cultivating an awareness of the challenges that can underlie that linkage is crucial to solving the critical problems with which Cook-Lynn has wrestled.

A SOVEREIGNTY READING OF *THE POWER OF HORSES*

The sense of an intimate relationship between mythic consciousness, land, and nationhood discussed at the opening of this chapter has led Cook-Lynn to create tribal-centered works of fiction and poetry that aim to support "a new treaty-based defense against dispossession of resources and lands" (Cook-Lynn, *Separate*, 189).[15] Indeed, as she has also argued with some frequency, a full understanding of the significance of her stories (even such short, enigmatic pieces as "Mahpiyato"—a word which refers to "the earth," the feminine creative divinity in Dakotah mythology) requires an awareness of the centrality of the law to her own thinking and to the history of her people. Cook-Lynn's reasons for placing written treaties with the United States at the heart of her writing are simultaneously philosophical, historical, and personal. As we have noted, skepticism regarding the utility of other legal technai as effective vehicles for pursuing sovereignty has been a key element. Her understanding of sovereignty as an expression both of tribal autonomy in governance and of indigenous knowledge rooted in a specific land base also intersects explicitly with the Dakotah experience of nineteenth-century treaty-making; the traumatic loss of the sacred site of the Black Hills (a crucial place serving as a repository of mythic consciousness) due to an illegal breach of treaty obligations of the part of the United States provides a central rallying cry in her work. Finally, the common misreading of the history of the American West as the "conquest" of the Plains Indians compels Cook-Lynn to invoke treaty history as a counter-narrative; this move is central to her efforts to challenge the controlling legal Doctrine of Discovery. One might say with some justification, then, that treaties are both the generative cause of and the essential context for her reading of material like the writings of Wallace Stegner, the writing of her own fiction and poetry, and her contemporary political engagements. The literary/critical erasure of Native peoples and their legal erasure/colonization, she would argue, are mutually constitutive. As such, a Dakotah discourse of sovereignty must oppose that erasure by being similarly broad in its scope, combining a consideration of legal and nonlegal texts.

To explore this conjunction, I will move back and forth between legal, critical, and literary materials in the discussion that follows. We will begin with the law, allowing Cook-Lynn to direct us to some of the more crucial texts. In the *Notebooks* she provides a reading guide to her fictional trilogy, *Aurelia*, which establishes the central importance of two specific treaties in the legal history of the Santee Sioux (her tribal community, whose homeland is now concentrated on the Crow Creek Reservation in South Dakota). Cook-Lynn first highlights the fact that the Santees signed the Treaty of Mendota with the U.S. in 1851 and then subsequently fought the Little Crow War in Minnesota in 1862, a war caused by the failure of the United States government to meet its treaty obligations for the payment of annuities and the preservation of some reserved territory along the Minnesota River for Dakotah use (*Notebooks* 42).[16] In the aftermath of that conflict in 1863 the Santees were relocated to the Crow Creek Reservation. It is the mythic geography of this reservation that Cook-Lynn depicts with great resonance in her creative work, both in the story collection *The Power of Horses* and in the subsequent cluster of novellas, *Aurelia: A Crow Creek Trilogy*.

Cook-Lynn also stresses the tremendous significance of the 1868 Fort Laramie Treaty between all of the tribes of the Sioux Nation and the United States. This document is of particularly central importance to properly understanding not just her own fiction and criticism, but also the entire modern history of the greater Sioux nation. The Treaty of Fort Laramie, signed April 29, 1868, concluded the 1866–1868 Powder River War fought between the United States and the Lakotas, Northern Cheyennes, and Arapahos. The American defeat in this conflict remains a source of considerable pride for present-day Sioux people. As such, the treaty represents, first of all, a refutation of the assumptions regarding conquest underlying the application of the Doctrine of Discovery in the U.S. Indian law. We should recall in this context John Marshall's explanation in *Johnson and Graham's Lessee* that "discovery gave an exclusive right to extinguish the Indian title of occupancy, either by purchase or by conquest; and gave also a right to such degree of sovereignty, as the circumstances of the people would allow them to exercise" (Prucha 35). As Cook-Lynn notes, the terms of the 1868 treaty clearly affirm that the Sioux were *not* conquered by the Americans, and it represents an agreement of purchase for only a limited amount of territory outside of the boundaries of the Great Sioux Reservation that it establishes. The reservation, the treaty stipulates, is "set apart for the absolute and undisturbed use and occupation of the Indians named herein" (110). In exchange for this recognition of territorial sovereignty, annuities, and other considerations, the Sioux agreed to allow the passage of settlers westward (though not along the Bozeman Trail, which was closed by this agreement), the construction of the transcontinental railroad contiguous to their territory, and the building of military posts south of the North Platte River. The Treaty of Fort Laramie, then, represents a validation of sovereignty.

Cook-Lynn clearly understands its subsequent violation by the United States (beginning in 1874 when gold was discovered in the Black Hills and culminating in an act of Congress in 1877 that seized the Black Hills and further modified the 1868 treaty boundaries) as a crime. The U.S. Supreme

Court has agreed on this point, finding in an 8–1 decision in *United States v. Sioux Nation of Indians* (1980) that the United States illegally obtained this territory. The monetary compensation offered to rectify the injustice has been rejected by the affected tribal communities, however, who continue to insist that the return of the stolen land is the only acceptable remedy. As Cook-Lynn might frame the issue, the sovereignty that was recognized by the United States in 1868 is not comprehended in an ownership concept of land that can be translated into a cash payment mediated by a controlling American legal authority. Rather it is tied to the *indigenous* possession of place that flows from the long tenancy of the tribe in a specific geography. As we can begin to see at this point, one facet of a treaty reading of Cook-Lynn's work involves the need to maintain an awareness that documents like the 1868 Treaty of Fort Laramie serve as the implied context for many other pieces of writing, even pieces that do not directly or obviously reference them. Treaty reading is a particular form of historicism, in other words, one that is related to Womack's discussion of asking of a text what jurisdiction is exercised in a particular place. "Mahpiyato," which I will discuss in more detail shortly, implicitly offers both a complement to the 1868 agreement (fleshing out the tribal understanding of their relationship and some of the territory in question) and a corrective to its subsequent interpretation in the courts (the land claims cases surrounding the Black Hills controversy). In this respect it participates directly, if obliquely, in a discursive battle over jurisdiction. Similarly, in much of Cook-Lynn's other poetry and short fiction the legal context of treaty history provides a necessary element for the reader who is responding to what might otherwise seem to be fragmentary or ambiguous musings.

The poetic prologue to *The Power of Horses* is illustrative.[17] It is a short poem about place, but once again place is apprehended through a distinctly Dakotah sensibility, deeply informed by the experience of colonialism. Without an awareness of that larger context, the text loses much of its nationalist resonance:

>   When you look East
>   from Big Pipe's place
>   you see Fort George; you look
>   south and see Iron Nation
>   and you sense a kind of hollowness
>   in the endless distance
>   of the river span
>   at odds
>   somehow
>   with the immediacy

of the steel REA
towers
stalking up and down prairie hills
(Cook-Lynn, *Power* 3)

Cook-Lynn carefully positions the reader in the landscape here, doing so in a way that registers, not primarily *physical* topography, but a particular historical experience of place. Again we might recall how Womack suggests opening a sovereignty reading of a text with the question, How can you locate it on a map? Cook-Lynn's poem, with its limited use of concrete imagery and physical description, leads its reader into a particular kind of mapping. Our awareness of place builds up gradually through tantalizingly partial details (the title itself providing no specific markers). We know right away that we are at "Big Pipe's place," presumably on a reservation. Allusively, the name Big Pipe might also orient us within in the world of Cook-Lynn's fiction and legal consciousness, but only if we have the benefit of having read her other work, much of which was published subsequent to *The Power of Horses*. It is fair to say, though, that much of Cook-Lynn's writing—similar to Vizenor's—urges the reader to make connections with a larger network of texts and narratives. Big Pipe is the family name of several significant characters in *Aurelia*, and it is also the pseudonym Cook-Lynn uses to reference the defendant in "The Big Pipe Case," protecting her anonymity. Being at Big Pipe's place, then, locates one simultaneously in a realm of tribal narrative memory and settler-colonial legal conflict.

Seeking more precise coordinates within the language of the poem, the reader might notice that the map has only two directions, east and south from the speaker's vantage point. Culturally specific symbolism is likely at play here, as the Santees often conventionally associate east and south with newness/rebirth and healing/growing, respectively. But the details of the poem also suggest that these directions are employed because they represent boundaries imposed through colonial conquest and dispossession. "Fort George" refers to the Benedictine mission Fort George Station founded in early 1913 (and closed in 1981) on the Crow Creek Reservation. "Iron Nation" references a recreational area/park (named after the great nineteenth-century leader of the Lower Brulé Sioux—one of the signers of the 1868 Fort Laramie Treaty) located adjacent to the Lower Brulé Reservation. At this point in the poem, then, we can locate ourselves in a more precise geographical sense on the edge of the Missouri River, on the Crow Creek Reservation, regarding the countryside around.[18] But what we *comprehend* about this place are not so much its physical characteristics, but rather its indices of settler colonialism. Remember, we only look east and south (as opposed to completing a full symbolic hoop). To the south the flow of the Missouri River contrasts with the Rural Electrification Agency towers cutting across traditional lands in much the same way that railroad and settler caravans of the previous century once did. From a Dakotah perspective, regarding the river flowing past the Lower Brulé territory conjures other difficult, and more recent, memories. What Cook-Lynn only obliquely evokes (but which would certainly be known to anyone familiar with local or tribal history) is that considerable portions of the Brulé lands were flooded in 1963 when the Big Bend Dam on the Missouri was completed.[19] The flooding triggered by the operation of this dam destroyed much of the fertile farmland on the Lower Brulé Reserve and covered traditional village sites. In the same spirit of "progress" represented by the REA towers, the water project disrupted the lifeways of the local indigenous population. Small wonder, then, that "you sense a kind of hollowness / in the endless distance / of the river span."

At this point I hope I am demonstrating that much of the content of the poem that I am evoking through this treaty reading is not, in fact, *in the poem*. Rather, much like the legal apparatus of colonialism itself, it surrounds the poem, rendering the content somewhat synonymous with the context. Reading Cook-Lynn's fiction requires far more than a cursory act of historicizing in this respect. The meaning of the prologue is generated by a combination of its obliquity and the external legal-historical context that intersects with it. *If* the reader succeeds in mapping him or herself into this Dakotah landscape altered by the jurisdiction of colonial law, however, that reader will encounter in the balance of the poem something different—a reassertion of indigeneity, of possession of the land rooted in mythic consciousness and proximity to the place in which that consciousness takes root:

> yet
> as your fingertips
> touch the slick leaves
> of the milkweed
> and roll the juicy leaves
> together
> it is easy to believe
> that this vast region
> continues to share its destiny
> with a people
> who have survived hard winters
> invasions
> migrations
> and transformations
> unthought of
> and unpredicted

and even easier to know
that the mythology
and history of all times
remains remote
and
believable
(Cook-Lynn, *Power* 3-4)

The turn in the center of the poem (signaled by "yet") marks a shift away from the colonialist political-historical mapping of the opening to something extra-constitutional, the historical experience of the Dakotahs, which embodies what Gerald Vizenor calls a spirit of "survivance" (survival and resistance). The vantage point of the reader modulates into a more concrete, tactile apprehension of place (represented through the touch of the milkweed), and through that experience emerges an awareness of not just secular but also mythic history from a tribal perspective. The remoteness of this memory is not intended to be an index of its loss or inaccessibility, but rather of its secure location reposited in the land, set apart from colonial ownership. Accessing it, we should recall, is for Cook-Lynn a central part of the vocation of the indigenous/nationalist writer, "the recovery of memory through writing" ("Fiction Writers" 80). The poetic prologue concludes, then, by implying that the stories to follow will carry out some of that work of recovery. Here, perhaps, those other Dakotah directional associations with east and south begin to assert their controlling influence on the piece.

What my reading of this poem is meant to suggest is that the process of developing a treaty reading of Cook-Lynn's work advances according to different protocols than formalist interpretation. What Cook-Lynn's work often requires of its readers is not simply close reading but also *supplementation*, an oscillation back and forth between law and literature, between context and content, to consider the significance and implications of the literary text for the assertion of sovereignty. (This kind of indigenous/new-historicist reading, it seems to me, is what she would prefer to see dominating that portion of NAS that is committed to literary study.) In this respect Cook-Lynn is urging us to read her written works *in the spirit of the oral tradition*—where the potentially variable meaning of an utterance is shaped by our sense of its performative context and its audiences and not simply by its manifest content.[20] To read in the oral tradition, if you will, is to be willing to secure the potential meanings of a text by asking questions like the following: What is the context I imagine for this text, and how does factoring context into my reading create for me a sense of the text's meaning? What seems to be the audience (or audiences) being addressed or constituted in the text? Does the text function in the same way for these different audiences? And finally, does the text direct us toward other material outside of itself to further develop its meaning? By encouraging these kinds of readerly questions, Cook-Lynn's writing functions performatively in a manner analogous to traditional storytelling; I think this is why Vine Deloria, in his jacket comment for *Aurelia*, commented that Cook-Lynn's fiction reminded him of "the way people used to talk."

Read along the lines I am suggesting, "Mahpiyato" provides another useful example of the complexity of the conjunction of law and literary aesthetics in Cook-Lynn's discourse of sovereignty. "Mahpiyato" has no plot in a conventional sense, and it may strike some readers at first as enigmatic. In less than five hundred words we are presented with a brief sketch of a grandmother (identified by the untranslated but contextualized Lakota word "[k]unchi") and her granddaughter walking toward an unnamed river to gather fruit.[21] As they walk, the shadow of a cloud falls over part of the river, creating an imagistic fusion of blue and grey in the water. The grandmother draws the child's attention to this phenomenon:

> "That is what we call *mahpiyato*, isn't it?" said the old woman to the child.
> "That is what *mahpiyato* really means." She stood as if entranced, her long fingers now touching the fringes of the blanket.
> "To say just 'blue' or 'sky' or 'cloud' in English, you see, doesn't mean much. But *mahpiyato* is that Dakotah word which tells us what we are witnessing right now, at this very moment."
> She pointed.
> "And you see, she is blue. And she is grey. *Mahpiyato* is, you see, one of the Creators. Look! *Look at Mahpiyato!*"
> Her voice was low and soft and very convincing. (Cook-Lynn, *Power* 6)

Despite its apparent simplicity (or perhaps because of it), to interpret this story—to consider what it means—using the standard tools of formal literary analysis is both difficult and limiting. It is hard to recognize what is happening before us, in other words. And yet, when approached more in the spirit of orality, and through a practice of treaty reading, the words of the page open up in remarkable and powerful ways as a manifestation of tribal-nationalist vox populi and an effort to assert sovereignty.

Let me start with the question of potential audiences, or addressees. We can produce a particular kind of strong nationalist reading of the text by focusing on what I will refer to as its constituent audience, an implied reader who identifies him or herself as a member of the Dakotah people. This is the Dakotah vox populi performed in the piece, in other words. Read in this way, the text *means* in particular ways. In very basic terms, "Mahpiyato" represents an affirmation that the sacred exists. Notice that there is nothing about the content of this short sketch that marks it as a fictional narrative. Within the collection of stories that it opens, it announces a belief in the accessibility of the mythology and history though a homeland that is suggested at the end of the poetic prologue. For its constituent audience, "Mahpiyato" would surely be resonant in additional ways, as well. Consider the relationships being modeled in this short piece—both across human generations and between the human and the sacred. Additional linguistic competence—noting that we are dealing with the child's paternal grandmother (kunchi) as opposed to her maternal grandmother (unchi)—might lead us to conclude that the story is teaching about the protocols of cultural transmission on a number of levels. One might notice, in this context, that the granddaughter does not speak at all in the piece, as she "knew from long experience about the moments when the stories came on and watched cautiously" (Cook-Lynn, *Power* 6). One might also attend to the structure of the grandmother's story teaching of the child. The teaching emerges organically from the experience of place (this visionary moment) and is equally rooted in the specifics of the Dakotah language.[22]

We might recall, in this context, Cook-Lynn's previously cited definition of "the indigenous view of the world—that the very origins of a people are specifically tribal (nationalistic), rooted in a specific geography (place), that mythology (soul) and geography (land) and inseparable, that even language is rooted in a specific place" ("Fiction Writers" 85). Kunchi models for the constituent reader the notion that the relationship between the human and the sacred is ongoing, mutually sustaining, and facilitated through language preservation, and in doing so draws that reader into a sense of indigenous solidarity needed to buttress separatist nationalism. Kunchi's sense of wonder in the moment depicted comes across as unfeigned, too, and her rhetorical question to the child ("That is what we call *mahpiyato,* isn't it?") indicates a shared experience of the process of expanding sacred knowledge across generations. This, too, resonates for the constituent reader as an invitation to participate in an ongoing process of nation formation by identifying with a particular form of political subjectivity. At this point, though, we are probably bumping up against the limits of this text as a discrete performance, as it seems to urge further consideration of how social being and sacred community are regularly reconstituted through the experience of place and narrative. This story, then, invokes the need for *more story,* for the continuation of an imaginative process of community formation and knowledge transmission through narrative. Cook-Lynn pursues that extension in her chronicle of the adult experiences of Aurelia Blue in her subsequent trilogy. For a constituent reader of this text, though, "Mahpiyato" represents an initial call to indigeneity, an invitation for Dakotah people to look at themselves from their own perspective. In this way, the story invokes its treaty context both by asserting the extraconstitutionality of Dakotah nationhood and by interpellating the people into a resisting community prepared to defend it, offering a model of political subjectivity for the purposes of decolonization.

I think what I have just presented is a reasonably persuasive, though surely incomplete, tribal-nationalist reading of this story. What I have attempted to do here is to put into practice Cook-Lynn's call in *A Separate Country* to develop and employ indigeneity as a category of analysis. What I take her to mean in this regard is that it is vital for a tribal-nationalist criticism to encourage and facilitate a process whereby Indian people are able to examine themselves and represent their world and experiences in a manner grounded in their own systems of knowledge, tied to place and language. In that spirit, the preceding reading foregrounds many of the ways that the text represents a forceful assertion of key elements of indigeneity and sovereignty through art. And yet when we approach the process of reading in the spirit of the oral tradition, we are enabled to recognize how easy it is to further reformulate the meaning and function of the text by altering our sense of audience and context. If one reading of what "Mahpiyato" is *about* foregrounds the demonstration and reconstitution of a particular Dakotah national ethos and voice of the people *for the Dakotahs*, surely there would be other potential meanings and significance of the tale for other audiences—for a broader, nonconstituent readership. Indeed, some of those other meanings are crucially important in light of the story's overall function in a context of treaty-centered nationalism. Put simply, there are (at least) two parties to any treaty agreement. If my reader will allow me to pursue the analogy, to grapple with the dynamics of international engagement that the treaty structure embodies *in a literary context* involves asking not just how to do a nationalist reading of an Indian text, but also how else a text might aim to interpellate readers who are not a part of the nation.

Departing a bit from Womack's formulation of sovereignty reading, then, I would suggest that treaty reading must also take into account the question of how the nationalist writer/critic negotiates the need both to write from a tribalcentric perspective and to cultivate necessary alliances and shared understanding outside of the tribal community (to ensure the recognition that is necessarily a part of the assertion of sovereignty). It is not my intention to reify an insider/outsider heuristic, in other words, but rather to show how different types of readers must be integrated in Cook-Lynn's discourse of sovereignty. A non-Dakotah reader surely has the potential to appreciate the belief system and social structure being invoked in "Mahpiyato," even if they are not his or her own. There is no contradiction between that idea and the point that a story like "Mahpiyato" is not intended to produce that same kind of nationalistic affirmation and impulse toward community formation in its constituent readers and its general readers. For an attentive and receptive general reader, the text's primary function is to produce an urge to pursue more of the tribal-centered knowledge needed to make it meaningful. Interestingly enough, it offers some clear guidance in how to engage in that pursuit.

As reader-response theory urges us to recognize, the range of ambiguities and textual gaps in the piece are functional. The story's enigmas are cognitively productive ones, as they push the reader to seek out supplemental knowledge. In "Mahpiyato" those textual gaps requiring supplementation range from the obvious (Mahpiyato is *one* of the Creators, but who are the others?) to the more subtle (we might wonder what knowledge is *not* being conveyed in a story that both makes a point regarding the limitations of English for conveying Dakotah knowledge and yet uses *only two* Dakotah words). The story also seems to cry out for more detailed mapping, similar to what we saw in the prologue, both in geographical and temporal terms. When and where this story is located surely matters to our sense of its overall meaning. To the extent that "Mahpiyato," in two short pages, can convey to a general reader the need to engage in considerably greater detail with Dakotah culture, then, it has the potential to transform that reader into someone more able to appreciate the justice and integrity of Dakotah claims to national and territorial sovereignty.

And yet there remains a strong possibility that "Mahpiyato" will remain for general readers a closed, enigmatic text, a vague sketch devoid of deeper meaning, or perhaps a bit of local color that depicts a fading ethnic past. Even if a reader is attentive to the textual gaps in the story, it is not clear that the text is easily able to dictate both its context and its interpretation in the way that Cook-Lynn and other nationalist critics might want. "If we accept the notion that ideas and the concepts of origin are essential elements of an indigenous text," Cook-Lynn has argued, "we are required as readers to look more deeply into the cultural translations that the story presents" (*Notebooks* 7). It is difficult, though, to facilitate readers' full engagement with this requirement. This dilemma, I would suggest, stands at the heart of the aesthetic problematic of Cook-Lynn's discourse of sovereignty, with its fused emphasis on treaty-nationalism and treaty reading. For there is a deep tension produced by the competing imperatives of Cook-Lynn's project: the need to resist recognizability and colonialist containment in nonindigenous textual forms, the need to cultivate a strong sense of indigenous national consciousness, and the need to facilitate a particular kind of interpretive exchange between the tribal nation and its treaty-making partner to advance the cause of sovereignty.

One sees throughout Cook-Lynn's writing an awareness of the problem posed by the fluidity of interpretive context. Consider her criticism of Wallace

Stegner. In many respects for Cook-Lynn, Stegner is simply a figure of a particular kind of historical blindness that erases the Indian presence from the history of the West. Where she sees in the Western landscape (the landscape of "Mahpiyato") a rich historical text, Stegner sees a blank canvas on which his own imagination can write a new history. They interpret the same places in radically different ways. Cook-Lynn thematizes this problem in "The Clearest Blue Day," another story in the *Power of Horses* collection. There, on the final days of a *wacipi* (traditionally, a healing ceremony, but here in the story and often now, a social occasion), three characters, "a young Indian dancer, a black Christian missionary woman, and an old singer of the Wahpekute," regard the Missouri river (Cook-Lynn, *Power* 57). Each one experiences something completely different in that landscape. Claude, the dancer, reflects on the departure of his lover and the changes in the land tied to the building of dams and the creation of recreational areas. The Christian woman, now bored with the missionary work that called her from her home in New Mexico, sees the splendor of the Missouri River, formed into a huge lake at the head of the dam. The old singer, tired and resting after playing a significant role in last two days of wacipi, does not see, but rather is framed in, a scene apprehended rather differently: "Behind the old man the whitecaps on the gray-blue waters flashed and dipped. The sun blazed, and it was the clearest blue day" (65). The significance of rendering the river in this way is only clarified in the final section of the story, where Cook-Lynn describes the sight of dancers streaming into the arbor occupied by the three principle characters: "Like a large, natural flow of water, the Dancers representing the People, the Dakotapi, poured into the dance arbor, each one brilliantly painted and adorned, carefully stepping in time to the drum, heeding the heartbeats of their own humanity and the humanity of all generations" (65). The depiction of these other wacipi participants as a natural flow of water—not *dammed* water—completes the portrait of the old singer in the previous section. He is a part of *this*, and the reader is able to discern the persistence of the sacred and mythic here, even in the context of a changed ceremonial form. But while even Claude is able, finally, to be caught up in this transformative experience of place (he forgets his lover, Julia, and "the disasters of the modern world" as he is absorbed in the drumming and dance), the unnamed missionary, paying scant attention to the dancers, is simply distracted by the wind before walking slowly away toward her car. In the end, then, the story presents all these characters in the same physical space, but in very different places of awareness and consciousness of that place.

So how does one ensure that one doesn't miss the river for the dams or end up with a Wallace Stegner type of (mis)reading of stories like "Mahpiyato"? One answer to that question, of course, would be to simply concede that it cannot be done. But this would be to despair that literature can have an impact on the struggle for sovereignty, owing to the vagaries of literary interpretation. Granted, there is some justification for this kind of pessimism (in which Cook-Lynn indulges at times). Consider the following comments from an online study guide to *The Power of Horses* produced by the South Dakota Library Association, written by an emeritus history professor from South Dakota State University: "The book begins with a 'Prologue,' which is a prose poem naming change and some of its consequences, and a prelude narrative entitled 'Mahpiyato,' which describes a grandmother speaking lovingly to her granddaughter about the beauty of the earth, encouraging her to look closely to truly see, and teaching her the language to describe what she sees" (1). Regarding "The Clearest Blue Day," we are given the following interpretive guidance: " 'The Clearest Blue Day' dramatizes the missionary presence among tribal people from a different angle of vision, as it portrays a young missionary woman with considerable sympathy and compassion. Both stories are vivid depictions of what logically occurs when one society attempts to impose its philosophies and values upon another society" (1).[23] I could take some time here to articulate why I think these comments constitute rather limited readings of Cook-Lynn's work, but that would be beside the point. What we see plainly here is the way in which, in the world of real readers, the process of making meaning from Cook-Lynn's stories can easily bypass her sense of necessary interpretive context. The author of this guide is clearly not offering a treaty reading, nor is he even making much attempt to consider the narratives from a Dakotah point of view (reading "The Clearest Blue Day" primarily through the lens of the missionary is striking in this respect).

Cook-Lynn is certainly aware of, and troubled by, the problem of this kind of reader, a problem that weighs heavily, I think, in her criticism of the high profile of "the ambiguity in literary studies" in NAS (*Separate* 20). And yet, at the same time, storytelling remains an essential vehicle for the production and transmission of knowledge in a Dakotah context; it is impossible to imagine a Dakota discourse of tribal nationalism that repudiates or bypasses it. What Cook-Lynn confronts, then, is the challenge of how to continue to create and transmit story in a way that simultaneously serves her tribal-nationalist project and effectively cultivates the kind of allied audience/reader that can engage in the form of treaty reading needed to support that decolonizing project.

Throughout her career as a fiction writer Cook-Lynn has employed a variety of strategies to address the problem of defining interpretive context and generating the kind of indigenous-centered perspective she sees as vital to advancing the cause of sovereignty in the political realm. Before looking at some of those strategies in more detail, though, it may make sense to pause and further elaborate *why* literary interpretation matters so much to this devotee of treaty-nationalism. The answer, quite simply, is that treaties, as texts, expose with particular clarity the relationships between literary and legal interpretation. Consider, in this context, another one of the crucial legal documents in Cook-Lynn's tribal archive—the 1825 Treaty of Prairie du Chien, which is the first written agreement between the United States government and the Sioux. This document, much like the later Treaty of Fort Laramie, represents a crucial strand in the history of Dakotah sovereignty, offering powerful evidence of the extraconstitutionality of Indian nationhood. For Cook-Lynn, again, the simple act of treaty making provides unambiguous evidence of the nation status of the various participants in the agreement. As we have seen, this argument has been made by other thinkers and writers in Indian country during the past century, and one can even argue that it has been tacitly acknowledged in the American legal system. When the U.S. Congress unilaterally forbade all subsequent treaty negotiations with Indian tribes in 1871, we should recall that it did so for the (questionable) reason that tribal communities *no longer* merited the designation of "national" powers, which made it ludicrous for the U.S. government to treat them as such. The underlying logic here, though, suggests that earlier treaties had indeed been negotiated with nations. Clearly, for Cook-Lynn, the Treaty of Prairie du Chien represents proof of the fact of nationhood. It is a foundation upon which subsequent assertions of sovereignty can be grounded.

And yet, it is quite clear when one considers the actual language of this document that the process of interpretation can be just as hard to discipline in the context of law as it is in the context of literature.[24] Even in such a fairly unambiguous document, a sovereignty-centered reading of the Treaty of Prairie du Chien is by no means an inevitability. Here is how the treaty begins:

> The United States of America have seen with much regret, that wars have for many years been carried on between the Sioux and the Chippewas, and more recently between the confederated tribes of Sacs and Foxes, and the Sioux; and also between the Ioways and Sioux; which, if not terminated, may extend to the other tribes, and involve the Indians upon the Missouri, the Mississippi, and the Lakes, in general hostilities. In order, therefore, to promote peace among these tribes, and to establish boundaries among them and the other tribes who live in their vicinity, and thereby to remove all causes of future difficulty, the United States have invited the Chippewa, Sac, and Fox, Menominie, Ioway, Sioux, Winnebago, and a portion of the Ottowa, Chippewa and Potawatomie Tribes of Indians living upon the Illinois, to assemble together, and in a spirit of mutual conciliation to accomplish these objects. (Prucha 43)

What do these words say about tribal nationalism? Do they provide, in themselves, unambiguous validation of the claim that Indian nations preexisted contact with the United States? This would be Cook-Lynn's claim. Read a bit differently, though, might they document the emergence/development of a new form of tribal nation, born out of contact between indigenous and Western powers? This reading does not absolutely conflict with the first one, of course, and it does allow for assertions of sovereignty, albeit formulated a bit differently. Based on his powerful argument in *X-Marks*, Scott Lyons might read the text that way, seeing it as evidence that the various Indian groups who were party to these negotiations were beginning a decades-long process of modernizing their ethnie by affixing their "x-marks" to a new kind of agreement (and entering into an Indian modernity). Even some readers working from a Euro-American legal tradition might be in partial agreement with that interpretation, viewing the Treaty of Prairie du Chien as a North American Westphalian moment, whereby out of a context of eclectic warring polities emerged a new tribal nation-state system. And yet we must also concede that other readers might see in our text confirmation of the very proposition that Cook-Lynn is most eager to challenge—the assertion of American legal superiority and dominance within the context of the Law of Discovery. It is fairly easy to glean from the passage above that the United States positions itself as a trustee of peace on the plains, stepping in to prevent its wards from doing harm to themselves and to American interests. It is worth noting, in this regard, that article 10 of the treaty contains language that explicitly invokes the ideology of Discovery: "All the tribes aforesaid *acknowledged the general controlling power* of the United States, and disclaim all dependence upon, and connection with any other power" (Prucha 42). Here we have the American government laying the foundation for the subsequent extinguishing of Indian title to desired lands and walling off interference from other colonizing powers, in precisely the way this had been done since the sixteenth century.

From the same words of the same text, then, emerge at least three different interpretations, all with different implications for tribal sovereignty. Clearly, to build one's discourse of sovereignty around treaties is not as simple as it might first appear. It is not simply a matter of holding up the documents as if they were deeds establishing clear title. A significant part of the political project of treaty-nationalism, then, needs to center around the cultivation of anticolonial interpretations of these crucial technai of sovereignty. This process involves a battle over the representation of the *intent* of the parties who signed them and the context in which the agreements were made, an attempt to recast those treaties (as Vine Deloria has suggested) not as unequal contracts but as enduring interrelational covenants. These are precisely the same issues that Cook-Lynn confronts in the realm of literary production and interpretation. Thus it is not surprising that, for her, the processes of reading and telling stories are deeply linked to the processes of the reading and interpretation of treaties. It is this deep linkage that makes treaty-nationalism become a kind of ideology that weaves its way through multiple disciplinary contexts to produce a discourse of self-determination. In this respect, I would once again submit that Cook-Lynn is wrong in declaring a general war against the big-tent interdisciplinarity of NAISA.

When we recognize that interpretation is a problem with equally important literary and legal consequences for Cook-Lynn, then we can better consider how and why she has set about trying to assert some hermeneutic control over her own work. Her strategies for doing so include (1) producing supplemental commentaries on her fiction to guide readers towards sovereignty-buttressing treaty readings based on awareness of legal context and indigenous content and (2) recuperating and reinventing the relatively moribund concept of intent as central to literary interpretation, in part by drawing on genre theory and employing the Dakotah form of the keyapi tale to guide the reading process. To see how she has tried to employ the first strategy, we might consider another piece from *The Power of Horses*, "A Visit from Reverend Tileston." This story, which depicts an intrusive group of missionaries making an uninvited visit to a house on the reservation to pray with the Indian family living there, will likely strike most general readers as a straightforward satire. One academic reviewer's commentary on the piece is representative here. In a review of the collection, Monique Ramune Jonaitis describes "A Visit" as

> a comical ten-page anecdote of one family's resistance through silence toward three traveling soul saviors. The clergymen who have come to 'spread the Gospel' forcibly impose 'fire and brimstone' biblical passages and church songs onto the community. To show just how relentless and unwavering the Catholic priest and his nuns are, Cook-Lynn throws in some comic relief, such that even the dog tries to 'detach from the oppressor' when he begins to howl and whine. (149)

The problem with this perfectly legitimate and sensible reading of the story, however, is that it misses much of the piece's intended nationalistic thrust. The fault here may be with the text itself, according to Cook-Lynn, who has described it as "obscure" (*Anti-Indianism* 47). To counter this textual problem, then, she has taken it upon herself to supplement the work with an extended commentary.

Cook-Lynn's discussion of "A Visit" models many of the components of a treaty reading of an indigenous text. In her view, the story contrasts intrusive Christian mythology with Dakotah culture in particular ways. The role of specific Dakotah knowledge in the piece is intended to situate it as an expression of critical indigenism, which Cook-Lynn has characterized as "a category of being and origin and geography, useful for refuting other theories of being and origin, such as what Christianity offers" (*Separate* 15). To grasp the specific critical thrust of the tale, though, requires us to be aware of the underlying mythic framework she is employing to structure the surface-level satire. "A Visit" turns on the knowledge that the Sioux, before they were the Buffalo People (Pte People), were the Star People. In her commentary Cook-Lynn references the traditional beliefs that the Sioux were created from water by a holy presence and then given the name *wicun* because they were supposed to be little suns to light the darkness of the world. This knowledge grounds Sioux cosmology and informs both a philosophy that emphasizes the exploratory nature of the journey into humanity and the idea that "creation is meant to be amiable and salutary, reflecting mirror-like onto the earth" (Cook-Lynn *Anti-Indianism* 48). This mythology also grounds Sioux "occupancy and possession of a specific geography on earth," a point that relates directly to Cook-Lynn's sense of the larger treaty context of her writing and her sense of how her fictions buttress assertions of sovereignty (48).[25]

Having established this context for the reader, Cook-Lynn explains how the myth underlies the narrative. The story ends after the departure of missionaries with a brief reminder about one of the star stories. After the youngest daughter watches the missionaries drive away, singing hymns loudly into the night, she "went to find Uncle, who would tell her a story about the star people and how the four blanket carriers once helped him to find his way home from a long and difficult journey" (Cook-Lynn *Power* 23). Cook-Lynn's explanation of her decision to do no more than mention this myth here highlights the story's subtle interpellation of a constituent reader; the myth is not repeated, she claims, because the Sioux know it as well as Christians would know the story of Mary and Joseph. In her commentary, though, Cook-Lynn registers her awareness of the need for her nationalistic texts to also cultivate allied, general readers, noting, "I've always thought that the little collection of short stories ... deserved a broader audience" (*Anti-Indianism* 46). So, for the benefit of that audience, which will not automatically recognize this invocation of Dakotah peoplehood, she explains that the specific myth referenced by the daughter is about the constellation often called the Big Dipper, but known to the Sioux as "man being carried into the sky" (*wicá akí yuhan pi*). The seven stars of the cluster are carriers of seven sacred rituals of the people. The four main stars are the four spirit people who assisted in the journey across the skies during the creation period, and this is recalled in the ritual of the Blanket Dance. With this in mind, the dog in "A Visit" is intended to recall the Sacred Dog (*shunka wakan*) who accompanied the Sioux on journeys in the present world. He is a protector, and in the story his whining saves the people from the Christians. The dog does not simply represent comic relief. That, at least, was Cook-Lynn's intent in the story. But as this discussion (as well as her own confession of obscurity) would indicate, "A Visit from Reverend Tileston" highlights the difficulty of producing a nationalistic text that accomplishes all of Cook-Lynn's narrative goals: galvanizing the Dakotah people as constituent readers, resisting incorporation into recognizable and cosmopolitan forms, buttressing extraconstitutional claims regarding the possession of place, and clearly defining a shared interpretive context that leads to the kind of recognition needed for effective assertions of sovereignty.

Part of the problem with the text's obscurity, ironically, may center on Cook-Lynn's commitment to a particular realistic aesthetic, central both to her anticosmopolitanism and her sense of what constitutes authentic indigenous expression. There is a strong cultural-conservative streak in Cook-Lynn, and she has seldom expressed interest or support in more avant-garde or experimental Indian writers. Speaking for herself, she says, "as a writer, I have come to the conclusion that it is not necessarily my overriding business to create new ways of looking at the world . . . but simply to remember the old ways and to tell my listeners about them" (*New Indians* 184). Her own literary models are largely older ones, then, writers such as John Joseph Mathews, D'Arcy McNickle, and even Ella Deloria. In contrast with what she calls an "old structural realism," Cook-Lynn opposes the literary influence of postmodernism and magic realism, which represent for her literary aesthetics that undermine the status of tribal knowledge and experience apprehended as *reality*, not as trope or image (52). Her suspicion of literary cosmopolitanism, then, is related to a sense that it supports this transformation of cultural realities into digestible tropes. Of course, no one would dispute Cook-Lynn's right to determine, for herself at least, the literary aesthetic that best advances her ideology. But it is worth pointing out that one of the advantages of alternative aesthetic discourses (like magic realism, postmodernism, or their tribal variants such as we find in the work of someone like Vizenor) is that they aggressively foreground the need for active interpretation, recontextualization, and critical thought in a way that is not always the case for more traditional, realistic works. In other words, it is not easy for the nonconstituent reader of "A Visit" to recognize the *need* to interpret the whining dog in relation to Dakota tribal roots. And it is probably fair to say that even a reader like the author of the aforementioned reading guide might recognize the need to engage in more sustained interpretive thought if confronted with, say, Stephen Graham Jones's *The Bird is Gone* or Gerald Vizenor's *Dead Voices* as opposed to "A Visit from Reverend Tileston." On this point, though, Cook-Lynn's commitment to anticosmopolitanism seems to have blinded her to the virtues of a more diverse Native literary canon.

In addition to articulating the mythic subtext of her story, in her commentary on "A Visit" Cook-Lynn gestures toward the second strategy she has tried to employ to cultivate sovereignty readings of her work—an appeal to specific ideas of genre. This is a more promising move in light of Cook-Lynn's interest in the treaty as a focal point for sovereignty discourse; according to one prominent understanding of the concept, genre functions as a type of contract between writer and reader whereby each agrees to follow a specific set of interpretive conventions in making texts meaningful.[26] In generic terms Cook-Lynn characterizes "A Visit" as a keyapi ("they say this") story, a narrative mode that she frequently employs in her writing. *Aurelia* is littered with both overtly declared and implicit keyapi moments. Keyapi stories typically begin with a long description of place and home. Following this pattern, before the noisy arrival of the obtrusive missionaries, "A Visit" opens with almost four pages of description of place: "Fifty miles from the nearest town of any size, deep in the bend of the Missouri River, where the *Dakotapi* had made history for generations, lived the Family" (Cook-Lynn, *Power* 12). The generic significance of this opening is missed in readings that see the piece only in satirical terms, for in that context the preliminary description would seem superfluous. As Cook-Lynn describes it, though, the keyapi story genre is about more than an expression of the geographical specificity of a people and culture. It is also a mechanism for signaling authorial intent in choosing to tell a particular type of story and for defining the larger context in which a narrative is to be placed. As Cook-Lynn puts it, a key characteristic of the keyapi form is that it provides a linguistic marker of the commencement of a purposeful act of narration. The comment "I will tell a story," she notes, is a common response to finding meaning in life and events *by connecting them to other, antecedent narratives* (perhaps mythic ones, perhaps shards of more recent historical memory). It signals, in other words, an attempt to employ a narrative text as a vehicle for reflection within some other, broader context that links together stories into a larger pattern. Cook-Lynn calls this "narrative's partnership with history" (*New Indians* 190). Equally significantly, she argues that in a Dakotah context there are very specific nationalistic implications for this act, as the transmission and connection of stories to present experience express the social structure of the band that is foundational for the tribal policy. Cook-Lynn notes that this "continuous overtracing of personal histories within the *tiyospaye* concept (defined as a societal/cultural/tribal organizational construct), which is based upon blood and ancestral ties and lineage and is so much a part of the storytelling process for the Sioux, is never put into the Third World theoretical lexicon simply because the professors are not much interested or are uninformed" ("Fiction Writers" 93). The invocation of genre in both the compositional and interpretive processes serves her, then, as a means of ensuring that readers do become interested in the relevant issues.

One final example from Cook-Lynn's short fiction represents perhaps her most successful attempt to create a nationalistic narrative, advancing the cause of sovereignty in a treaty-centered context and addressing the interpretive problems I have laid out. In the title story of the collection, "The Power of Horses," we have a narrative that exemplifies Cook-Lynn's discourse of sovereignty with remarkable economy, providing a clear indication of the real potential to achieve a powerful fusion of law and literature along the lines she has envisioned. As is the case with the balance of the collection, the realism of "The Power of Horses" marks it as an aesthetic throwback to the short fiction being produced by American Indian writers in the late nineteenth and early twentieth centuries, but Cook-Lynn employs those realist strategies to particularly good effect in this piece. The story opens with a depiction of tension between an unnamed Indian mother and her daughter, Marlene, tension that is largely sublimated in a scene where the two of them work together cooking, peeling, and canning beets. At first, we seem to have a typical story of adolescent conflict with a parent (Marlene sullenly resists having to do the hot, uncomfortable work), but other details soon suggest additional levels of meaning. Shortly after she and her mother begin their work, Marlene notices her father outside conversing with a white rancher and grows apprehensive. "They always want something from him," she thinks, clearly signaling an awareness of her family's defensive position in a settler-colonial landscape. With her sense of protectiveness toward her father roused by the sight of the unfamiliar, but vaguely threatening, white man, Marlene reflects on the tensions between her two parents. She has been manipulated by her mother into watching her father for signs of infidelity, shaming him in a way that is just as damaging to him as his present tendency toward drunkenness. Memories of this shame lead, in turn, to a recollection of her own discomfort in confessing this "history of acrimony" to a priest (depicted with a faint hint of sexual predation) at the mission school she attended (Cook-Lynn, *Power* 70). Deploying a minimalist, realist aesthetic and skillfully employing Marlene as the focal, point-of-view character, then, Cook-Lynn begins to create a map for the reader where family tensions are interwoven with the history of colonialism. Through this map the power of horses gradually emerges.

In the story horses have tangible, physical reality, symbolic resonance, and mythic significance and power. They first appear as a literal, threatened family possession. Marlene divines that the white man has come to buy the horses from her father, and we can further assume that the bargain struck in his drunkenness is an unfavorable one. The literal threat of loss here functions as a synecdoche for the broader history of settler-colonial dispossession. This point becomes clearer when Marlene opines to her mother that her father must be selling most of the horses (excepting only her horse, two brood mares, and a special black-and-white gelding that she calls *Shōta*, or "smoke" in Dakotah). The mother responds with a story from her own childhood that contextualizes the present moment and Marlene's efforts to come to terms with it, while also linking both of their memories to a larger mythic history through the keyapi form. "I used to have land, myself, daughter," the mother begins, "and on it my grandfather had many horses. What happened to it was that some white men from Washington came and took it away from me when my grandfather died because, they said, they were going to breed some game birds there; geese, I think" (Cook-Lynn, *Power* 72). The specific explanation of how and why this dispossession took place is strategically left out of the story, urging the reader/interpreter to engage in a full treaty reading—to ask jurisdictional questions and provide supplemental context.

There are no dates in "The Power of Horses," so, as in the prologue the reader must piece together a temporal and geographic map. Stephen Mission, the school Marlene had attended, refers to a town and mission founded on the Crow Creek Reservation in 1886–1887 (the beginning of the allotment era). We also have a reference to Fort George, so we have a clear sense of where to place the story. The darkened house at dusk, the lack of other signs of rural electrification, Marlene's knowledge of her grandmothers' having made paths to gather plants along the riverbank, and the discussion of the heat and drought that has left grass too short for the horses offer temporal clues that allow us to locate the present moment the story in the mid-1930s, probably 1934. This was both first year of the dust-bowl droughts of the era and, interestingly, the year of the IRA legislation, which in Cook-Lynn's view would only serve to further undermine traditional Dakotah political autonomy and sovereignty. These markers, in turn, help us locate the loss of Marlene's mother's land in the context of the implementation of the allotment policy (by unilateral legislation, we should note, not by treaty) in the wake of the passage of the Dawes Act. Her grandfather's death opened the door for the expropriation of addition familial surplus land to non-Indian speculators. "There was no one to do anything about it," Marlene's mother notes, "there was only this old woman who was a mother to me, and she really didn't know what to do, who to see, or how to prevent this from happening" (Cook-Lynn, *Power* 73). The specific history of the dispossession of tribal lands through allotment, in violation of treaty rights, emerges as an important supplemental context for the narrative in "The Power of Horses," then. As the story shrewdly implies, this history is largely invisible in the settler-colonial narrative of the West. Not surprisingly, though, Cook-Lynn counters the "Wallace Stegner" interpretation by directing her reader to pose different questions about the history of this place. These are sovereignty reading questions: How do you map this place? What jurisdictions are operative here? How did the events depicted in this story come to be? Answering them requires effort on the part of the reader, of course, but unlike in "A Visit," "The Power of Horses" provides sufficiently concrete markers to allow the nonconstituent reader to supplement the text without remaining mired in obscurity. We are directed, effectively, to reinterpret the colonial history of the West—a move that we have seen is crucial in Cook-Lynn's view to the political agenda of a properly engaged NAS.

Marlene's mother's narrative about her land does more than simply register loss and guide the reader toward a recognition of colonial history, though. In the end the story is not just about the land. It is about the horses who have lived on it, the way those horses have historically linked the Dakotahs to each other and to the land (through the tiyospaye concept), and the potential for Marlene to use that knowledge to cope with present-day challenges. "Among the horses there on my land was a pair of brood mares just like those two out there," the mother tells Marlene (Cook-Lynn, *Power* 73). In addition, "there was also another strange, mysterious horse, *su'ka wak a,*" a word that Marlene notes means "mysterious dog" in Dakotah (73). We might recall the discussion of the guiding and guarding "Sacred Dog" in "A Visit." Both mother and daughter connect this mystery horse with the present-day horse, Shōta, but in the mother's memory it is also linked to an important mythic narrative with deep significance for tribal consciousness and a sense of the possession of place. This story, shared with her by her grandfather (Bowed Head), is of "a primordial time when an old couple of the tribe received a gift horse from a little bird," a horse "that produced many offspring for the old man and woman, and the people were never poor after that" (73). Of equal significance to the end of poverty here is the horse's nation-building role in the creation of the people: "I wish this tribe to be strong and good," the mysterious horse had told the old man, "and so I keep giving my offspring every year and the tribe will have many horses and this good thing will be among you always" (73). In this respect the mythic history of the mysterious horse of the Dakotahs represents a reminder, both for Marlene and for the constituent reader of Cook-Lynn's story, of that extraconstitutional, indigenous consciousness needed to underpin tribal nationalism and facilitate the resistance toward ongoing threats of dispossession and loss. The mother's vitality, both in telling the tale and confronting the challenges of the present, are foregrounded in the narrative, and those early hints that mother-daughter conflict might be the major theme fade away.

In offering her own horse story to Marlene, the mother frames it as a keyapi tale ("it is an old story"). In doing so, she invites Marlene to take it up as a tool for her own process of knowledge formation and to continue to supplement it in her own way. In this respect Cook-Lynn's story offers to its Dakotah audience specific characters who serve as models of political subjectivity congruent with her own treaty-centered vision of tribal nationalism. At the same time, the manner in which the narrative itself is written signals non-Dakotah readers that something special and significant is happening here, in genre terms, something that needs to be *recognized* for the story to be complete. Marlene herself notes the "abruptness with which the story seemed to end," leading her to ask her mother about the fate of those horses on grandfather Bowed Head's land. "What happened to those horses?" she asks. "Did someone steal them? Did they die?" (Cook-Lynn, Power 74). Despite her mother's response "after a long silence" of "Yes, I suppose so," it is fairly clear to the reader that as a power (as narrative, as myth, as memory, etc.) the horses cannot die. They survive, just like the Dakotahs themselves, a people whose blood both stains and flows through this landscape (a point symbolized in the story by multifaceted image of the red beet juice fallen on the drought-stricken ground). Recognizing this, on some subconscious level, Marlene moves beyond her fear of the present to take up the story she has been given.

Marlene herself adopts the keyapi mode in an effort to find the knowledge and fortitude needed to help her father overcome the circumstances that have rendered him "a man of grave dignity . . . comic and sad and helpless" (Cook-Lynn, Power 76):

> Keyapi: Late one night, when the old man had tied the horses near his lodge, someone crept through the draw and made ready to steal them; it was even said that they wanted to kill the wonderful horses. The mysterious gift horse called to the sleeping old man and told him that an evil lurked nearby. And he told the old man that since such a threat as this had come upon them and the people of the tribe, the power of the horses would be diminished, and no more colts would be born and the people would have to go back to their miserable ways. (76)

That Marlene extends her mother's story in this way is instructive, for that gesture cuts in two directions. On one hand, a story about a threat to horses can be seen as an effort on her part to employ traditional Dakotah knowledge to both explain and cope with the present threat of American colonialism. There are, it is clear to her, ongoing efforts to steal the horses (efforts that hearken back to the theft of the Black Hills themselves and the violation of the Treaty of Fort Laramie). At the same time, Marlene suggests that discord *within* the community is also a fundamental factor undercutting its strength and leading to poverty, a point with particular resonance in light of her own ongoing family story. This becomes a major theme in Cook-Lynn's subsequent fiction in *Aurelia*, which explores in greater detail the different models of political subjectivity and resistance that have been advanced in Sioux country from the 1930s to the present.[27] When Marlene thinks to herself that she "must look . . . into the past for the horse that speaks to humans," she is seeking a narrative power both to impel her own community toward the solidarity of peoplehood and to reveal a specific path toward resistance.

It may be mere serendipity, but Cook-Lynn's story implies that something more mysterious and sacred is involved when, the morning after these reflections, Marlene is awakened by her sober and focused father, asking for her help. With her aid, he leads the bulk of his horses into the hills, the same hills "to which the people had come when the Uprising was finished and the U.S. Cavalry fell to arguing with missionaries and settlers about the 'Indian Problem'" (Cook-Lynn *Power* 77). This is a reference to the 1862 war, where the Santees rose up in violence to challenge the failure of the United States to honor treaty obligations, an event of tremendous significance for the self-consciousness of present-day Dakotah people. In those hills, which both call to mind that history of resistance and stand for Marlene as "repositories of sacred worlds unknown to all but its most ancient tenants," father and daughter release the horses into the wild. The Shōta horse, that link between present experience, familial history, and myth, leads the herd away, creating a moment, if not of unambiguous triumph, then of fidelity to community and heritage. It is unclear whether the horses will survive the drought conditions on their own, and the family will clearly be impoverished by their loss. But in releasing them rather than selling them to the white rancher, Marlene's father has reclaimed his dignity and autonomy, resisted in some way the colonial power's enrichment of itself at his people's expense, and reestablished continuity between his family's experience and its tribal heritage. It is significant, too, that each member of the family has contributed to this outcome— her mother in invoking mythic history, Marlene in grasping and extending it, and her father in applying it. This ideal of a resurgence of tribally specific gender roles, with women as the story keepers and males as the more overt political actors, will become another of the major themes of *Aurelia*.

The function of a narrative like "The Power of Horses" in a context of treaty nationalism is clearly complex. It picks up on many of the central themes of Cook-Lynn's critical writings. The story itself is built around, and advances, the core principles of indigeneity (origination in a specific place indexed through myth, memory, and language) and political sovereignty (assertions of the independent authority of the Dakotah nation as a kind of extraconstitutional polity) that she values. It invokes a broader legal context and encourages a reconsideration of American history as settler colonial, rewarding the application of the principles of treaty reading. It cultivates a nationalist constituent readership of Dakotah people while also seeking, through a variety of textual strategies, to engage allied readers in a kind of interpretation that recognizes Dakotah perspectives. This masterfully written story resists the impulse that Cook-Lynn finds in much postcolonial writing to merely thematize colonialism or position a cosmopolitan reader to speak for the Indian. Rather, it pushes readers to *see* the world from a Dakotah perspective. In this respect, "The Power of Horses" is a literary act that resonates with Cook-Lynn's most optimistic appraisals of the transformative power of the written word: "It is my business to remember . . . to remember the past and recall the old ways of the people. . . . Literature and art, myth and history have always been the way to shape a new world" (*Notebooks* 14).

As I've tried to suggest here, Cook-Lynn's own work provides ample justification for her vocational commitment to literature and criticism as a vehicle for pursuing sovereignty. "As a writer and professor," she has written, "I am more certain than ever before that writing is at the ethical core of the nation building that is occurring on our homelands these days" (Cook-Lynn *Notebooks*, 64). Reading attentively, with a focus on pinpointing her specific vision of sovereignty, we can appreciate the discernment behind the following critical pronouncement: "Put simply, the importance of the word, the book, the literature, and the daily news of any society cannot be underestimated as carriers of ideology" (Cook-Lynn, *New Indians* 178). Here Cook-Lynn alludes to the complex discursive interplay between law and aesthetics in her work, which truly emerges in its full clarify only through a process of treaty reading. A bit ironically, then, Cook-Lynn's literary work suggests the need for NAS as a field to continue to develop in the opposite way from what she advocates. To the extent that texts ranging from traditional Dakotah stories about place to written documents laying down agreements between tribal nations and the United States stand at the heart of the struggle for sovereignty, the field will only fulfill the promises of its foundational years by drawing on the techniques and insights of multiple academic disciplines. The challenge of avoiding becoming a hodge-podge of unrelated, parochial inquiries is a real one. But as Cook-Lynn's own work shows us, when we work to reorient the critical questions that confront us in relation to the problems of sovereignty, we discover that many of the problems that literary professionals comprehend with particular clarity are directly related to the more pragmatic ones that nationalist writers have sought to put at the center of the field.

In conclusion, it is probably also worth reiterating my sense that this process of reorienting the field in relation to sovereignty must also involve a recognition that the discourse of sovereignty is not a simple or narrow one. There are many strains of political thought, technai of sovereignty, and aesthetic approaches that should be taken into account as we think through these difficult critical problems. This is probably the most significant limitation in Cook-Lynn's project, for her almost exclusive advocacy for the treaty as the centerpiece of sovereignty struggles overlooks the fact that other forms and approaches are necessary in the struggle for decolonization. The fact that some indigenous communities in the United States lack an archive of treaties upon which to build a modern political struggle for sovereignty never really registers in Cook-Lynn's writing. Her direct rejection of constitutionalism and constitutional reform also overlooks another key facet of what it happening in Indian country today. To the extent that she writes as an advocate for her own Dakotah community, Cook-Lynn may be entirely justified in her strategic emphasis. But when she seeks to translate her tribal-specific vision into a general platform for NAS in general, greater caution is warranted. With this in mind, in the next chapter I will offer a different but complementary example of how law and literature can be pulled together in a rich discourse of sovereignty. In the critical, legal, and literary work of Gerald Vizenor we can see how a constitutional praxis has opened a different kind of door for further decolonization in the case of the White Earth Anishinaabeg.

CHAPTER 6

Gerald Vizenor's Constitutional Praxis

TRICKSTER HERMENEUTICS AND THE WHITE EARTH CONSTITUTION

Among the major figures in contemporary American Indian literature, there may be no one whose work has been more misunderstood due to narrow applications of the concept of sovereignty than Gerald Vizenor. While some scholars have mounted compelling defenses of Vizenor's writing against his critics (who are often particularly skeptical about its political utility), those defenses have often been primarily literary in focus, exploring Vizenorian aesthetics in isolation.[1] In this chapter I begin with the presumption that a debate about whether political concerns should trump aesthetic ones in our assessments of Vizenor would be misguided. For, as an architect of a richly realized discourse of sovereignty, Vizenor's aesthetics are deeply political (just as Womack's and Cook-Lynn's are). His recent foray into the realm of legal technai (as the principle drafter of the new constitution of the White Earth Anishinaabeg) provides us with an ideal opportunity to explore that claim.[2] Through an examination of some of Vizenor's nonfiction criticism and his constitutional writing, I hope to demonstrate that a *functional* approach to understanding his work (one that emphasizes the effects of his language on readers and what that language does in a performative sense) helps to uncover his praxis. With its striking and innovative linkage of legal and literary concerns, Vizenor's constitutional criticism represents another compelling example of the emergence of sovereignty discourse in the present moment.

As with Cook-Lynn, when evaluating Vizenor's oeuvre in the context of contemporary struggles for tribal self-determination, it is useful to begin with his theoretical work. In his relentlessly dialectical critical essays Vizenor has consistently challenged attempts to define and constrain Indian people within the frameworks of Western legal and scientific discourses. His approach to doing so, however, is rather distinctive among contemporary indigenous writers. Vizenor invites his readers into an interpretive process that emphasizes the mobility of concepts and the performative nature of words themselves. In this respect his prose seeks to interpellate a kind of ideal reader/political subject who will be resistant to the language effects of settler colonialism. Vizenorian critical praxis, then, is a complex synergy of aesthetics and politics, a synergy that appears most clearly when we focus our attention on the issue of interpretation in his work. As we shall see, trickster hermeneutics (Vizenor's term for the reading practices of his ideal reader) has profound implications in the realm of constitutional law, where debates over the meanings of words and the canons of textual interpretation are central preoccupations. And Vizenor's recent foray into constitution writing (the production of a text whose manifest purpose is to be interpreted, with very real consequences) usefully refocuses our attention on the political implications of his other belletristic work, implications that I would argue have always been there, even if sometimes they have been hard to discern.[3]

Finding a discrete entry point from which to begin discussing Vizenor's criticism can be difficult, especially as a typical Vizenorian text regularly directs its reader's attention away from itself—to works by other writers, to other works by Vizenor himself, and so on.[4] One particular essay appearing in *Manifest Manners* offers as concise an overview of the concept and experience of trickster hermeneutics as one might hope for. For that reason, I want to indulge in a somewhat detailed lexical and syntactic analysis of that piece, "Postindian Warriors," in order to discuss the experience of reading it and also to highlight how it renders certain key theoretical concepts meaningful.[5] Those concepts, in turn, will underpin my subsequent analysis of the new White Earth Constitution. The opening lines of "Postindian Warriors" may be taken as representative of the style of much of Vizenor's critical nonfiction. Invoking the Lewis and Clark expedition of 1804–1806, Vizenor observes that this journey "would become the most notable literature of tribal survivance" ("Postindian" 1). Such a seemingly paradoxical statement arrests the reader immediately, focusing our attention on the importance of individual words as loci of meaning in Vizenor's writing.[6] And considering just two of those words can help begin to illustrate some of the key performative dimensions of his prose style.

Even though it is one of Vizenor's now well-worn neologisms, "survivance" is a word that defies straightforward definition. Vizenor implies a legal etymology for the word in his preface to *Manifest Manners* where he remarks that "survivance means the right of succession or reversion of an estate, and in that sense, the estate of Native survivancy" (vii).[7] Legal dictionaries do not include the term, however, employing instead the word "survivorship" to express a related concept of property inheritance. The link between Vizenor's use of "survivance" and traditional legal discourse is metonymic, then. Understanding his word as a legal concept requires a lateral movement between texts and discourses. That kind of mobile thinking encourages a range of simultaneous varied translations of the quotation above. We might, on the one hand, take Vizenor to be saying that the Lewis and Clark expedition marks the origin of the settler-colonial experience for western tribes, necessitating survivance in its wake. On the other hand, we might read the sentence as a way of taking the historical event of the journey and allegorizing it, creating a more theoretical statement. A few sentences later Vizenor locates the essence of the expedition in Lewis and Clark's desire to be seen by Indian people (more on this shortly). That gesture encourages us to retroactively gloss "survivance" as the act of being recognized. Such a move might lead us to understand survivance as the political act standing at the heart of sovereignty itself—the act of asserting autonomy and having that autonomy acknowledged by others. And this, in turn, takes us back to the original sentence again, which we can reread now as a comment on the fact that the expedition initiated a struggle of competing assertions of sovereign recognition and legal regimes.[8]

The word "notable" is capable of various interpretations here, as well, and in the case of this term, we can see that neologism and intertextuality are not Vizenor's only strategies for suggesting the multiple significations of individual words. Context and syntax are what render "notable" polyvalent. "Significant" is one possible gloss, of course, but our word's appearance in a sentence discussing Lewis and Clark's journal suggests that "notable" might also connote something related to record keeping, quotation, or the abstracting of information. Especially in light of Vizenor's avowed interest in poststructuralism, then, "notable" begins to signify something like "iterable," the state of being repeatable and capable of redevelopment and reinterpretation through recontextualization.[9] Such a reading makes sense, especially in light of the preceding discussion of survivance. Settler-colonial history and law have reiterated the story of the Lewis and Clark expedition many times, but so have tribal literatures (oral and written). "Notable," in this sense, can clearly be linked back to the previous comments about this journey as a key moment in an ongoing struggle for political and legal recognition, a moment capable of being revisited and transformed through subsequent interpretation. This reading locates Vizenor's work in a longer tradition of indigenous reinterpretation of Western texts and concepts (like those of Vine Deloria).

I could continue on in this vein (we might ask what happens if we read the sentence ironically), but one should by now be able to see how in less than twenty words Vizenor is able to introduce his readers to an interpretive universe where the meaning of words and concepts is highly mobile. This is Vizenor's primary debt to post-structuralist theory—especially Derridean deconstruction—and the difficulty of his prose style derives from its perhaps grotesque exaggeration of these hermeneutic possibilities. Making sense of a text like "Postindian Warriors" requires a reader to be willing to follow the traces of Vizenor's language through, and sometimes across, texts (both his and others').[10] And it requires an awareness that the precise meaning of a term or concept can vary depending upon its placement in a specific context. Still, as I hope my examples reveal, Vizenor does not engage in an unending form of regressive linguistic play; the meaning of words in his prose is multiple, but not indeterminate.

The broad understanding of the relationship between reading (or, in an oral context, listening) and meaning making that I have sketched here stands at the heart of what Vizenor, throughout his work, calls "natural reason." Natural reason is essentially a form of dialectical thinking, which Vizenor believes characterizes traditional tribal consciousness and the trickster discourse that modernizes and reexpresses it today. For Vizenor, the natural reason of tribal consciousness involves a rejection of the premises of formal logic, especially the presumption that things/concepts must be *either* identical *or* different from one another, in absolute terms, but never both.[11] Formal logic begins with an attempt to set and fix definitions of terms/concepts, while dialectical natural reason seeks to emphasize how a single term may take on different meanings depending upon the set of relations it is placed in. This is a useful way of comprehending language if part of one's project involves decolonizing a concept like sovereignty and removing it from a Western-versus-Indian binary. The kind of reader Vizenor's critical prose calls for, then, is one who is comfortable setting aside a desire for a priori, prescriptive definitions and is instead willing to work at the production of meaning throughout the reading experience. A text like "Postindian Warriors" interpellates a naturally (dialectically) reasoning political subject as its ideal reader. Vizenor seems to intimate that we need both indigenous and nonindigenous versions of that type of subject.

Returning to the text of Vizenor's essay with these ideas in mind, we should note that the focus of "Postindian Warriors" is to engage its readers in dialectical thinking about three interrelated concepts or relations—survivance, simulation, and postindian. After the paradoxical opening sentence discussed above, Vizenor continues his exploration of survivance, doing so primarily through strategies of juxtaposition and implication. As mentioned before, the reader is told that Lewis and Clark reported in their journals that "they wanted to be seen by tribal people on their expedition," a comment that seems to gesture toward a fixed definition of survivance as *the act of being seen by others* (Vizenor, "Postindian" 1). However, the ambiguity produced by Vizenor's syntax and the mobility of meaning at the level of individual words draws the reader on in a search for greater conceptual clarity. *Seen* in what sense, we might wonder? And how does the context of seeing affect the meaning/signification of the act?

The fact that the Lewis and Clark expedition was a colonial voyage of legal discovery is not lost on Vizenor, and he clearly recognizes that not all forms of being seen are equal in such a context.[12] In that light, the essay's immediate juxtaposition of an unexpected supplementary example—Luther Standing Bear's journey east to attend the Carlisle boarding school in Pennsylvania during the allotment era—comes across as an intriguing gambit to advance and complicate the interpretive process. Standing Bear's willingness to expose himself to the colonizing gaze of the other was obviously also a form of *being seen*, but the reader will likely feel compelled to ask, *how is this, too, survivance?* Surely there is a difference between Standing Bear's experiences and those of Lewis and Clark, encountering the Mandan or other western tribes. Vizenor's urging of his reader to work through the commonalities and contradictions between the two experiences (he notes that both "created simulations that would honor their survivance in literature") is a classic invitation to dialectical thought ("Postindian" 1). We are driven to consider how Standing Bear and Lewis and Clark are simultaneously the same and different, how their experiences signify survivance differently owing to their different contexts. It would seem that each asserts sovereignty in some sense (for example, each engages in a process of trying to be seen and recognized by others), but sovereignty cannot mean the same thing for both of them because of the different contexts in which those assertions take place. Puzzling this out fully, however, requires the introduction of the next relational term.

It is clear from numerous references throughout Vizenor's work (including "Postindian Warriors") that "simulation" is a word he adopts from post-Marxist thinker Jean Baudrillard. As Baudrillard uses it, of course, simulation refers to the hegemony of artificial imitations of the "real" in late capitalist/mass media society.[13] Indeed, Baudrillard's use of term often veers into the melancholic or fatalistic—as he sees the real being displaced by artifice in a manner that is not liberating. In reading Vizenor's work, especially "Postindian

Warriors," however, it seems clear that he is not using the term "simulation" with precisely those connotations. Simulation, in Vizenor's dialectical use of the term, does not necessitate the destruction of the real (of, for example, tribal consciousness). Again comparing Standing Bear and Lewis and Clark, Vizenor notes that their expeditions were more than "mere simulations of savagism and civilization" ("Postindian" 2). "How so?" the reader asks, sensing again that "simulation," like "survivance," means differently depending upon its context. Here is one possible answer: Lewis and Clark were simulations in the sense that they represented/embodied "civilization" (as a legal fiction) on a state-sanctioned voyage to *discover* and *possess* savage lands. Another way to say this would be to note that Lewis and Clark's voyage and journals were a form of legal representation explicitly designed to further the development of imperial sovereignty in nineteenth-century America. And yet Lewis and Clark were also men whose autobiographical experiences, as documented in their journals, somehow exceeded those legal roles and discursive functions. Standing Bear, as a celebrity, was a somewhat different kind of simulation, one who represented a different kind of legal fiction (the "assimilable Indian") for many Americans during the allotment era. And yet his autobiography also hints (often through irony) at other levels of experience and enduring tribal consciousness.

Sorting out the valences of "simulation" in this way requires considerable engagement on the part of the reader. Vizenor's textual reconstructing of a process of natural reason demands that we continually set aside our desire for static definitions, engaging instead in the progressive play of ideas and examples off of one another. It is this seeming open-endedness, of course, that understandably troubles some readers. And I would concede that continuing with the kind of dramatization of a hypothetical reader response that I have been offering here risks making Vizenor's writing seem needlessly tedious or circular; parsing Vizenor's critical prose can be a bit like writing an extended explanation of why a joke is funny. The essential point will have been made, though, if my own reader has a sense of the kind of interpretive process Vizenor's text elicits. Again, this is what I mean in saying that Vizenor's prose interpellates a specific kind of reader/political subject. It is also important to recognize that this interpretive process, which Vizenor labels "trickster hermeneutics," is built on the premise that concepts become meaningful through a provisional process of definition and redefinition, positioning and repositioning. Engaging in trickster hermeneutics involves being wary of rigidly authoritative statements and being open to the prospect of the evolving significance of key terms/concepts. Each time one encounters a critical term in Vizenor's writing, one must consider the possibility that its meaning has shifted somewhat because of the new context in which it has been placed.[14] This use of language is politically significant, for trickster hermeneutics is directly opposed to the interpretive canons of the common-law tradition that underpins Anglo-American colonialist discourse. A fluid sense of meaning is also central to Vizenor's understanding of nature of the struggle for sovereignty.

At this point, I would like to set aside this sentence-by-sentence reconstruction of the readerly experience of trickster hermeneutics in "Postindian Warriors" to instead offer a more sweeping statement regarding the significance of the third key relational term in that essay—postindian. If one surveys the series of dialectical statements defining the postindian warrior in the essay, the first thing one notices is Vizenor's refusal to offer stable nominative claims pinning down what such a person *is*.[15] To the extent that he does define terms, those definitions are fluid and context-bound—relational in the dialectic sense. Indeed, we should note that Vizenor seems primarily concerned with defining postindian in terms of functions—what one *does* as opposed to what one *is* in some ontological sense.[16] So what is it, then, that the postindian warrior does? The figure derives its existence and form, at least in part, from the ongoing control of literary and political discourses by the colonizers. In that sense, to the extent that we can designate it as a thing, the postindian is really a historically contingent rhetorical position or storytelling pose defined by its primary function—resistance. There is nothing in Vizenor's writing to suggest his sense that some type of postindian identity represents the inevitable future for or essence of tribal people in the wake of colonialism. "Postindian" does not coincide with a tribal "real," in other words (here we see its intersection with his use of the term simulation).[17] Instead, it may be more useful to think of postindian as a way of describing resistant reading and writing practices that form the basis for a specific model of political subjectivity. Postindian, in its Vizenorian sense, signifies either (1) a kind of performative mask that allows a writer or activist to engage in an evolving dialectical contest with the colonizing institutions and discourses that "invent" Indians in order to dominate them or (2) an approach to reading that is attentive to this dialectical contest. This is part of what Vizenor seems to mean when he positions "postindian simulations" against the "simulations of manifest manners." For a writer to function as a postindian warrior, then, is to engage in simulation that negates the invented "Indian" of the colonizer, but to do so in a way that avoids being pinned down, in turn, as a simplistic and binary "anti-Indian"; this point highlights why it is so difficult to define postindian warrior as a static thing or a comprehensive category that defines identity. And if, as I am suggesting, the phrase refers to both a rhetorical posture and a set of hermeneutic practices that push back against whatever forces would prevent tribal people from being seen or recognized in their own terms, we can see how all three key terms I have been discussing—postindian, simulation, and survivance—interact with one another relationally. The essence of survivance for Vizenor, then, is the act of nurturing the postindian creation of counternarratives and the employment of reading practices that clear away colonial simulations to create a space for the re-creation of the real, the sovereign right of indigenous people to determine how, or how much, they are *seen* by others. An unfolding form of survivance, in this respect, can be the composition of an innovative constitutional text that makes particular interpretive demands of its readers, demands with the potential to facilitate this vision of sovereignty.

When one examines the text of the Constitution of the White Earth Nation (which I will abbreviate throughout as CWEN), one can readily perceive an attempt to reimagine postindian critical practices into the realm of law—to draft a legal document of survivance, in the sense that I have just been using that term, that moves us toward a full flowering of a discourse of sovereignty.[18] Overtly, the text engages with and reworks its key source texts, particularly the Revised Constitution and Bylaws of the Minnesota Chippewa Tribe (hereafter referred to as the Chippewa Constitution), an IRA-era document that the CWEN is intended to supplant.[19] We also see clear evidence of postindian rhetorical strategies in the CWEN's approach to defining White Earth Anishinaabe political subjectivity. Not surprisingly, though, considering what we have already seen regarding the qualities of Vizenor's prose, the CWEN also encourages trickster hermeneutics in more subtle, implicit ways, interpellating the same kind of dialectical, naturally reasoning reader we noted in the preceding discussion of "Postindian Warriors."[20] Taken together, then, all of these textual features reveal the CWEN to be an intriguing legal experiment that asserts Anishinaabe sovereignty in, at times, strikingly aggressive and innovative ways, while also maintaining a degree of engagement with the dominant legal discourses of the Anglo-American tradition.

The preamble of the CWEN immediately foregrounds many of the key features of Vizenor's postindian rhetoric. Preambles to tribal constitutions, especially in the past few decades, are commonly the places where some type of definition of the nation or polity is offered.[21] The preamble, then, is also typically the most explicit statement of Native political subjectivity—the clearest expression of the vox populi—that one will find in the entire text. It is also the place where some suggestion regarding the spirit in which the text is meant to be read might be offered. It is interesting in this regard to note the language of the CWEN preamble and to contrast it with the opening of the earlier Chippewa Constitution:

Revised Constitution and Bylaws of the Minnesota Chippewa Tribe, Minnesota

Preamble

We, the Minnesota Chippewa Tribe, consisting of the Chippewa Indians of the White Earth, Leech Lake, Fond du Lac, Bois Forte (Nett Lake), and Grand Portage Reservations and the Nonremoval Mille Lac Band of Chippewa Indians, in order to form a representative Chippewa tribal organization, maintain and establish justice for our Tribe, and to conserve and develop our tribal resources and common property; to promote the general welfare or ourselves and our descendants, do establish and adopt this constitution for the Chippewa Indians of Minnesota in accordance with such privilege granted the Indians by the United States under existing law.

The Constitution of the White Earth Nation

Preamble

The Anishinaabeg of the White Earth Nation are the successors of a great tradition of continental liberty, a native constitution of families, totemic associations. The Anishinaabeg create stories of natural reason, of courage, loyalty, humor, spiritual inspiration, survivance, reciprocal altruism, and native cultural sovereignty.

We the Anishinaabeg of the White Earth Nation in order to secure an inherent and essential sovereignty, to promote traditions of liberty, justice, and peace, and reserve common resources, and to ensure the inalienable rights of native governance for our posterity, do constitute, ordain, and establish this Constitution of the White Earth Nation.

First of all, we might notice that the Chippewa Constitution created a federal system linking together various bands of Anishinaabe people (identified here, through the colonial-era label "Chippewa") in a manner that is both paternalistic and assimilationist. This reflects much of the ambivalence inherent in the IRA constitution drafting process itself. The emphasis on the development of tribal resources and property, which is picked up even more strongly in article 1 ("the purpose and function of this organization shall be to conserve *and develop* tribal resources and to promote the conservation *and development* of *individual* Indian trust property" [my emphasis]) underscores the nature of this 1934 document; the Chippewa Constitution is, essentially, a business plan for the confederated bands. The clear acceptance of U.S. plenary power in the final sentence of the preamble is, likewise, a far cry from the kind of assertion of sovereign nationhood we may have come to expect from more recently drafted constitutions (those written since the mid-1970s). Rather, it is more of a reflection of early twentieth-century attitudes regarding the limitations on tribal sovereignty within the framework of U.S. Indian law.[22] The Chippewa Constitution is an "Indian" constitution in the sense that

Vizenor would use the term. Even insofar as it represents a progressive move away from the extreme assimilationism of the allotment era, the document still reifies a simulated identity for tribal people that relegates them to a subordinate position in a colonialist hierarchy. This, to be sure, is the kind of constitution that Cook-Lynn rejects as an unacceptable surrender of tribal sovereignty.

With this image of the immediate constitutional precedent, it becomes easy to see that one of the functions of the preamble of the CWEN is to ironically reimagine the earlier written document. I use the term irony in its broad, rhetorical sense here, to designate the idea that the meaning of the new text emerges, in part, from awareness of a larger context, which includes its predecessor document. In other words, irony is a key element of Vizenor's form of sovereign reading and historicization, and it strikes me that we might see some similarity here to what Cook-Lynn was referring to, both in her comments about the emancipatory potential of ironic discourse and also in her focus on context in her development of the protocols of treaty reading. When we consider both what the CWEN preamble says (its content) and how it says those things (its performative or functional dimensions), we see how the new document offers a strikingly different approach to defining Anishinaabe political subjectivity. The preamble approaches the topic of national peoplehood in a classic Vizenorian manner—employing neologisms, complicated syntax that troubles our sense of denotative meaning, performative (as opposed to nominative) statements of definition, and invocations of other texts whose presence supplements the meaning of what is on the page before us. Designating the Anishinaabeg as "successors of a great tradition of continental liberty," for example, is both a radical departure from the Chippewa Constitution's focus on blood quantum (an awareness of the earlier text produces at least some of the ironic meaning of the new one, in this respect) and a complex provocation to the reader in its own terms. What is the "great tradition of continental liberty" referenced in this foundational document? Is this to be taken as an invocation of a pan-Indian democratic sensibility, predating colonial contact?[23] Is this an embrace of at least one important strand of American (United States) constitutionalism? Vizenor cites the U.S. Constitution as another one of his model texts, we should remember, and the second paragraph of the preamble certainly echoes its U.S. counterpart.[24] Perhaps it is an attempt to position the CWEN as a text in the tradition of Native survivance, looking back to the writing of turn-of-the-century figures such as Charles Eastman, Zitkala-Ša, or the clearly admired Standing Bear? Or perhaps, better than all these alternatives, we should see the text as doing all of these things—making a complex point that Anishinaabe subjectivity and nationhood, in the present moment, combines multiple strands of historical and conceptual experience, that (in legal terms, at least) the Anishinaabe polity is best defined dialectically (that is, relationally and situationally).

Other phrases in the opening paragraph of the preamble reinforce this impression. "Totemic associations," we can readily infer, signifies clan structure as a basis for social and cultural organization.[25] But is "native constitution of families" simply a reiteration of the other term, or something else? Syntactically, the answer is ambiguous, but clearly the choice of the term "constitution" itself here is provocative and pregnant with multiplying possibilities of meaning. If, for example, "constitution" *denotes* "creation" in a manner that *connotes* something about the way that webs of interrelationships in complex kinship structures function, does that very connotation have the potential to reshape, dialectically, the meaning of the White Earth *Constitution* itself? Is the preamble gesturing (inconclusively, we must add) toward a subtle reformulation of our understanding of how to read a constitutional document—rendering such a document a textualization of interrelational identity? This strikes me as a move similar to what Deloria was calling for in *We Talk, You Listen* in proposing a radically new way of reading the U.S. Constitution through the lens of the group, or even Mark Rifkin's arguments about the queering of sovereignty. Clearly, the CWEN preamble approaches the definition of Anishinaabe nationhood, and thus sovereignty, in a radically different manner than the business-committee model of the Chippewa Constitution.

Another intriguing aspect of the CWEN preamble's approach to national self-definition involves the text's functional emphasis, its delineation of the Anishinaabe political community primarily in terms of what the constitution calls on it to *do*—create stories. We should also note here, though, that the precise nature of that storytelling cannot be pinned down solely by reference to the CWEN itself—another example of the political dimensions of Vizenor's emphasis on intertextuality as an essential aspect of interpretive practice. A useful way grasp this is to imagine a tribal court judge endeavoring to read the CWEN preamble while preparing an opinion in a case bearing directly on Anishinaabe sovereignty or constitutional law. This hypothetical judge would reasonably conclude from the text in front of her that part of the story of Anishinaabe nationhood involves the promotion of the right of representative self-governance and the preservation of public order. However, neither *Black's Law Dictionary* nor the standard legal fictions and precedents of U.S. Indian law would enable said judge to easily make sense of terms like "natural reason" or "survivance." Indeed, even formulations such as "native cultural sovereignty" and "reciprocal altruism" become problematic terms for legal interpretation. (The latter term, we should note, commonly appears in the field of evolutionary biology, but not law.) In moments like these, then, notwithstanding the fact that it opens a text that has some formal relationship with Anglo-American constitutionalism, the CWEN preamble clearly directs a reader's interpretive thinking outside of itself and away from the discourse of U.S. Indian law. Vizenor's writing cannot be read in good faith, I would argue, without moving beyond a Chippewa legal-historical framework and examining alternative indigenous sources of meaning. These would include, interestingly enough, Vizenor's own literary and critical oeuvre (the most obvious place to look for definitions of neologisms like "survivance") as well as the broader discourse of Native American studies, where "survivance" has been adopted as a term of art. In other words, we can discern the beginning of the emergence of a full discourse of sovereignty around this legal text. The potential transformative power of this postindian preamble is clear in this respect.

The full text of the CWEN (not just the preamble) approaches the definition of Anishinaabe subjectivity in other manners broadly consistent with Vizenor's postindianism. Throughout the document multiple signifiers are used to designate the community as a whole and its individual members. While some variation of this kind is inevitable, the CWEN's use of such variation is unusually extensive, a point that recalls Vizenor's debt to post-structuralist thinking and its emphasis on the contingency and context-driven nature of meaning. The prior Chippewa Constitution, even in seeking to create an economic federation of multiple Anishinaabe communities, nevertheless used only two labels for its subjects—the Minnesota Chippewa Tribe and Members of the Minnesota Chippewa Tribe—a textbook example of the kind of colonial simulation that Vizenor has consistently challenged throughout his career. Even a much more assertive, contemporary constitution—that of the St. Regis Mohawks, or Akwesasnes—limits itself to one phrase, the "Saint Regis Mohawk Tribe" (or "members of . . ."), to designate its subjects. In contrast to this precedent, the CWEN uses eight different phrases to signify White Earth Anishinaabe political subjectivity, with different terms seeming to connote different facets of Anishinaabe legal experience. The CWEN references the Anishinaabeg of the White Earth Nation, highlighting the simultaneity of White Earth's political autonomy and its larger affiliation with other tribes (in both the U.S. and Canada). Phrases like "the White Earth Nation" and "citizens of the White Earth Nation" signify in a narrower way a primarily local definition of political selfhood. Elsewhere the expressions "the people," "no person," and "citizens" are used in those parts of the CWEN focused on civil rights, suggesting an interplay between a more liberal experience of individual rights and community authority. Add to this list expressions such as "the Anishinaabeg and their descendants" (a phrase that picks up on the aforementioned retreat from blood quantum) and an interesting alternation between cultural positions in designating the chief executive alternately as the "President" or the "White Earth Chief," and we find a document that seems to be using textual variation to emphasize that the experience of legal subjectivity at White Earth is richly various and implicated in a range of contexts and discourses. The CWEN strains to avoid interpellating a single type or model of Chippewa subject. Instead it implies that to be a member of this political community is to function at times as a part of a culture that transcends lines of political governance, at other times as an individual enmeshing in the rights of talk and the liberal ideology of the modern United States, and at still other times as a part of a community whose sovereign independence from that American modernity is paramount. Significantly, in this respect, the CWEN innovatively registers a particular vision of the real complexity of the indigenous political life *in our present historical moment*, doing so through its embodiment of Vizenor's thinking about postindian subjectivity.[26] And in doing so it addresses some of the problems with which Womack struggled in *Red on Red* in his efforts to produce a pragmatic model of Creek national subjectivity that avoids being trapped in a reifying politics of identity.

The inventiveness of the CWEN extends even beyond its striking acknowledgment of political complexity as well. Especially significant in light of the arguments I have been advancing in this book, the document incorporates a variety of strategies to shape the process of reading itself. First of all, the CWEN is organized through a provocative use of a generic trope in order to immediately signal its difference from other constitutional texts. The CWEN is divided into chapters, not articles (the term article is reserved for subdivisions within the chapters), a move signaling that the Anishinaabe law-ways being codified here in writing also participate in a larger narrative or storytelling tradition. Such a point is picked up in other ways throughout the text, as in, for instance, the explicit commitment to the practice of restorative justice in tribal courts (a central theme in contemporary indigenous jurisprudence), or more idiosyncratically in explicit guarantees of the "freedom of thought and conscience, academic, artistic irony, and literary expression" (phrases that obviously originated with Vizenor). Another indication of the text's implication of its reader in a specific hermeneutic universe is its creation of both community councils and councils of elders to advise the legislative council and president. These political structures explicitly link this written document of constitutional governance with Anishinaabe cultural practices and oral traditions. The community councils' charge is to "promote, advance, and strengthen the philosophy of *mino-bimaadiciwin* [the good life]" and the councils of elders are expected to "provide ideas and thoughts on totemic associations, traditional knowledge, . . . native survivance, . . . etc." And here we see, once again, the document's most subtle, and perhaps most important, innovation—its persistent direction of its users' interpretive thinking, even as it mandates behaving as a nation in a manner that far exceeds domestic dependence.

In a document that so frequently and variously raises the issue of interpretation, it should probably come as no surprise, then, that the CWEN establishes a potent and multilayered Anishinaabe judiciary. This is in direct contrast with the typical IRA-era constitutions, which emphasized centralized executive authority to a much greater degree and often lacked any independent judicial branch at all. This multilevel court system is assigned both original and appellate jurisdiction, as well as the power of judicial review over any legal matter of the nation. Such provisions, when put into full effect, will place tribal interpretive bodies at the center of White Earth political life and governance. At the same time, in doing so the CWEN urges those engaged in its interpretation to look both inward and outward in the process of meaning making in this new national narrative. The document explicitly notes, in chapter 4, article 17, that its inspiration incorporates not just inherent and tribal sovereignty but also the "rights and provisions provided in the articles and amendments of the Indian Civil Rights Act of 1968 and the U.S. Constitution."[27] And in this respect, the full text of the CWEN complements the complex, situational definition of Anishinaabe political subjectivity discussed earlier.

In the end, then, we can see that the CWEN (and the people it represents) has been "invented" (rhetorically) in a way that would seem to guarantee that it will need to be interpreted using sources outside of itself. We can also infer, based on the performative dimensions of the text that I have been discussing, that its interpreters are expected to approach the text in the same spirit of trickster hermeneutics that underlies Vizenor's criticism. The ideal reader/political subject interpellated by the CWEN will be a "natural reasoner" aware of the multiplicity and relations of Anishinaabe political subjectivity within a web of relationships and legal discourses, and able to function as a postindian warrior who strategically advances the causes of liberty and sovereignty. This is, of course, a high burden to place on readers of this constitutional text, a point that is reinforced in the document's explicit standards for Anishinaabe judges. Those key interpreters must (1) be graduates of a law school accredited by the American Bar Association; (2) be admitted to the bar to practice law in Native communities and in state and federal courts; (3) be experienced lawyers, magistrates, or judges; and (4) have knowledge of Anishinaabe cultural tradition and general history. Interestingly the text does not explicitly mandate that those judges be fluent in the Anishinaabe language. But if the bar is high for these most crucial professional readers of the newly codified fundamental law of the Anishinaabeg, this is because

Vizenor is placing an equally high degree of faith/hope in the power of readers and reading to effect practical change. Indeed the central theme and performative function of all his critical and legal writing is the demonstration of the fact that the most profound transformations of consciousness occur in the process of encountering and making meaning from texts. Even in his commitment to a strong form of rights consciousness, Vizenor acknowledges that texts (be they the U.S. Constitution, the UN Declaration of Human Rights, or a tribal governance document) cannot deliver on their promises of liberty without active readers and a vigorous democratic process.[28] This, I think, would be his final response to the concerns raised by Alfred and Barsh regarding the difficulties in indigenizing Western legal concepts and forms.

This reading of the CWEN is intended to foreground the potential of a discourse of sovereignty emerging from postindian thinking and writing to intervene meaningfully in the project of decolonization. Vizenor's key legal contribution here involves his sophisticated challenge to the common-law thinking that has frequently not served indigenous people in the United States well. Since the founding of the United States, Indian peoples endeavoring either to resist colonialism or to achieve true decolonization have been forced to reckon with the common-law roots of America's legal and political systems—systems that combine in the potent discourse of U.S. Indian law. The tremendous power of American judges to either make or overturn law through the power of judicial review, combined with the canons of interpretation that guide that process (most notably *stare decisis*—precedent), has often made it particularly difficult for tribal peoples living within the United States to effectively and consistently assert their sovereignty.[29] The external struggle for tribal sovereignty (the direct contest between tribal communities and federal or state courts and governments) has been frequently waged in the shadow of the rigid precedents of canonical legal fictions (for instance, "domestic dependent nations") or against interpretations of Indian law based upon disadvantageous new readings of precedent.[30] I would also note that internally (within tribal communities themselves) the struggle over sovereignty has often involved an ambiguous legacy of both strategic and unreflective borrowing from Anglo-American legal constructs on the part of tribal courts and governments.[31] This partly explains why writers like Taiaiake Alfred argue for a total disengagement from Western forms and legal discourse as a condition for true sovereignty.

It is here, however, that the postindian language of the CWEN reveals some of its potential to be of service in the process of decolonization. The canons of judicial interpretation that buttress common-law thinking (which is central to U.S. Indian law and regularly infuses tribal law) are grounded in the practices of formal logic.³² Rigidly fixed precedents are not dialectical concepts; slavish obedience to stare decisis is not natural reasoning. To the extent that the CWEN—in its interpellation of a different form of ideal reader, in its relational exploration of key terms, in its explicit address of alternative interpretive practices—represents a kind of text that resists inflexible common-law interpretive reasoning, then, it can also represent a substantive contribution to the struggle for sovereignty in both the external and internal senses. The text urges its readers (judges, legislators, and citizens, both inside and outside of the White Earth) to read, think, and reason in new ways—to decolonize themselves in this respect. Thus, even granting the legitimate point that there is no guarantee that the CWEN will work as a performative act (that those who engage with it will allow themselves to be interpellated as postindian readers and political subjects in the way the text seems to intend), the constitution's functional opposition to the hermeneutics of the common-law tradition surely represents a form of political praxis no less legitimate than Elizabeth Cook-Lynn's treaty-centered politics and reading protocols. Pragmatically minded critics should notice that the CWEN seeks to engage with and transform Western law in a subtle but immediate way through its embodiment of a postindian praxis. It seeks instead to redefine aspects of Western law (certain forms of rights consciousness, for example) within the context of mino-bimaadiciwin (the good life), for example, and it works to redefine Anishinaabe legal and political subjectivity dialectically in a way that speaks to the realities and contingencies of the present moment.

While it is now ratified and in the process of being implemented, hopefully the preceding discussion has made it clear that we should not regard the CWEN as a finished text. Within the Vizenorian oeuvre, it is also clearly supplemented by a range of literary works, and it is in this conjunction of the legal and the literary that we can further discern the contours of Vizenor's discourse of sovereignty. As with Womack and Cook-Lynn, Vizenor has long sensed deep continuities between the processes of reading and interpretation that underlie decolonizing forms of political subjectivity and the work of literary production. Coincident with his work on the CWEN, then, it should not be surprising that he has produced in rapid succession a series of novels and essays and a long poem that buttress his legal and critical writing on behalf of Anishinaabe sovereignty. This material, which we might refer to as Vizenor's White Earth Narratives, functions in a manner analogous to that of Elizabeth Cook-Lynn's *The Power of Horses* and *Aurelia* to constitute the literary side of Vizenor's discourse of sovereignty. With that in mind, I want to turn now to a detailed consideration of one of those narratives, Vizenor's brilliant novel *Shrouds of White Earth*.

A POETICS OF RECOGNITION: IMAGIC MOMENTS IN *SHROUDS OF WHITE EARTH*

> The Mediterranean sun has something tragic about it.
> —Albert Camus, "Helen's Exile"

In his recent work Vizenor has frequently expressed a sense of affinity toward Albert Camus, whom he characterizes as a kindred spirit in exile.[33] His 2008 novel, *Father Meme*, is in many ways a retelling of Camus's *The Fall*, from which it borrows a number of themes and formal devices. And in the essays collected in *Native Liberty* (2009) and in the American Book Award–winning novel *Shrouds of White Earth* (2010) Vizenor regularly invokes Camus the essayist—particularly his classic meditation on artistic consciousness and political engagement, "Helen's Exile." It is Vizenor's recognition of a shared ability to engage in the dialectical thinking characteristic of postindian consciousness that best explains this sense of connection with Camus. For him, what Camus calls exile is, in fact, the vantage point from which the modern artist engages in the creative philosophical and narrative work that allows him to balance local and global consciousness in a politically engaged manner. Vizenor's own term for this condition and vantage point is transmotion.[34]

For a brief initial illustration of what I mean here by linking Camus's notion of exile with transmotion, we might consider the line from "Helen's Exile" in the epigraph, specifically the phrase "the Mediterranean sun" (186). What exactly is the vantage point from which one might perceive the Mediterranean sun? It might be Algiers, of course, or Oran, Tipasa, or southern France, to list of few of the Algerian-born-exile Camus's vantage points. Similarly, as readers of the 1948 essay will know, one might also be looking from the perspective of an aggressively instrumentalist modernity or from a Heraclitean philosophy of the limit, to list a few of Camus's intellectual concerns. Perhaps, though, the deeper significance of the phrase lies in its dialectical linkage of all of these locations—the particular and the general, the local and the cosmopolitan, the historical and the imminent—all in mutually constituting relations. To stand in the streets of Algiers and contemplate the Mediterranean sun, not merely the Algerian sun, involves an expansive (Vizenor might say visionary) perspective, built on an initial dualism but rapidly transcending it. One can certainly see the Mediterranean sun from a particular locale, in other words (indeed one *must* see from some locality), but one can only see that sun *as* Mediterranean by imagining the relationship between that locale and a larger totality. Paradoxically, one finds oneself "at home" through the dialectical consciousness of exile, or if you prefer, transmotion.

In his recent White Earth Narratives Vizenor has embraced the notion that the creative artist, through the dialectics of transmotion, is particularly empowered to envision analogies between the local and global (one is tempted to substitute "tribal" and "cosmopolitan" here in light of current debates within Native American studies) without collapsing those terms into one another. For Vizenor the creative power of transmotion has been central to the production of a praxis of survivance. Exile, reformulated as transmotion, becomes a positive concept, not a tragic lack (or a terminal creed, as Vizenor might say). Transmotion is the position from which analogical thinking occurs, and it serves as a synonym, perhaps, for what recent scholarly discourses have begun to call transnationalism. It is also, I would argue, the position from which it is most likely to achieve the types of reciprocal recognition necessary for the realization of self-determination. The literary cultivation of transmotion, then, is a necessary complement to the constitutional form in Vizenor's discourse of sovereignty.

Perhaps owing to his work on the CWEN, Vizenor's recent fiction and criticism have advanced his earlier thinking about these issues with its more thorough articulation of the specific events that crystalize our experience and consciousness of transmotion. His current term for the transformative experience of visionary, analogical thinking characteristic of transmotion is an "imagic moment." This concept looms particularly large both as an intellectual preoccupation and as a formal device in the White Earth Narratives. In those texts Vizenor self-consciously foregrounds a series of imagic moments that articulate the relationship between his own transnational aesthetics and his evolving understanding of Anishinaabe sovereignty. Focusing in this discussion on *Native Liberty*, *Shrouds of White Earth*, and the CWEN, then, I want to highlight how Vizenor's consciousness of transmotion enables his engagement with tribal and cosmopolitan materials, bringing those elements into clear analogical relationships that seek to avoid the deleterious pressures of both assimilationism and globalization. For Vizenor, the transmotional subject position becomes a "fourth-person space" from which sovereignty can be asserted *and recognized* in philosophically authentic and politically viable forms.

In his essay "Ontic Images" Vizenor offers two specific examples of imagic moments. The first involves author Greg Sarris's (Pomo/Miwok) discovery of his Indian identity and subsequent transformation from disaffected youth into celebrated author and tribal political leader. Sarris describes the experience in his biography, *Mabel McKay: Weaving the Dream*, a narrative that is structured around his realization that his own effort to comprehend the life of his mentor and friend was intricately linked to the discovery of his own identity.[35] As Vizenor retells it, at the age of twenty-seven Sarris "discovered a picture of his father, a student at Laguna Beach High School," triggering a transformative reconfiguration of his entire life narrative, "one dominated up to that point by his adoption and adverse experiences as a youth in suburban Santa Rosa, California" ("Ontic" 167–168). Vizenor's second exemplary imagic moment is W. S. Penn's (Nez Perce/Osage) account in his essay collection/memoir *All My Sins Are Relatives* of how Native identity in the modern world is creatively "found in a lonely vision" ("Ontic" 169). Penn notes that even though he grew up knowing he was Indian, because of the dynamics within his own family (in particular his non-Indian mother's ambivalence about her marriage to his assimilationist father), he was never truly aware of "how Indian" (Penn 61). His transformative, imagic moment, then, involved the discovery of a photograph of a previously unknown ancestor in the archives of the Brooklyn Museum, "a picture of me taken in 1877 in Osage, Oklahoma—a me named Albert Penn, then, but me nonetheless, and wearing the Anglo name that in an instance of simultaneity I had given the narrator and protagonist of my first novel" (53–54). As with Sarris's experience, the "me" in Penn's case is an "other" in whom he perceives an image of self that causes him to abruptly reconstitute his identity and life narrative. As Vizenor describes it, W. S. Penn's ontic image, his analogical "me" was an "archival, tenuous ancestor" through whom "the author created an imagic moment . . . and boldly announced a surname connection to the Osage of Oklahoma" ("Ontic" 170). In Vizenor's account, then, looking across time and space, both of these exiles (Sarris and Penn) discovered and recreated themselves as Indians in a manner that is both aesthetic and political. Sarris, for example, has gone on to become the tribal chairman of the Federated Indians of Graton Rancheria (Coast Miwok and Southern Pomo) a position he has held since 2005. It is not difficult to see, too, how their experiences suggest further analogies with Vizenor's ontic acts in his own literary and political practices.

To better grasp Vizenor's sense of how these ontic processes of re-creation work, it may also be useful to consider the way in which he employs the concept of modernism as a bridge between his more abstract theoretical musings and his fictional practice. Vizenor opens "Ontic Images" with the following claim: "Native American Indian personal and cultural identities have always been strategic maneuvers, and in that sense *modernist*, names and singularities that arise from and are created by both communal nominations [names], collective memories [stories], and by distinct individual, visionary experiences [imagination]" (159; glosses and italics added). This modernist maneuver of identity formation is effected through the processes of analogical thinking, a term Vizenor adapts from Barbara Maria Stafford's book *Visual Analogy*. Analogical thought may be characterized by both its "uncanny visual capacity to bring divided things into unison or span the gap between contingent and absolute" and its "move to *tentative* harmony" in that process (qtd. in "Ontic" 159; emphasis added). Such a formulation draws attention to the affinities between analogical thought and dialectics. This tentative, transformative, gap-spanning process is modernist insofar as "modernity" signifies *any* moment in which our reality is altered as a result of a shift in our paradigms for organizing/thinking about it.[36] Framed slightly differently, a new critical concept can retroactively restructure the entire historical narrative that precedes it; a scientific paradigm shift can totally alter our sense of the natural world and cosmos; a new form of constitution can change the broader legal nomos in which it operates.

Vizenor sees this modernist impulse as deeply embedded in Native traditional cultural practices, noting that Indian stories "have always been the imagic moments of cultural conversion and Native modernity" ("Ontic" 161). He makes this point explicitly in "Ontic Images" through the example of Crazy Horse—the Oglala leader who spent much of his life on the move and living among the Brulés, Cheyennes, and Hunkpapas (162). In the spirit of Crazy Horse, Vizenor notes, Native "storiers" have always evinced an openness to encounter the new and to move toward a tentative harmony with it in a way that allows for a perpetually modernizing sense of self. Most suggestively, Vizenor grounds this claim in a general ethnographic assertion regarding the customary transnationalism of tribal peoples: "natives have always been on the move, by necessity of sustenance, and over extensive trade routes. Motion is a natural right, and the stories of visionary transformation are a continuous, distinctive sense of sovereignty" (162). Significantly, then, we begin to see how Vizenor relates sovereignty to the ability to create one's stories/identity through a process of analogical encounter with others—through an openness to the ontology of the imagic moment.[37] "Native identities are stories that arise from the common tease of cultures," Vizenor notes (163). I would suggest that the consciousness of transmotion represents, for him, the ultimate vantage point for that teasing.

Shrouds of White Earth may be Vizenor's most sophisticated expression to date of the transmotional tease of cultures, most notably in the way that it intricately links the aesthetic and the political in a discourse of sovereignty, albeit in a less abstract manner than we find in his critical prose. *Shrouds of White Earth* explicitly develops the connections between the trope of exile, the visionary perception and creative power of transmotional consciousness, and the assertion of sovereignty as a phenomenon of mutual recognition. It achieves this remarkable fusion through an extensive series of imagic moments linking its first-person narrator (White Earth Anishinaabe painter Dogroy Beaulieu), Dogroy's interlocutor/narratee (an unnamed and fictionalized, but clearly recognizable, version of Gerald Vizenor), and the great

Russian-Jewish expatriate painter Marc Chagall. There are, to be sure, many other analogical figures in this complex novel; Anishinaabe painter George Morrison's work and biography are referenced in a variety of ways, as are the lives and works of figures ranging from German expressionist painter Otto Dix to Albert Camus. Nevertheless, the aforementioned trio forms the central core of the novel. The effect generated by the imagic links between Dogroy-Vizenor-Chagall is a kind of narrative triptych (one of Chagall's and Dogroy's favorite compositional forms) that highlights Vizenor's understanding of the ways in which sovereignty is asserted and effectualized. Dogroy's claim that "I have no native state but my visionary portrayals in art" should be taken as classic example of Vizenorian wordplay, in this regard, with "native state" referring to both a personal and national ontology (3).[38]

It is striking to notice that the CWEN (which the narrative treats as having been ratified and taken effect, even though this had not taken place at the time of the book's publication) provides the impetus for the plot of *Shrouds*, while also setting up the first of the novel's imagic moments. Dogroy Beaulieu opens the book by noting, "I was exiled from my home and studio in spite of the specific article in the new constitution that clearly prohibits banishment" (Vizenor, *Shrouds* 3).[39] This component of the constitutional text clearly references Vizenor's own career-long discomfort with the application of this punishment to individual members of the nation for specious reasons and his interest in reincorporating displaced urban Indian exiles back into the cultural and political fabric of Anishinaabe life at White Earth. The novel registers this emphasis (forging links between Dogroy and Vizenor) in a number of ways, most notably perhaps in Dogroy's retelling of the story of Marlene American Horse's alienating experiences in Minneapolis, a narrative Vizenor had previously related in *Wordarrows*.[40] The metafictive invocation of the CWEN also reinforces another suggestive imagic moment, set up through one of the novel's epigraphs taken from Edmond Jabés's *The Book of Questions* ("I am in the book. The book is my world, my country, my roof, and my riddle"), for Dogroy continues his account of his banishment noting, "This, a charter irony, was a political contravention, more than a censure of an artistic composition, *as you know, my friend, because you were the principle writer of the article in the constitution that prevented banishment*" (Vizenor, *Shrouds* 4; emphasis added). In a metafictive moment like this, Vizenor's aesthetic and political strategies in the novel begin to become clear. What is being invoked clearly is the idea that while Vizenor's political subjectivity and sense of sovereignty are both indeed symbolized *in the book*, the book is not a closed and finite thing. Rather, "the book" of White Earth is an expansive network of texts and analogical relationships (encompassing written constitutions as well as novelistic fictions), the understanding of which demands of the reader that he or she position him or herself as a kind of transmotional exile. This point should remind us of the earlier discussion of the performative nature of the CWEN itself in the context of Vizenor's trickster hermeneutics. Vizenor is looking at the same issue from another vantage point.

If an initial ontic image of Gerald Vizenor emerges from this clever use of narrator/addressee to invoke the CWEN, the process of relational or analogical self-definition continues in a variety of ways throughout the novel, focalized through the figure of Dogroy. Taking into account just a few of these, we might note first how Dogroy's surname, Beaulieu, recalls not just a place but also Vizenor's own ancestors (key figures in the history of Anishinaabe print culture), who have been subject to considerable reflection recently in the essays of *Native Liberty*; Vizenor writes repeatedly there about their work in publishing the weekly newspaper *The Progress* on the White Earth Reservation beginning in 1886.[41] Significantly, Vizenor's discovery of this family history (tied to tribal print culture, we should note) when he was pursuing graduate studies at the University of Minnesota in the early 1960s represents one of his own personal imagic moments (analogous to Greg Sarris's and W. S. Penn's). As he describes it in the essay "Native Liberty," "I was inspired by the dedication of the editor, and the news stories created a singular sense of native presence. . . . *The Progress* has forever been in my imagination and sense of native liberty. . . . I was transformed, inspired, and excited by a great and lasting source of a native presence and survivance" (36). The associative chain (both direct and metonymic) that links Vizenor to Dogroy here is amplified in a variety of other ways (formal and content-based) in the novel as well. Elements of Vizenor's life enter into the novel through Dogroy's storytelling: Vizenor's work as a community activist between 1964 and 1968 in Minneapolis, his relationships (both positive and ambivalent) with figures ranging from American Indian Movement activist Clyde Bellecourt and civil-rights lawyer Douglas Hall, and other biographical details (his father's murder, for example).[42] Dogroy either appears as a companion/witness to some of these events or he seems to have experienced them himself. Finally, to cement their analogical, shared identity, Vizenor more or less directly invokes the trope of "blood memory," employed to such great effect in N. Scott Momaday's memoir *The Names* and analyzed perceptively by Chadwick Allen in his book *Blood Narrative*.[43] In recounting how he and the addressee, "Vizenor," grew up together, Dogroy fairly explicitly blends their experiences and memories: "My father laughed as he watched us build a brick wall near the street. We carried one brick at a time from the building to the sidewalk. We must have been very serious about the job. . . . My native memories, like yours, are communal, not separate traces of the past. I know, we were about two years old, and now we share these memories and stories of our families" (Vizenor, *Shrouds*

30–31). What we have here is, of course, a textbook example of an imagic moment calling to mind the passage quoted earlier regarding how modernist Native identities "arise from and are created by both communal nominations, collective memories, and by distinct individual visionary experiences" (Vizenor, "Ontic" 159). The interaction of names, stories, and imagination is clearly central to the mutual constitution and the recognition of identity between Dogroy and Vizenor.

This, then, is one side of the triptych, with Dogroy, "Vizenor" the interlocutor, and Vizenor the extratextual presence progressively reinforcing each others' identities through a proliferating series of analogical, imagic moments. Far from being a dilution of self, though, the mobile form of intersubjectivity shared by this trinity actually has the effect of strengthening or amplifying it while providing a clearer sense of aesthetic purpose and beginning to point toward new articulations of sovereignty. But it is only when the third side of the triptych—the figure of Marc Chagall—begins to weave itself through the narrative of *Shrouds* that we truly grasp how aesthetics and politics fully coalesce. The named influences on Dogroy's art (figures who, not surprisingly, are regular subjects for appreciation and reflection in the essays of *Native Liberty*) include George Morrison, David Bradley, Otto Dix, and Albert Camus. Dogroy also references Native ledger art, the primitivist realism of the Santa Fe Indian School (under the direction of Dorothy Dunn), Anishinaabe Midewewin birchbark scrolls, and Japanese Shunga paintings and woodcuts as inspirations. Far exceeding all of these, though, is the figure of Chagall. But why him? In what ways do Dogroy and Vizenor find in him and his work another series of imagic moments?

Any doubts about the significance of Chagall in the novel are easily dispelled when one notes that there are nearly forty discrete references (by my count) to the painter in the 150-page novel.[44] Chagall plays almost as large a role in *Shrouds* as Dogroy himself, then. Numerous particular imagic moments in the text connect the two (or three, if we again think of Dogroy-Vizenor as part of the triptych) figures together analogically. Significantly for my argument here, both are presented as exiles, and this shared exile consciousness is deemed central to the artistic consciousness of each: "Chagall, his dreamy abstract creation of characters in flight, was an inspiration to me, along with the color of floating horses in native ledger art. We were banished by the secular and tradition fascists from Vitebsk and White Earth, the Pale of Settlements" (Vizenor, *Shrouds* 15).[45] In a similar vein, Dogroy notes, "Marc Chagall creates visionary scenes over his hometown, Vitebsk, in Russia, on the Pale of Settlement. Beaulieu is my Vitebsk, a settlement on the Pale of the White Earth Nation" (6).[46] Right from the start of the novel, then, Dogroy and Chagall appear as analogous creative figures whose aesthetic productions are clearly linked to related (but not identical) political experiences—Dogroy's banishment for his opposition to tribal casinos and casino politics and Chagall's semivoluntary exile for his resistance to the dogmatism and secularism of soviet art and the Proletkult movement in the 1920s.[47] Both share the same transmotional exile consciousness that I traced earlier in my brief treatment of Camus's "Helen's Exile," and both might also be linked to the experience of Vizenor's own tribal community with settler colonialism.[48] Beaulieu and Vitebsk form the core subjects of their art, but their consciousness of these locales and representational strategies for depicting them ("shrouding" them, in Dogroy-Vizenor's case) derives from a mobile exile consciousness. To repeat my earlier formulation, then, each finds himself at home in the paradoxical consciousness of exile—where one is both rooted in place and inclined to constantly re-view that place from alternate vantage points.

Building on this initial depiction of a common exile consciousness, *Shrouds* offers readers a larger series of biographical and aesthetic parallels between Dogroy and Chagall. These range from rather subtle (the implicit parallels between Dogroy's muse, Cimone—one of his seven "women of the creature arts"—and Chagall's muse, Bella—his first wife and the frequent subject of his paintings) to much more overt. For example, Dogroy connects his birth with Chagall's in a manner that recapitulates bits of the opening of Chagall's autobiography, *My Life*: "Chagall declared in his autobiography that he was born dead, and during a great fire in Vitebsk on the Pale of Settlement. I was born dead almost fifty years later in Beaulieu on the Pale of the White Earth Nation" (Vizenor, *Shrouds* 58). Both "dead" babies are revived through a dash of cold water, a serendipitous parallel that prophesies the later aesthetic connection between the two, though Dogroy does tease himself for this small moment of narrative modernism:

> Do you suppose, my friend, that because we were first born dead, and bluish, that by seconds we became artists and created abstract creatures and figures that are blue? No, not really, because our figures are green, blue, red, and many other colors, and so are the horses of native ledger artists, the heavenly blue liberation of Wassily Kandinsky, and the creatures of Franz Marc. Even so, blue is the most common color mentioned in *My Life* by Marc Chagall.[49] (59)

The "even so" looms large here, however, and this textual moment is important (and representative) in the framework of *Shrouds* for several reasons. More than just a simple reiteration of the imagic moments and analogies that link Dogroy-Vizenor-Chagall, this passage demonstrates something fundamental about transmotion and the relationship between aesthetics and sovereignty, amplifying a point I made earlier. We should note the connection between Chagall and Native ledger art (a link that comes up elsewhere in the novel) and its pairing with the connection between Dogroy and Euro-American painters such as Kandinsky, Marc (one could plug Otto Dix into the list), and of course Chagall. In this web of analogies we see something of the dialectics of transmotion, as these figures are placed in mutually defining, constitutive relations where they enter into each other in fundamental ways without collapsing into each other. One might put the matter this way: Chagall *is* in some sense a Native painter, but only in the same sense that Dogroy *is* a European painter. Better perhaps to say that Chagall's Nativeness is refracted through his Europeanness, and Dogroy's Europeanness is refracted through his Nativeness. The true subject position of each artist is, in fact, a transnational one, a state of motion between various locations. And of particular significance is the fact that this very mobility and fluidity is what allows them to *recognize* each other and define their sense of liberty (a point related directly to the discourses of sovereignty and constitutionalism, to which I will turn at the end of this discussion).

The concept of liberty forms the linchpin between the aesthetic and the political for Dogroy and Chagall, as indeed it does for Vizenor. We see considerable evidence of this in the essays of *Native Liberty* and in *Shrouds of White Earth*. Dogroy comments, "Marc Chagall inspired me, as you know, to create an art of visionary liberty," and that phrase, "visionary liberty," (which recurs throughout the novel) represents a clear fusion aesthetics and politics (Vizenor, *Shrouds* 70). So what characterizes the visionary liberty of Dogroy and Chagall as exiled artists and transnational Natives? First, of course, is the break with realism in favor of a more figurative, metaphorical, and perhaps idiosyncratic artistic idiom. Significantly, when considered specifically from the location of an American Indian artist, this becomes a potent decolonizing gesture. As Dogroy notes, "Marc Chagall inspired me more than any other painter by his dreamy, bold colors, and flying figures. You see, when *tutored* or cultured artists create colored creatures in flight, the scenes are considered inspirations of primitivism, . . . but when a native visionary artist creates creatures in bold colors on papers, canvas, birch bark, and on rocks, the images are pronounced primitive" (16; emphasis added). Here Dogroy is implicitly contrasting the aesthetic of the Santa Fe Indian School style of painting, under the influence of Dorothy Dunn (which dominated the Indian art scene from the 1930s through the 1950s), with a Chagall-style folk art that reinterprets the "primitive" through the lens of modernity. Readers familiar with Chagall might think of that artist's assimilation of certain technical features of, say, Cubism, which he nevertheless harnessed for distinctly non-Cubist ends.[50] What Chagall inspires in Dogroy (and what he, Dogroy, and Vizenor share) is the notion that one can take a powerful personal sensibility, rooted in tradition and Native ground, and work with and through conventions and forms from other places, cultures, and even languages to modernize oneself. This is, in many respects, what a legal document like the CWEN also represents. Similar to the way that Vizenor has, throughout his career, transformed simulated (or tutored) Indianness through his concept of the postindian, Dogroy testifies to the possibility of uncovering/reviving the "storied presence" of the past (which Vizenor has recently come to refer to as a fourth-person perspective in art) and creating a new, authentic, liberated Native art through imagic moments of contact with others.

Dogroy describes the dialectical process generating this art, which he calls "cosmoprimitivist," in the following way: "Some of the salon artists of Paris, London, and Germany were roused by primitivism, and their art has been ennobled by historians, collectors, curators, and sold at pricy galleries. The perception and sway of native visionary artistic practices have reached around the world and return at this moment to our very conversation in the Band Box Diner [one of the unorthodox locations where Dogroy's own art has been displayed and circulated]" (Vizenor, *Shrouds* 17). Put in a slightly different way, what Dogroy-Vizenor is describing here is the experience of transmotion, rooted in the transnational aesthetics of survivance, and effected through the modernizing force of imagic moments. It is no accident, in this context, that Dogroy refers to Chagall as "the crucial artist of survivance" (62). We might paraphrase the process in the following way (producing a narrative, I would venture, that will seem quite reasonable to many scholars working today in Native American studies): Native peoples were colonized and then "invented" as "Indians." In time, Indian art was invented through the mediation of the colonizers, but traces of the Native persisted in and through that art. This art traveled, and travels, to others (to the colonizers in particular) who reinvent themselves through this imagic encounter. This reinvented art has been, in turn, re-reinvented by Native artists who modernize and assert their Nativeness through it. And strangely enough (even granting that it takes place in a charged colonialist political context), through this continuous process of reflection and transformation the artists/subjects within this cultural field not only come to know themselves in new ways, but they come to *recognize each other* in powerful new ways.[51] Dogroy attests to this throughout the novel, for he not only stresses what he has learned about creating his own, authentic Native art through the ontic image (and images) of Marc Chagall, but also intimates the ways in which this process leads Chagall (or would lead him, were he still alive) to also know Dogroy himself. This explains another odd textual feature of the novel, with Dogroy interspersing reflections on his own biography and experiences with comments such as these: "Chagall would have painted this devout story," (87); "Marc Chagall should hear that story"

(11); and "Marc Chagall would surely believe my story" (127). Such comments clearly suggest a kind of reciprocity of invention and reinvention that exceeds the structures of colonial or neocolonial dominance and tutoring. The ontology of transmotion breeds mutual recognition in a forward-moving process of transformation, a point with clear implications for the theorization of sovereignty. For what Vizenor is writing about here is not only relevant for art, but also for law.

At this stage, it should be clear that in *Shrouds of White Earth* Vizenor is quite self-consciously trying to describe and promote a dialectical process that leads from decolonization to a kind of model of sovereignty built on the experience of transmotion and the power of mutual recognition. In his essay "Mercenary Sovereignty" Vizenor offers further insight into this vision of sovereignty. He begins with a fairly obvious point—that the modern, post-Westphalian system, built on the foundations of "territorial border security and state sovereignty," has historically been no boon to indigenous peoples (Vizenor, "Mercenary" 103). "Native American Indian communities . . . were not secure by mere treaties of peace and sovereignty," Vizenor notes. "Natives, already under colonial siege and disease, were decimated by the first fatal contact with the domination of 'globalization'" (105). As a consequence, he maintains (drawing on Peter Singer and Giorgio Agamben, and echoing Vine Deloria), "state sovereignty must be re-conceived to protect human rights around the world." (106). Such a vision is clearly related to such international and transnational structures as the United Nations Declaration on the Rights of Indigenous Peoples and the United Nations Convention on Genocide (the latter of particular interest to Vizenor recently). And it demands an abandonment of the absolute idea of state sovereignty (and of the state conceived as solely in formal terms) that has come to dominate Western legal thought.

Beyond the obvious failure of the Western nation-state system to respect the rights and sovereignty of indigenous peoples as a matter of external relations (think here of the broad history of colonial conquest and dispossession), Vizenor also notes that we find similar problems *within* the constitutional borders of the United States, in the context of the Doctrine of Discovery and the mechanisms of settler colonialism. He contends, "the United States Constitution has seldom served or protected the rights of natives" (Vizenor, "Mercenary" 109). While this is, admittedly, an oversimplification of a complex legal history, it is essentially correct to note the precarious, unstable position of Native peoples (such as the White Earth Anishinaabeg) within the American constitutional order, and also to recall that this position has involved constant contestation and struggle in the courts and legislative venues.[52] It is noteworthy, in this regard, to recall that Vizenor even offers a mildly ironic, analogical reflection of this problem in *Shrouds of White Earth*, suggesting that even the CWEN is unable to guarantee the protection of rights as a matter of formal certainty. Dogroy, we should recall, is banished from White Earth, despite the prohibition against banishment in the constitutional text, as political maneuvering and intertribal hostilities and rivalries come to determine the application of the text. So, then, if constitutional forms are not inherently able to guarantee sovereignty or protect individual rights, what is the relationship between constitutionalism (to which Vizenor has clearly committed himself, having written a constitution for White Earth) and Native liberty? The answer to that question hinges, I think, on Vizenor's understanding of politics itself as intersubjective—on his commitment to foregrounding transmotion as the vantage point from which a constitutional text should be not only drafted but also read, interpreted, and effectualized.

In "Mercenary Sovereignty" (and elsewhere) Vizenor juxtaposes the idea of transmotion (which he will also sometimes refer to as "continental liberty") to the post-Westphalian state as the locus of sovereignty. In doing so he both makes a move to deterritorialize the concept of sovereignty in positive ways and also places a qualified faith in the messy, democratic processes of transnational recognition. There are, we might note, certain similarities between this vision and Vine Deloria's advocacy for a tribalist politics of multiple, intersecting groups as a way of redefining American constitutionalism. What Vizenor's approach entails, in part, is a recognition that sovereignty is a function of ongoing relations of reciprocity and recognition, not just formal structures. Indeed, Vizenor holds that sole reliance on the conventional liberal nation-state form more or less guarantees the structural maintenance of conflict and the fragility of cooperation (Vizenor, "Mercenary" 113). The state, conceived as a reified thing, cannot protect sovereignty or defend rights in stable ways as long as sovereignty is considered a formal attribute of the state itself, as it is today (113). In contrast to these reified, formal national conceptions of sovereignty, then, Vizenor offers "native interdependence, transmotion, visionary rights, and liberty"—in short, a reconceptualization of the very subjects who invent and employ the forms (113–14). What is needed, beyond the existence of a constitutional text, Vizenor intimates, are subjects of that constitutional order who recognize the own identities through the same ontology of analogic thinking and exile consciousness that we find in *Shrouds of White Earth*. This, inevitably, leads to a reconceptualization of the nation-state itself, for a fully conscious transmotional subject cannot easily commit to the ontology of the Westphalian model. Again, we might note certain similarities here with Deloria's insistence that the legal forms of sovereignty can be transformed through the redefinition of the peoples who constitute and mobilize them. What is needed to assist in this process of reconceptualization, though, is a type of constitution that participates in the aesthetics of survivance and is congruent with the network of mutual recognition that we see in *Shrouds of White Earth*, a constitution that comprehends the Vizenor-Dogroy-Chagall triptych. Literature and storytelling thus enter into an integral relationship with the legal techne of the constitution, a process that yields a fully formed discourse of self-determination.

For Vizenor, I would argue, the power of the CWEN resides not only in its practical applicability to the immediate technical problems of internal governance, but also in its capacity (in conjunction with other stories) to promote transmotional consciousness and political subjectivity on the part of those inside and outside the formal structure of the tribal nation. The CWEN, in this sense, represents a kind of ontic image that furthers the cause of self-modernization and mutual recognition that Vizenor regards as central to the advancement of liberty. It is not difficult to view specific elements of the document in this way, considering the text as an ontic image of the U.S. Constitution, other tribal constitutions, and even the UN Declaration of the Rights of Indigenous Peoples.[53] Considered in this way, we can see that the CWEN aims not only to realize Anishinaabe political subjectivity in a particular form but also to generate potentially transformative imagic moments across political and national boundaries (to influence the self-awareness of the subjects who read and use it, in other words). The earlier discussion of the CWEN, I believe, reveals it to be precisely this kind of text—a document that both responds to and invites a specific kind of reader as political subject. At this point I would like to revisit the preamble once more in order to direct our attention back to some of the supplementary uses to which the CWEN is put in *Shrouds of White Earth*.

The text of the preamble, we should recall, reads as follows in English (though it has also been translated and published in Anishinaabe):

> The Anishinaabeg of the White Earth Nation are the successors of a great tradition of continental liberty, a native constitution of families, totemic associations. The Anishinaabeg create stories of natural reason, of courage, loyalty, humor, spiritual inspiration, survivance, reciprocal altruism, and native cultural sovereignty.
>
> We the Anishinaabeg of the White Earth Nation in order to secure an inherent and essential sovereignty, to promote traditions of liberty, justice, and peace, and reserve common resources, and to ensure the inalienable rights of native governance for our posterity, do constitute, ordain, and establish this Constitution of the White Earth Nation.

It is readily apparent that the two paragraphs of the preamble mirror each other, but they do so with a particular kind of force (one with which readers of *Shrouds of White Earth* should be quite familiar). The second paragraph, of course, tracks very closely with the language of the preamble of the United States Constitution, forming an easily recognizable image evoking that legal and political location. The first paragraph, on the other hand, provocatively evokes another, tribal, vantage point. The relationship between the two is not one of critical comparison or parody, however, as one might think at first glance. Instead, what the preamble intimates through its juxtaposition of these two vantage points is that Anishinaabe political subjectivity exists in a dialectical state of transmotion—relating, but not collapsing, the two locations. The further implication is that a full awareness of each tradition (tribal and American) is achieved through the dialectical relationship between them. Each has the power to modernize and change the other over time, in other words. This is not fundamentally different from the fictional and essayistic examples of transmotion I highlighted earlier. What we see in the preamble to the CWEN, then, is an extension of the aesthetics of survivance employed throughout Vizenor's other White Earth Narratives, one that has for at least one goal a modernizing re-redefinition of Anishinaabe national identity and perhaps as another the gradual transformation of the American legal nomos.

It seems clear to me, then, that Vizenor believes that this kind of ontology of imagic moments can have liberating, transformative effects for both the colonizing culture and the colonized. The audience of the CWEN (or of *Native Liberty* or of *Shrouds of White Earth*) is a cosmopolitan, transnational one, and Vizenor's gambit seems to be that through the analogical thinking provoked by imagic moments, profound shifts in the dynamics of mutual recognition essential for sovereignty to be realized and maintained can be achieved. Two concluding examples should suffice to illustrate this. The first involves the indigenous creation of an imagic moment to transform (albeit briefly and provisionally) the colonial order—Vizenor's often-told story about Charles Aubid's day in federal court. As Vizenor relates the tale (most recently in the essay "Aesthetics of Survivance" in *Native Liberty*), Aubid was called as a witness in a federal case regarding the regulation of the wild rice crop in Minnesota.[54] Aubid testified that as a young man he witnessed federal agents telling another tribal member, Old John Squirrel, that the Anishinaabeg would enjoy control over the harvest in perpetuity. Aubid also offered this testimony as evidence that "the Anishinaabe always understood their rights by stories" (Vizenor, "Aesthetics" 87). Significantly, though, when the judge in the case ruled that such testimony was inadmissible as hearsay, saying, "John Squirrel is dead, . . . and you can't say what a dead man said," Aubid countered with a gesture at the legal books on the bench, wondering why he should believe what these dead white men say when the judge won't believe John Squirrel. Producing a powerful imagic moment in the courtroom in this way,

Aubid altered the course of the case—modernizing the court, we might say, in ways that led to new forms of mutual recognition. "Judge Lord was deferential," Vizenor tells us, "amused by the analogy of native stories to court testimony, judicial decisions, precedent, and hearsay. 'You've got me there,' he said, and then continued with the testimony of other Anishinaabe witnesses" (87). Granting that a single imagic moment like this does not represent an overcoming of the structures of colonialism (it might be taken in a patronizing way, as well) surely we can imagine a *network* of such images achieving substantive ontological change (not just for the Anishinaabeg, but for non-Indian Americans). What Vizenor highlights with this story is the potential impact of imagic moments on the consciousness and capacity for mutual recognition of individuals who are acted on, and act through, legal forms. The cause of Native liberty (and sovereignty) is advanced by the utopian power of imagic moments to pull us into an awareness of transmotion, an awareness that can change those who have come, reflexively, to view themselves as divided from each other by essential legal, political, or cultural binaries.

If the Aubid story offers us a hint of how the consciousness of transmotion has the capacity to transform the colonizer, it also suggests some ways in which Vizenor believes it to be essential for indigenous peoples as well. Vizenor describes Aubid's conjuration of the figure of John Squirrel as central to the "practice of survivance, the storied presence of a fourth person." I want to conclude with this interesting phrase—fourth person—as a final example of Vizenor's reflection on the discursive conjunction between the aesthetic and the political—between literature and law. In "Aesthetics of Survivance," Vizenor compares the court's initial inability to recognize the "other" (John Squirrel, the validity of the oral tradition as testimony, etc.) and modernize itself through an encounter with the other to "monotheism" (87). Turning back to *Shrouds of White Earth*, it is noteworthy to recall that Dogroy characterizes his own imagic art as a "natural tease of monotheism." Dogroy's, Vizenor's, and Chagall's mutual reconstitution of identities and artistic vision represent, in this context, a simultaneous liberation of both self and other, the creation of a new vantage point—the fourth-person perspective. Significantly, from this vantage point (one that I think is legitimate to see as essentially synonymous with Camus's positive formulation of exile and the notion of transmotion), the colonized person seems finally able to transcend the historical and psychological burdens of the colonial experience. The fourth-person perspective is an extension of the concept of narrative point of view where the political subject is understood to grasp his or her own position dialectically, ironically, as something defined through the mutually constitutive interaction between the locality and totality.

Vizenor thematizes this point in *Shrouds* through his treatment of museums, or perhaps more broadly, in his treatment of the spaces in which the visionary products of Native imagination are located and experienced. As my formulation here should suggest, the museum for Vizenor represents not just a literal institutional form but also a metaphor for the location, or vantage point, from which Native subjectivity is performed and perceived.[55] Throughout the novel Dogroy draws our attention to a variety of these sites—the range and complexity of which speaks again to his own transnational subjectivity and transmotional perspective. He opens the novel with a poignant question (one reflecting his banishment from White Earth and from his studio at Beaulieu): "Does anyone ever experience a native state, a secure place of stories, solace, and sentiments that never torments the heart and memories?" (Vizenor, *Shrouds* 5). Lest we think Dogroy is succumbing to a tragic sense of exile here, though, he quickly follows up with a comment to the interlocutor-Vizenor. "Yes, of course, my friend, you create marvelous literary scenes and stories of the reservation, and yet your characters are always in flight from the mundane notions of reality. You write not to escape, but to evade the tiresome politics of native victimry" (5). Significantly, and despite his initial exile, Dogroy attests throughout the novel to his own ability to find spaces from which to view himself, and from which his artistic visions can be viewed, an ability that allows an evasion of victimry and a sure, confident sense of self-worth. Dogroy's mobility (and mobile consciousness), in fact, ensures his survivance, as he locates his artistic career in sites ranging from his home studio to the notorious Native bar Hello Dolly's (razed to make way for a public housing project), to the Band Box Diner (where many of the conversations that compose the novel take place), and to the Galerie Orenda in Paris (to which Vizenor is connected through his nonfictional friend, the artist Pierre Cayol—who illustrated *Shrouds*, and who in this sense represents a kind of ontic image for Dogroy himself). In all of these locations Dogroy's analogical thought and aesthetic are able to flourish and his art is likewise able to circulate effectually. For in each of these sites (however odd or ironic) a process of recognition of a Native presence is able to take place.

It is striking, though, that the novel culminates with a visit Dogroy makes with his muse, Cimone, to the Musée du Quai Branly in Paris, an unusually ambiguous museum location. The Musée du Quai Branly (which was enthusiastically supported by former President Jacques Chirac and opened in 2006) is an anthropologically oriented museum of indigenous art. That formulation is a bit misleading, though, as what it actually contains are a large number of fairly typical artifacts (masks, ceremonial objects, and the like) displayed in an aesthetic manner with great attention to lighting and color context. The museum is wildly popular but has also been the subject of considerable criticism. Many view it as a place that perpetuates stereotypical primitivist images of indigeneity (its garden aesthetic strikes some as advancing a jungle theme, for example). In this respect, the museom would seem to be a classic example of the institutional depiction of the invented Indian (in Vizenor's sense). And yet, in the very architecture of the place we find a hint of some alternative potential—the potential for transmotive re-reinvention that I described earlier in this piece. The Musée du Quai Branly is built in the form of a great bridge spanning the trees of its exterior garden. It has no rooms or doors, instead being constructed as an enormous flowing space (a gradually sloping ramp takes visitors through its collections). The museum is also the product of a conjunction (or perhaps a collision) of artistic and creative visions: the structure designed by the French architect Jean Novel; the gardens by Gilles Clement; the vegetative covering of the buildings by artist Patrick Blanc; and, of course, the contents created by indigenous people from throughout the world over a period of millennia. A bit like a constitution, then, the museum is an ambiguous form, suggestive of the potentiality of transmotion on the one hand, but also quite clearly capable of reinscribing a colonial ideology. In the end, it is the perspective of the user that determines the actual function of the museum.

In the novel's account Dogroy and Cimone bring to the Musée du Quay Branly the type of consciousness needed to transform its meaning—for them at least—from something limiting, tragic, or terminal to something liberating and pleasurable. Entering the museum with their own fourth-person perspective of exile consciousness intact (developed through long experience with the potency of imagic moments) they are able to reexperience the space in powerfully subversive ways. Dogroy notes that "the native names, cultural categories, ethnographic comments, and even the ordinary nonsense documents of discovery were scarcely significant," which is to say that the museum's formal intention in defining indigeneity failed to function for him. Instead, viewed from the perspective of a transmotional artist, "the native objects in the museum became an entity of faint voices" (Vizenor, *Shrouds* 136). These fourth-person voices penetrate through even Dogroy's own initial intention: "we were actually there to critique the 'strangeness' of the museum, but instead the union of chance changed the moment and our sense of presence" (136). "Union of chance," we should note here, is both the title of the final of the chapter of the novel, and a phrase Dogroy uses to describe his imagic relationship with Chagall.[56] Instead, confronting the museum's invention of the "Indian" (which they are fully able to comprehend owing to their own mobile forms of consciousness) Dogroy and Cimone are able to perceive instead the Native traces beneath its forms. They hear voices, "real, ceremonial voices," that were "the native presence of a fourth person associated with the objects in the museum" (139). And the encounter with these voices facilitates an erotic overflow, as Cimone and Dogroy mutually masturbate (a trope for imaginative pleasure and creativity for Vizenor) among the displays. In doing so they, in some sense, reverse the fetishism of dead objects (which museums use as stand-ins for the vanishing or vanished Indian) and replace it with a display that signals the ongoing life and presence of Native people. Having decolonized themselves in this way, they simply leave the museum, unburdened of its form and legacy. Dogroy then returns to his art and, suggestively, finds that his banishment from White Earth has been rescinded.

While an allegorical depiction of onanism might seem an odd gesture to end a novelistic meditation on Native liberty, I think what we see in Vizenor's culminating depiction of the Musée du Quai Branly is, in fact, a powerfully suggestive account of the ways that imagic moments and the consciousness of transmotion might facilitate the development of precisely the kind of sovereign self-consciousness that allowed Charles Aubid to modernize the federal courtroom. And it is, in this respect, just another example of how the path of the Indian exile, paradoxically leads back home to Native ground. The transmotional political subject (whose consciousness emerges in the novel through the Dogroy-Vizenor-Chagall triptych) can, in the end, be neither banished nor erased. The presence of that subject reveals the promise (albeit a bit of a utopian one) of a transformation of the politics and forms of constitutionalism. Drawing attention to this fact strikes me as one of the central contributions of the kind of constitutional criticism that has been pioneered by Vizenor and also is being performed, in some sense, through the rich textual effects of his other work. Vizenor's discourse of sovereignty, then, moves back and forth between the CWEN and his White Earth Narratives, then, forming a powerful conjunction that others can access through their own acts of reading. In his project we find a parallel image, if not a completely ontic one, of Craig Womack's and Elizabeth Cook-Lynn's work. And between these three writers, we can trace many of the contours of an emergent discourse of self-determination that has the potential to radically change our understanding of Native American literary studies going forward.

CHAPTER 7

CRITICAL PROSPECTS

Sovereignty in the Cahuilla Storyway

The relationship between the postindian literary practices of trickster hermeneutics, the CWEN, and the ontology of imagic moments that I traced in Gerald Vizenor's work may be more complicated than the relationships between law and literature in the works of Womack and Cook-Lynn. I want to remind readers, though, that it has not been my intention to set up a hierarchy of writers. Throughout this book I have attempted to illustrate the existence of a set of continuities between the literary and political projects of a range of major contemporary American Indian writers. The figures that I have considered have the common ability to link law and literature together in a discourse of tribal sovereignty, a fact that I have sought to highlight and advance here. One of the central elements of the next phase of American Indian literary criticism, I believe, will involve the emergence of more critical and aesthetic practices designed to fully take up the pragmatic challenges raised by nationalist criticism. These new practices will need to continue in order to develop our understanding of the complementarity of legal forms and literary works in advancing the cause of sovereignty. In this book I have attempted in my own way to contribute to that emergence by exploring and demonstrating some of that variety. My sympathies are with big tent critical approaches, and I hope that I have been able to suggest that the intellectual work of decolonization requires considerable mobility and innovation in our thinking. In this vein, I must also stress again that this book has not been intended to be proscriptive in its arguments or panoptic in its view. I am not suggesting that the projects pursued by Womack, Cook-Lynn, and Vizenor represent a totality of the potential approaches to crafting a discourse of sovereignty;

they are merely particularly rich examples of such approaches. To bring this study to a conclusion and to amplify that point, then, I would like to offer a final example of how the diverse local realities of the experience of colonialism on the part of American Indian people necessitate committing to a diversity of literary/critical practices, interpretive strategies, and legal forms. My focus will be on my own state of California, an understudied and particularly complicated site in which to consider the problem of sovereignty, both from its legal and literary sides.

In 1987, during a campaign by Bishop Thaddeus Shubsda of Monterey to advance the canonization of Franciscan Father Junipero Serra, Rupert Costo and Jeannette Henry Costo published a series of documents and essays intended to challenge the romanticized history of California's mission system and its famous architect. *The Missions of California: A Legacy of Genocide* gathered the testimony of a range of witnesses, writing both on Serra's behalf and in opposition. It reveals a great deal about the challenges faced by California Indian peoples in their ongoing efforts to claim and protect their sovereignty. On the one hand, we find clear evidence of how California Indians have struggled for more than two centuries with the need to confront a history of genocide that continues to be denied by many Californians. This creates a striking irony, of course, when today's Indian communities—which must necessarily maintain a clear focus on the assertion of their continued political existence and vibrancy—must also engage in the paradoxical act of demonstrating to skeptics the degree to which their ancestors were destroyed by colonizing powers. At the same time, California Indians today are faced with a series of presumptions regarding the degree to which they have willingly assimilated into mainstream American society. Many of these originate with the mission apologists, who express bewilderment at the idea that heavily outnumbered enclaves of Spanish priests and soldiers could have built the mission system without the eager and willing participation of their Indian converts. Other similar arguments emerge in the context of tribal gaming, where outsiders sometimes see the economic success of particular tribal communities as evidence that Indian people persist in California as privileged corporate entities, only masquerading as separate polities. The fact that many California Indian communities lack federal recognition, let alone the economic infrastructure of a casino, is lost on many of these critics. But even the successful "casino tribes" find their actual legal and political situation regularly misunderstood in the context of these public debates. The fact that many Indian people living in California are not, in fact, *California* Indians only adds another level of complexity to the overall picture.

While the Serra canonization debate was not specifically an argument over tribal sovereignty, it is worth referencing some of the specific views offered by the scholarly experts who were interviewed by the Monterey diocese regarding the historical experience of the Indian people indigenous to California. The defense of Serra and the mission system offered by the church in the 1980s reveals how Indian people in California often continue to fight many of the discursive battles of the nineteenth century even as they seek to assert their sovereignty using the tools of the twentieth and twenty-first. In the opinion of Harry Kelsey (chief curator of history at the Los Angeles County Museum of Natural History), for example, mission history tells us that California Indians voluntarily accepted Spanish religious and secular authority in a manner that reflects a "human condition" whereby "people in general are dissatisfied with what is going on" and "want things to change" (Costo and Costo, *Missions* 207). Though it is unclear what specific evidence leads him to his particular Hobbesian conclusions (which are perfectly consistent with the Law of Discovery), Kelsey confidently asserts that "the Indians were delighted to come into the missions," for up to that time "they had been living on the bare edge of existence" and in a state of "constant warfare." By ushering their Indian wards out of this state of nature (where a concept of Indian state-sovereignty would hold no meaning), Father Serra and the other missionaries fortuitously "came in and rescued them from extermination" (209).

Other experts cited by the diocese take further pains to locate the California tribes in a nineteenth-century narrative of cultural hierarchy and evolution. Michael Mathes (professor of history at the University of San Diego) opines that the assimilation of Indian people into a more advanced Western culture was inevitable. "Considering colonial systems as inevitable," he notes, "the Spanish system, for all its faults, was the best available at the time: The most humane, the most progressive in the sense that it was designed to integrate a society" (Costo and Costo, *Missions* 210). Such a view of the history of settler colonialism in California positions Indian survivance as hopelessly compromised from the very start. From the perspectives expressed by Mathes and Kelsey, the survival of any Indian peoples into the present day only serves as proof of the fact that they were, indeed, ushered out of "primitive" tribal life and assimilated into modern society. Had they not assimilated, in other words, they would be dead.

Lest Indian people today are inclined to reverse this assimilative trend by reasserting some sort of precolonial political sovereignty, we can find other experts eager to explain to us that precontact California Indians possessed none of the attributes of nations on which a claim might be based. Doyce B. Nunis (professor of history at the University of Southern California) tells us that it was the introduction of Catholicism that "for the first time dignified the individual" in Indian society. Further, in his view, "up to that time, the Indian had no sense of fidelity to each other, there was no spirit of loyalty.

There was no spirit of commitment. You stayed together out of necessity rather than appreciation. In other words, *they had no idea of a social compact*" (Costo and Costo, *Missions* 220; emphasis added). If Indian people apparently lacked the sense of corporate identity necessary for meaningful communal life (for peoplehood in a political sense), let alone for a nation built on the liberal model of the social contract, it is not surprising that they would also be seen as lacking a sense of specific territory (another key element of nation-state status). "You must understand something about the Indians of North America, that was true of the Indians here in California," Nunis concludes. "They had no sense of land ownership. It was communally owned. And since the Indians of California were not agrarians, but rather gatherers, *they had no sense of place. Only a sense of area*. You know, in the winter we go here because there is something there, and then in the spring we go here because there is something there, and in the summer we go here because there is something there, and so on" (222; emphasis added).

It is not my contention that the opinions expressed by this particular cohort of pro-Serra scholars represent a consensus view in academic circles. Nevertheless, I trust that the fact that these positions were advanced so confidently, and by multiple sources, in the context of a fairly recent debate of considerable significance for the master narrative of California history will help to reinforce two key points in the present study: (1) the contemporary discourse of Indian sovereignty must be a varied one, precisely because of the persistence and protean nature of colonial legal systems and their master narratives, and (2) an understanding of the conditions driving that variation are necessary if we are to evaluate the connections between literature and law in the development of discrete discourses of sovereignty. I want to offer an example of these ideas by focusing on issues that are, for me, quite literally close to home. Thinking about what sovereign reading might involve in a Southern California Indian context underscores, for me, the potential problems created if scholars seek to designate one particular form of critical praxis as *the* solution to the pragmatic problem of linking literary study with political activism. My illustrative act of textual analysis will focus on a particular Southern California community, the Agua Caliente Band of Mission Indians (Cahuilla), and a particular text from that community, Francisco Patencio's 1943 *Stories and Legends of the Palm Springs Indians*. In order to set up my discussion of that work and elaborate on of some of the approaches we might take to situate it within the broader discourse of tribal sovereignty in a California context, however, I want to offer first a general overview of the complex position of a band like the Agua Calientes in relation to the contemporary struggle for sovereignty.

In some respects Indian country in California bears little resemblance to Indian country in the territory of relatively large tribal communities such as the Diné (in Arizona) or the Cherokees (in Oklahoma). According to the 2010 census, there are 108 federally recognized tribes located within California's borders, along with one recognized by the state but not by the federal government, the Juaneño Band of Mission Indians. The sizes of the California tribes range from as few as five people to as many as four thousand. In addition to these disparately sized entities that are recognized, there are some seventy-eight other groups currently petitioning for recognition. These unrecognized Indian communities are unable to hold reservation lands collectively in trust under U.S. law. The recognized California tribes, however, have nearly one hundred separate reservations or rancherias. Again, though, there is considerable variation in the nature of these sovereign territorial spaces. Some are as small as six acres in size. Some, like the Agua Caliente Reservation, are located in the middle of urban centers (Palm Springs, in this case). Some (particularly in northern California) are rural and relatively isolated. And finally, we should note that there are also numerous individually held trust allotments throughout the state. These facts create considerably different conditions than those faced by large nations like the Dinés, whose reservation covers more than 24,000 square miles and is occupied by more than 170,000 of their own people (over half of their total population in the United States).

The overall Indian population in California is not small, of course, but we must recall that this population is also much more diverse than in many other parts of the county. According to the 2010 census, counted individually, California actually has the largest population of American Indian/Alaskan Native (AI/AN) people of any state (362,801). California also has the largest mixed-blood population (AI/AN along with some other identified ethnicity) in the country, totaling more than 720,000. Despite this large Indian and mixed-blood population, California has relatively little tribal land (trust land) within its borders, and less than 3 percent of its total AI/AN population lives on a reservation or rancheria. Part of the reason for this is that more than half of the Indian people living in California are members of tribes located outside of the state. But many members of tribes indigenous to California also live either without a reservation land base or off reservation.

Clearly, bearing this kind of data in mind, it is difficult for most, if not all, California Indian tribes to effectively make claims for full political sovereignty. In general, to rely on claims like those made by Cook-Lynn's Dakotahs would be a complicated proposition. Many California tribal communities lack a bounded territory large enough to sustain a sizeable permanent population today. Many also lack a population that could function effectively as a fully autonomous polity along separatist lines. In addition, many of the common metrics used to define sovereignty in group-centered cultural terms (such as those used by Vine Deloria) can be difficult to apply in contemporary

California contexts, owing largely to the particular history of settler colonialism in the state. At least fifty indigenous languages that were spoken in California before the arrival of European settlers have become extinct, and of the roughly fifty that remain, many are on the verge of extinction (Hinton 27). Conservative estimates of language preservation suggest that in the mid-1990s the largest cohort of indigenous speakers located within the borders of California was the Quechan people living in the southeastern corner of the state, who still had approximately 150 fluent language users at that time. Among the Serrano people, in whose traditional territory I live and work, however, the number of fluent speakers at that time was two. Among the neighboring Cahuillas, that number is only slightly higher. There are efforts underway throughout the state (some at my own institution) to preserve and teach endangered languages to younger generations of California Indian people. And many communities still maintain their songs and traditions, though it is not uncommon for a singer from a California tribe to confess that the specific meanings of specific words being sung have been lost and forgotten, or for tribal communities to share singers/songs to make up for gaps that have developed in their own cohort of practitioners. But in the final analysis, as Deborah Miranda (Chumash/Esselen) has noted in her recent memoir, *Bad Indians*, the experience of many indigenous Californians today in interacting with their traditional cultures is one of reconstruction and reconstitution, often involving fragments of knowledge and tradition (sometimes embedded in the archives of the colonizing power).

If demographics reveal particular challenges facing California Indian people in their struggle for sovereignty, we should also note how some of the most important legal technai employed elsewhere in that struggle have been rendered less effective for many California tribes, owing to the specific patterns of colonial history in the state. When compared with other Indian people within the borders of the United States, California Indian peoples first encountered European colonialism relatively late. Despite this fact, they have found themselves confronted with the need to endure a bewildering variety of traumatic colonial encounters. The Spanish colonization of Alta California commenced in 1769 with the expedition into what is now San Diego County led by Gaspar de Portolá and Junipero Serra. This date marks the commencement of the mission system that would eventually extend from San Diego to Monterey. The goal of the missions (universally conceded, even by those critics who still dispute the degree of coercion and violence in the system) was the conversion and assimilation of the indigenous population. The joint church-state program of *reducción* (reduction) aimed to gather California Indian people into concentrated communities located near the missions where they could be instructed and supervised (as well as employed as a source of cheap labor). This displacement, not surprisingly, had the ancillary benefit of opening up tribal lands for use by the colonizing power. Even if, in theory, the missions were merely holding some of these lands in trust on behalf of their new wards until they had reached the necessary point of cultural maturity, in actual practice they facilitated a process of dispossession. While no more than one-third of the Indian population living in the vicinity of the missions was ever brought under their supervisory control, the disruptions they brought to traditional tribal lifeways were still extensive and traumatic. And no stable legal foundation for *international* relations was established between the Spanish and the Indians at this time. To date we do not have a universally recognized archival history of treaty negotiations or enforceable documents from the Spanish colonial period on which California Indian people can later draw in reasserting their sovereignty. The mission-era Spanish, we should recall, never treated this population as independent polities in formal terms. Rather, they were viewed as (primitive) *individual* converts and subjects of the Spanish crown.

The changes wrought by the Mexican Revolution on the situation of tribal people in California would also be difficult to characterize in positive terms. When the Mexican Republic was formally proclaimed in 1824, the official policy of the government was to render all inhabitants of the former territory of New Spain (including Indians) citizens of the new nation with equal civil rights. We should note first of all, though, that even in the most ideal situation, this move to grant individual citizenship to California Indians would not constitute a recognition of corporate political identity or sovereignty. While theoretically effecting a liberation of sorts for Indian peoples from the control of missions, Mexican policy must still be characterized as assimilationist and colonialist. In practice, of course, even this ideal vision of colonial policy failed to be actualized. During the period of the secularization of the missions (which commenced with the 1833 Statute of Secularization and continued up to the beginning of the war with the United States in 1846) the Mexican government attempted to convert the missions into pueblos and allot their land holdings. The Indian wards of the missions were to be emancipated, with male heads of families given lands and agricultural implements to allow them to live as independent farmers or ranchers. Indians were prohibited from selling their lands, though, or from entering into independent contracts, restrictions which often drove them into poverty and landlessness (Costo and Costo, *Natives* 192–93). As in the case of the later U.S. policy of allotment, the effect of secularization was to impoverish and dispossess the Indian population that had gathered around the missions. Non-Indian settlers grabbed up surplus and "abandoned" land, with the final divestment of mission property happening in 1845 through public auctions decreed by

Governor Pio Pico (the last Mexican governor of California). The nominal citizenship of California Indians did little to protect them from what Rupert Costo refers to as a "period of plunder" (195).

The history of California's incorporation into the United States as a state in 1850, following the Mexican-American War of 1846–48, reveals the continuing vulnerability of California Indian people in the face of an aggressive colonizing enterprise. Technically speaking, the 1848 Treaty of Guadalupe Hidalgo should have granted California Indians, along with other Mexicans living in California, citizenship in the United States. Taking possession of California just as American imperialism was heading into its peak period, though, the U.S. government refused to recognize California Indians as included within the terms of the treaty. Federal authorities were thus complicit in the political erasure effected by the new California state legislature. With the passage of the California Indian Indenture Act in 1850 some indigenous people were put into a condition of de facto slavery, and many California Indians would remain disenfranchised until the passage of the Indian Citizenship Act of 1924, which made *all* Indian people in the country U.S. citizens. With California Indians positioned in an even more extreme position of domestic dependency than usual, the U.S. government moved to negotiate a series of treaties that would define the limits of their territories and gain significant concessions of lands. Between 1850 and 1852 the American commissioners negotiated eighteen treaties with various tribal communities throughout the state. Owing in part to protests from the new California delegation to Congress, however, these were never ratified by the Senate. But the Indian people who negotiated these agreements were not informed of this fact. Encouraged by federal agents, and in many cases suffering from starvation and homelessness, many Indians moved unilaterally to their new reservations, freeing up their old lands for settlement. In the end these reservations were created through executive order, not through the mechanism of the treaty. The result of this, of course, is an unusual situation in Indian country, in which California Indian people can assert with some justification that they entered into a treaty relationship with the U.S. government, but at the same time, the U.S. government is technically correct in claiming the opposite. The end result is that the treaty functions as an ambiguous techne of sovereignty in a California context. Treaties between the U.S. government and California Indians may have ethical weight, but they lack formal potency.

Without a ratified and functioning treaty system around which sovereignty claims could be built, California Indian peoples' control over their lands during the balance of the nineteenth century was tenuous at best. Statutory land-claims mechanisms were the initial tools used by the United States to further Indian dispossession in the 1850s. In 1851 Congress passed the Land

Claims Act, which directed all individuals in California claiming title to lands under the authority of either Spain or Mexico to confirm those claims with supporting evidence within two years. Any lands not claimed with a title deemed valid during this period would enter into the public domain. Through this mechanism all of the lands "abandoned" by Indian people during the period of secularization, or as part of their good-faith execution of the provisions of the unratified treaties, were efficiently acquired by the United States. In 1853, then, Congress passed another act opening public lands in California to preemption claims (squatters rights), which transferred more than 8 percent of the state's lands into private, non-Indian hands. Indians, as noncitizens, were not eligible to make such claims, even if they had been aware of the mechanism (Costo and Costo, *Natives* 259–60). The federal government did put into effect a short-lived military-run reservation system in California at this time, though that system was largely an effort to manage displaced, often starving Indian populations in the northern and central parts of the state and to protect them from a settler population increasingly bent on violently eliminating them from the landscape. The documentary evidence of this genocidal period of California history coinciding with the gold rush makes for grim reading.[1] The five military reservations established in the state during the 1850s were quickly overrun by the pressures of settlement, and California Indian people found themselves pressed into ever-shrinking land bases throughout the state. Eventually small reservations and rancherias were set aside for some California Indian people, though these were created by executive order of the president or legislative action (with no treaty regimen on which to base them). For many non-Indian Californians, though, by the end of the nineteenth century the commonly held assumption was that California Indian people were on the verge of extinction, if they had not already vanished.[2]

By 1920 the U.S. government had established roughly 110 rancherias (in the northern part of the state), 38 reservations, and 4,000 individually allotted Indian homesteads throughout California (Costo and Costo, *Natives* 313). From this period through the 1970s the struggle for tribal sovereignty involved (1) an effort to induce the federal government to compensate Indian communities for the treaty debacle of the 1850s and (2) a battle to fend off the allotment of lands and the termination of the tribes persisting on already-small land bases. The antitermination battle was a national one, and we have already addressed it sufficiently elsewhere. The trajectory of the claims process merits a bit more explanation. Starting in the 1920s, growing discontent over the failure of federal authorities to help address problems confronting their communities led California Indian people to begin to look to the court system and Congress for redress. In 1928 Congress passed the Jurisdiction Act, which allowed California Indians covered by the eighteen unratified treaties from the 1850s to sue the federal government for compensation. These lawsuits were prosecuted until a final settlement was reached in 1944. After the federal government deducted its expenses in creating subsequent reservations, however, this settlement amounted to a payment of $150 per capita to approximately 36,000 individual California Indians paid out in 1951. By that time, under the auspices of the federal Indian Claims Commission (created in 1946), attorneys had filed many additional petitions on behalf of other California tribes. These were consolidated into a single docket in the 1960s, and in 1968 nearly 65,000 Indian people were again deemed eligible to divide settlement money (amounting to about $600 per person). This small settlement obviously was not satisfactory to the vast majority of the litigants, and it certainly did not bring to a close the legal battles over land and sovereignty between California tribes and the government.[3]

It is remarkable that despite this colonial history California Indian tribes have indeed endured (and in some cases prospered). Their tactics of survivance, however, have been shaped by the particular forms of settler colonialism that they have confronted. Lacking sizeable land bases, large populations, and ratified treaties around which to construct and assert claims of sovereignty, then, California Indian tribes' engagement with the U.S. legal system and other forms of political negotiation with state and local authorities has continued to prove to be the most viable strategy for tribal communities in the state. In other words, the primary foci of California tribes have been on claims of legal sovereignty and on lobbying to influence non-Indian public opinion in the state. This pattern persists into the present even for the affluent casino tribes. Their efforts to realize their sovereignty and autonomy on the land often involve employing their resources to provide economic opportunity for their communities and generally take up many of the practical functions of local governments. These efforts typically take place in a context of intense political activity: lobbying the state and federal government for favorable legislation; negotiating with local and state authorities; providing charitable contributions and public outreach to the non-Indian community; and, not-infrequently, beginning litigation. Not surprisingly, other Indian communities sometimes look on with concern at the strategic moves made by California tribes, fearing that their tactics may have negative consequences for others.[4]

It is worth noting, also, that many Southern California tribes continue to operate under older-style constitutions adopted in the initial period after the passage of the IRA; there is no widespread movement for tribal constitutional reform in California at the present time. The operative Agua Caliente Constitution was ratified in 1955 (and amended in 1957). Significantly, too, the tribe itself characterizes its by-laws and constitution as having "[launched] the Agua Caliente tribe as a *modern-era business and political entity*" (emphasis added).[5] This language does not foreground the kinds of assertions of sovereignty that we find in the works of a writer and activist like Vizenor. And yet at the same time it seems to me important that we acknowledge it to be an assertion of *some form* of sovereignty, one which, of course, may not represent the final limit of what California Indian communities might achieve, but which at the same time represents another type of pragmatic effort to make the best use of the tools available to advance the process of decolonization.

Reading Francisco Patencio's narrative in the shadow of California's particular settler-colonial history highlights the value of having a diverse set of protocols for sovereign reading. *Stories and Legends of the Palm Springs Indians* is a book whose contents Patencio (the Agua Caliente clan leader, or "Net") narrated to Margaret Boynton (a former governess who lived in a house on land he owned) in 1939. It was published in 1943 under the imprint of the Los Angeles Times-Mirror, but it has never been reprinted or widely circulated. The Agua Calientes reference the work on their web page as a source for some of the traditional stories that are reproduced there. It is also mentioned occasionally in ethnographic scholarship on the Cahuilla people. In that context, however, the significance of Patencio's book is often questioned, or at least qualified. Ethnographers often lament the text's "corruption"—its failure to reflect the false ideal of precontact purity valued in the salvage ethnography of its time. Such readers prefer the more condensed versions of the Pass Cahuilla origin story to be found either in Lucille Hooper's 1920 monograph, *The Cahuilla Indians*, or in William Duncan Strong's 1929 *Aboriginal Society in Southern California*. Those texts are valuable, to be sure (the Agua Calientes also cite them approvingly), but I would suggest that the Patencio volume offers something that the other two do not. For in *Stories and Legends of the Palm Spring Indians* we have a work that intricately maps the jurisdictions (to use Womack's term) of the Pass Cahuillas of the Palm Springs area at a crucial time in the mid-twentieth century. This is the period when the Agua Calientes were actively developing their legal strategies for resisting federal interference in their lives (specifically to fend off plans to allot tribal lands that bitterly divided the community) and struggling to maintain control over as much of their territory as possible.[6] Patencio's book provides us with an example of how a place-centered, traditional indigenous narrative from Southern California was deployed to assist in the modern struggle for sovereignty.

Stories and Legends of the Palm Springs Indians is divided into two parts. First we have "The Creation," which contains a series of traditional Pass Cahuilla narratives about the origin of the world and the migrations and deeds of the early people, or *Nukatem*.[7] The second section, "Patencio's Life," combines more conventionally autobiographical and historical materials with a range of highly specific references to Cahuilla place-names in the Palm Springs area. Both are preceded by a brief forward in which Patencio directly addresses his audience. It is worth noting, in this respect, that he explicitly presents himself as the "writer" of the text—never raising any of the standard concerns about his book being an "as-told-to" narrative. Boynton, for her part, never registers a presence in the text in any way other than being mentioned on the title page. Her influence on the form and content of the book appears to be minimal.

In his forward Patencio explicitly identifies three types of readers who he thinks might value the book: (1) "ones who have an interest in new things"; (2) "men of science who study the world"; and (3) the Cahuilla people themselves, who are in danger of losing or forgetting their own traditions (ix). The depth of what is in the book greatly exceeds this modest list of its potential contributions and audiences, however. There are many ways to read *Stories and Legends*, all of which speak to sovereignty issues confronting the Cahuilla people, both in the 1930s and today. I would like to touch on three of those potential reading approaches—one rooted in our understanding of genre, and the others built around a pair of critical tropes that also speak to the concept of sovereignty. We can consider Patencio's book as a whole, first as an autobiography, then as a map (with direct implications for the struggle over allotments and land claims), and finally as a reminder of the treaty as a potential tool for decolonization in Southern California contexts.

Particularly in light of recent theoretical work on the nature of autobiographical narrative, we should resist the impulse to read the two parts of Patencio's narrative as rigorously divided from one another; the mythic narratives of the Cahuilla creation and the historical material later in the book are deeply connected. Recent work in autobiography studies also reminds us that we would do well to approach autobiographical texts as constructed narratives whose meaning and form are driven as much by the contexts in which they are produced as by the contents which they recall. For those who appreciate the nature of storytelling in an oral tradition, this is not a foreign concept. Reading Patencio's text *autobiographically*, then, leads us to consider, first, what concerns specific to 1939 influenced the choices he made regarding what to include in his relation to Margaret Boynton, and second, what the text's formal construction—its organization as a narrative—suggests about its meaning.

In the late 1930s the Agua Calientes were in a period of considerable political and cultural upheaval. The year 1937 saw the incorporation of Palm Springs as an independent city, an event that took place within the broader context of the federal government's attempts to allot the Agua Caliente reservation and alienate its surplus land. Active tribal resistance to allotment dated back to the 1910s, but tensions surrounding the implementation of the policy continued to build into the 1930s. In fact, 1937 saw the temporary arrest of the Agua Caliente tribal leadership (including Patencio) and a full federal takeover of the reservation. Earlier in that same year Patencio had visited Washington in an attempt to advocate for Agua Caliente land rights.[8] This contention over land claims would go on for decades, only becoming relatively settled with the Equalization Act of September 21, 1959 (Public Law 339), which finalized individual Indian allotments and set aside certain other lands for tribal use and cemeteries. However, even today the Agua Caliente Reservation is a textbook example of the post–Dawes Act checkerboarding of tribal lands. Paradoxically, of course, this has also led to the fact that the Agua Calientes are also the largest landowners within the city limits of Palm Springs itself, a situation which the tribe has leveraged for its economic benefit.

It is in this historical context that Patencio chose to set down a series of traditional Cahuilla narratives that emphasize both his community's understanding of the natural facts of sudden and eruptive change and their capacity to survive and adapt to that change. Patencio channels the Cahuilla vox populi, then, through the retelling (in print) of traditional stories, applying those tales to provide a model of Cahuilla peoplehood going forward. A central theme in Cahuilla cosmology is the relative unpredictability of creative power (referred to as *Um Naw* in Patencio's text). We see this theme developed in great detail through Patencio's narration of the core creation cycle stories involving the rivalry and tension between the cocreators, Mo-Cot (Mukat) and Mo-Cot-Tem-Ma-Ya-Wit (Temayawit).[9] These twin divinities bicker and compete throughout the extensive process of the initial creation of the first people (Nukatem), and their conflict culminates in Temayawit departing the world with his own (double-faced and duck-footed) creations. Temayawit's descent into the earth with his Nukatem unleashes a series of geographical cataclysms, raising mountains and changing the land. Later in the cycle Mukat proves an equally significant agent of disruption himself, provoking the Nukatem into bewitching and killing him after he sexually violates their beloved teacher Moon-Maiden and introduces war and death into the world. Through these and other elements of the core creation stories we can see how the Cahuilla worldview and collective ethos has traditionally been grounded in the recognition that power is both orderly and disorderly, creative and destructive.

Patencio highlights how Cahuilla tradition stresses the ability of the Nukatem (and the less powerful people who have come after them) to cope with this experience of flux. This point is explicitly made in the second, more overtly autobiographical, half of the book. Patencio recounts the living memory of changes in the land, such as the drying up of springs and water sources after earthquakes in the late nineteenth century. Significantly, too, in this same context he also mentions changes brought on by the missions. Here in the text a great deal of meaning is created by context and placement rather than by direct authorial commentary. Patencio offers some broad reflections on the process of the transmission of knowledge in Cahuilla culture, which he calls the "council-fire tradition." He defines that tradition as the sum total of the things that people know to be true and of the prophetic knowledge in which they have confidence, handed down from father to son. The council-fire tradition might be thought of, then, as an expression of the Cahuilla nomos (the normative universe in which the community operates), and it thus encompasses the constitution, or fundamental law, of the Cahuilla people. Patencio makes a point of highlighting the fact that everything that represents what might be labeled Cahuilla law is embedded in the oral tradition. When members of the community acted in a way that was deemed transgressive or outside of the bounds of cultural norms, it would be said that "the song is against them." Patencio also stresses that the knowledge of this law is "not [simply] in the [ceremonial] Songs and Stories" (xi). This is a key assertion of survivance in light of the undeniable historical fact that colonial contact disrupted traditional lifeways in a variety of forms. Rather, the council-fire tradition constitutes a range of literary forms in which may be found "our history of people and places, not only the people of the First People, but many things of the plain people; things they have done to help their people" (74). Here, then, Patencio implicitly defines the book he is dictating as a part of that tradition. *Stories and Legends* becomes a legal text, albeit in a different form from the ceremonial songs and stories.

It is significant, too, that Patencio locates a central theme emerging from this living council-fire tradition in the understanding that Cahuilla history is dominated by a pattern of apocalypse (that flux of creative power) *and rebirth* (75). Patencio tells us that Um Naw (the power of creation) "allows people and animals to live for a time—much time, and then He destroys." This change often comes suddenly: "A few moments and then world changes to a new condition" (76). Patencio's decision to integrate his discussion of the mission fathers and their interactions with tribal communities into this part of his telling suggest the breadth of his understanding of change. Structurally, his narrative conveys the idea that colonial contact represents just another type of change (albeit noninstantaneous) that the Cahuillas can also confront through their repository of traditional knowledge and law. As an artfully constructed autobiographical recitation, then, Patencio's book draws attention to the links between present experience (no matter how difficult) and the internal, communal resources with which to confront it.[10]

Reading Patencio's text autobiographically in this way can draw our attention to the second heuristic I want to advance—treating the book as a map.

Here, again, we might begin by considering choices regarding content. Patencio's version of the creation cycle has considerable similarities to the earlier versions collected by Hooper and Strong. The primary difference is that his telling includes much more material. This extra story largely constitutes the aforementioned corruption that has troubled some ethnographers. When one looks closely at the added material in Patencio's version, however, especially with attentiveness to its extensive use of Cahuilla language-markers, one sees that what he has done is present a rigorously localized form of this creation story, an assertion of Agua Caliente jurisdiction, in Womack's language. He puts down a version of the creation, parts of which would be shared universally by Cahuilla people throughout Southern California, but parts of which are particular to the Agua Caliente band and their experience of place. Once again, the development of that story extends across both halves of the book.

Stories and Legends offers its readers a series of migration narratives, beginning with an account in part 1 of "some of the early people," a people of power who could rise through the air through the power of prayerful song but are now gone from the earth. These ancestral people, called by Patencio the *Mo moh pechem* (which he translates as "moaning in pain" people), lay down a series of territorial markers throughout what is, essentially, the overall territory of the Cahuillas in Southern California. Originating in an unidentified pass to the north (and west), the Mo moh pechem fly, in turn, to San Fernando Mountain (in the San Gabriel range northeast of Los Angeles), Cucamonga Mountain (the highest peak in that range), San Gorgonio Mountain (northeast of the San Gorgonio Pass into the Coachella Valley), San Jacinto Mountain (south of and overlooking Palm Springs), Palm Canyon, the end of the Santa Rosa Mountain range, and finally to the San Filipe Valley (southwest of Temecula and Palomar Mountain, near the Anza-Borrego Wilderness Area). After these general markers have been laid down, Patencio then includes narratives of other ancestral culture-heroes and more recent leaders, gradually narrowing our focus until we are mapping, not a broad swath of Cahuilla territory, but specifically the lands of Patencio's Fox clan.

The story of the ancestral clan founder (Evon-Ga-Net, or "The Fox") follows his route as he travels through, marks, and names some twenty-three specific places that define the outer borders of Agua Caliente land. These include such vital locations as Tahquitz Peak and Palm Canyon, and Patencio is meticulous about identifying these places in the Cahuilla (and occasionally Serrano) language.[11] This is a powerfully suggestive act, especially when we recall that white settlers in the Palm Springs area had been engaged for years in efforts to have these spaces designated as national monuments, removing them from tribal control.[12] Finally, in part 2 of the book he connects these earlier stories to more recent migrations and, implicitly, to the present-day battles over land rights. In an extensive section designated "The Rightful Owners of Palm Springs" he relates the migration of another ancestor of the Fox clan lineage, a headman named Ca wis ke on ca (Fox's Horns). The story of Fox's Horns recounts him leading his people from an area south of Palm Springs to their present homeland, which he recognized based on the marks left by Evon Ga Net. "Where he [Evon Ga Net] went," Patencio notes, "he always put the name of the places, so that his people could follow him" (95). As Patencio himself follows Fox's Horns through the process of narrative memory, he is able to generate his own picture of the land, providing a photographic negative contrasting the municipal grid that was being imposed upon it by the newly incorporated city of Palm Springs.

These examples highlight how Patencio's storytelling generates the textual equivalent of a (political) boundary map, asserting Cahuilla (and more specifically Agua Caliente) jurisdiction over this territory. In the process, his recitation also functions as an appeal to the vox populi, both calling into being and buttressing a collective Cahuilla political consciousness and working to create space for the kind of mutual recognition needed for effective sovereignty claims. In this respect, *Stories and Legends* can be read productively through the lenses provided by much recent scholarship about visual and narrative forms of place making in indigenous communities.[13] When we do so, another theme that emerges is the importance of sharing space—of recognizing the presence of others, over time, in a mutually occupied landscape with overlapping jurisdictions. It is in this respect that we can also begin to see the value of approaching the text through the third heuristic mentioned earlier—the trope of the treaty, which I would argue functions for Patencio as the foundation for future relations.

Patencio recounts a number of stories that focus on the movements of others through Agua Caliente territory, not with the intent of undermining tribal land claims, of course, but rather in acknowledgment of the fact that multiple groups' senses of historical memory track through the same spaces. One good example of this is Patencio's rendering of the migration story of "Eagle Flower" (or Aswitsei, his name given by Strong). Eagle Flower is one of the Mo Mo Pechems who slept for thousands of years while the ancestral people were migrating from the north. Finally awakened by the barking of his dog, he tries to follow the path taken by the others, eventually coming through the San Gorgonio Pass and Palm Springs and moving down to Indian Wells. There, recognizing the palm trees as his people, he attempts to change himself into that form, but Um Naw (the creative power) will not allow this to happen. Eagle Flower then continues on to Indian Wells Point, where he leaves a mark on a rock (a petroglyph) as well as indentations on another hilltop from his chin, elbow, and knees. Seeing a group of Indians living in a nearby valley, he goes to live with them and marries into their community, eventually fathering three sons. Those sons quarrel with each other, leading to a diasporic migration of many of the "Eagle Flower people" out of the area.

Patencio offers his audience a pair of morals for this story. He notes that because of internal strife, the Eagle Flower people came to be divided from one another by place and language. This division is also exacerbated by their lack of knowledge of certain ceremonies and customs (such as the "fiesta for girls"—a Cahuilla puberty ritual), caused by the fact that Eagle Flower "slept and didn't learn." It would be a mistake, however, to read the Eagle Flower story as having *only* a didactic function within the overall structure of Patencio's narrative. Patencio's older brother Alejo (the Agua Caliente Net before him, from the late 1890s until 1930) related a somewhat shorter version of the same tale to William Duncan Strong in the 1920s. Alejo's version is more explicitly framed to document and honor the historical presence of a different Cahuilla clan (the Atcitcems) that had once lived in Indian Wells, but whose members had either moved away or been absorbed into the Fox clan. Bearing this in mind, and in light of other textual features we have noticed, it strikes me as plausible to suggest that Patencio's choice to include this material in his own telling reflects both a consciousness of the layered history of place and an ethos that demands the recognition of the presence of others in the landscape, not their erasure, as the basis for sovereignty claims.

I find it equally striking, and suggestive of these underlying cultural values of reciprocity and recognition, that Patencio even takes the time to draw an "American" presence into his map—highlighting the possibility of respectful and sustaining relationships between Indian and non-Indian communities. This is a pragmatic way of beginning to reconceive the problem of sovereignty in a California context, where the interaction and overlapping of groups in urban spaces is often an unavoidable reality. In part 2 of *Stories and Legends* Patencio recalls the activities of several pioneers in the Coachella Valley: Hank Brown, who established early stagecoach stations through the area after the end of the pony express; Jack Summers, an agent at Palm Springs who employed local Indian people in gathering feed for horses; and Bill and Frank Smith, stage drivers who took the time to learn the Cahuilla language and enjoyed good relations with the local population. In an interesting gesture that mirrors his charting of Cahuilla territory, Patencio also maps the route of the stagecoaches and their stations through the area, noting fourteen specific places, some with Cahuilla names, and commenting on the fact that the marks of the old stage road are still visible throughout the valley.

Quite unlike the colonial palimpsest approach to historical memory—writing over the past and erasing others from the landscape when new owners take possession—Patencio offers a vision where some form of shared history of place is possible. The key to this is both a willingness to recognize the legitimate claims and ongoing presence of the other and a commitment to keep covenant with those others through agreements forged over time. Patencio notes that Hank Brown made, and always honored, agreements with Indians for water and land. Consequently, the Indians found no fault with him. It seems no accident, then, that while recounting his own recollections of these more honorable pioneers, Patencio foregrounds his own sense of the legal and ethical centrality of the treaty for the future of the Cahuilla. Unlike in Cook-Lynn's case, though, where a history of ratified treaties between the United States and the Dakotahs exists as a solid foundation for sovereignty claims, for Patencio this is a more aspirational statement, looking ahead to future engagement with the U.S. government. He notes that his own desire to learn English at a young age was tied to his recognition that the "time of the bows and arrows and guns was gone. Now it was paper with the names written, that my people had to do" (63).

Among the papers that matter most, of course, are the papers on which have been written the various treaties, grants, and contracts between Indian peoples and outsiders. We should recall here that it was these papers that provided the basis for the land claims process begun in the 1920s to which the Agua Calientes and their leadership committed themselves. Not surprisingly, then, Patencio notes, "I know about all the Treaties from the time of the Missions and Spanish Grants. All the agreements since Spain, Mexico, and United States have taken the land" (63). Knowing this history, of course, Patencio knew that none of the eighteen treaties negotiated with California tribes in the early 1850s, which would have formally recognized their lands, were ever ratified. Partially as a result of this legal history, the Palm Springs Indians in the 1930s were confronted with an even more difficult set of challenges in rendering themselves and their relationship to their territory visible and recognizable to an aggressive settler-colonial society as well as in pushing their own land claims suits. Nevertheless, *Stories and Legends of the Palm Springs Indians* aims to counteract this process of erasure, offering both an alternative model of Anglo-Indian relations and an alternative form of evidence to buttress the tribe's pursuit of legal sovereignty through legislative mechanisms opened up by the Jurisdiction Act. At this point, the specific legal valences of Patencio's politically charged act of storytelling become even more apparent. Even if he was not fully theorizing his activity, Patencio was actively engaged in creating a Cahuilla discourse of sovereignty, linking legal and literary concerns in new and innovative ways. He pursued this work in a particularly constrained context, to be sure, one where some of the tools and strategies employed by Cook-Lynn and Vizenor were simply not available to him. But Patencio's imaginative act does not represent an ending point in a Cahuilla tradition of political and literary thought. It simply indexes a point of development of a different branch of the modern discourse of sovereignty in Indian country.

My sovereignty reading of *Stories and Legends* highlights just *some* of the ways that California Indian literatures might be employed to support the future development of sovereignty discourse in the state. Today, with the early emergence of new norms in international law (through UNDRIP), it seems very likely to me that demonstrations of indigenous understandings of place like those that we find in *Stories and Legends* will begin to underpin new forms of decolonization. We are clearly not at this stage yet in the United States, owing to our government's current framing of UNDRIP as an aspirational text. But it is equally clear that Patencio's narrative lays the foundations for potential future claims to land, both in relation to the "right to cultural integrity" (tied to the ability of groups to maintain and develop their cultural identities) and to the recognition of forms of property that arise from the "traditional or customary land tenure of indigenous people" (these phrases appear in the text of UNDRIP). In addition to the examples I have discussed already here, *Stories and Legends* contains a rich textual archive of traditional knowledge, indexing the specific historical connections between Cahuilla identity and the physical geography, flora, and fauna of the Coachella Valley region.[14] As international legal norms and structures evolve in the future, these kinds of archives might be deployed in new ways.

Granting that the internationalization of sovereignty discourse in Indian Country in the United States is in its nascent stages, I would also emphasize the ways that important current shifts in federal legislation (the passage of the Native American Graves Protection and Repatriation Act, for example) and innovations in state law (as seen in California Senate Bill 18) suggest other areas where a text like Patencio's can be applied in the pursuit of legal sovereignty. The ability of tribal communities to effect the repatriation of ancestral remains and cultural property is tied to those communities' ability to demonstrate a historic link to the places where those remains have been found or from which they have been removed. In California the Native American Graves Protection and Repatriation Act overlaps in some ways with the California Environmental Quality Act, which sets up a framework for the study of the environmental impact of land use and development. When development or land-use projects uncover potential cultural property, the developing entity typically calls in its own archeological experts to determine which tribal group needs to be consulted as part of the project. Lacking clearly defined cultural/historical maps to guide this process, however, there is a clear potential for interested parties to selectively identify tribal groups who may or may not be the most directly concerned in the cultural site. Texts like

Patencio's, when publicized as "maps," can help to ensure that the correct tribal communities are, in fact, able to assert their control over ancestral remains and sites.

We can see the further relevance of sovereign readings of texts like Patencio's in the context of potential new legal instruments such as Senate Bill 18, which carves out protections for Traditional Tribal Cultural Places, or TCPs, in the local planning and zoning process. TCPs are a new legal concept/category, but they hold considerable promise to allow tribal communities to intervene and protect their sacred sites *before* those sites encounter the direct pressure of development. Bearing such examples in mind, Native American literature scholars would be justified in better attending to archival and oral texts that can help (1) to generate place-making maps of tribal lands and (2) to spur dialogue that advances the possibilities of mutual recognition within shared historical and geographical space. Looking forward, such critical projects can have as much a place in the field as examinations of treaty-centered literary nationalism or constitutional criticism. Indeed, I believe they will be central to the struggle for sovereignty in a context like California, where other models remain difficult to apply.

This concluding consideration of sovereignty in the Cahuilla storyway has hopefully foregrounded the need for scholars working in NAS to do more to appreciate and elucidate the value of divergent strategies for decolonization. We need to develop critical models that tap into the various emergent forms of sovereignty discourse available to American Indian people today. We need to avoid the cultivation of exclusionary approaches and need to question the tendency to insist that discrete models or political strategies (which may be extremely effective for one tribal community) must become the centerpiece of a panindigenous politics. A related problem, of course, remains how to organize and sustain the kind of larger political alliances and movements (like the recent "Idle No More" protests radiating out from Canada) that are necessary to struggle effectively against still powerful settler-colonial state structures.[15] It seems to me, though, that this is why sovereignty will continue to maintain its tremendous force as the dominant political signifier in Indian country for some time to come. It is the most powerful and useful threshold concept that we have at our disposal. As a feature of contemporary American Indian politics and literature, the fluidity of sovereignty is not just a desirable strength; it is an absolute necessity. Nevertheless, as I have tried to show throughout this book, precisely because of this fluidity, when used as a literary-critical concept and as an organizing principle for tribally specific tactics of decolonization, sovereignty works best when locally specified and refined. When we do so, we see clearly how the discourse of sovereignty functions as a threshold concept, connecting not just tribal communities and the

United States government but also the various thinkers in the big tent of NAS. Employing the hermeneutic practices of a sophisticated and fully historicized form of sovereign reading strikes me as one of the most promising ways that Native American literary studies can continue to play a central role in the field it helped to build. But as long as literary critics respond *in some way* to the push toward ethical commitment and political relevance that has shaped the critical discourse of the last decade, we will continue to have enormous opportunities to contribute meaningfully to the next stage of the struggles for sovereignty throughout Indian country.

Notes

Introduction

1. A more complicated version of this formulation would be Carl Schmitt's controversial definition of "the sovereign" as the entity who has the power to decide on the "state of exception," the power to unilaterally suspend the normal rule of law and impose different conditions. Schmitt's theories are viewed by some as a realistic critique of the naive idealism underpinning traditional liberal political theory and by others as a dangerous justification of fascism. See Schmitt, *Political Theology*, and Schmitt, *Concept of the Political*.

2. *This Is Not a Peace Pipe* predates the passage of the United Nations Declaration on the Rights of Indigenous Peoples, but Canada's relationship to UNDRIP is sufficiently equivocal to grant his point continued validity.

3. The term "middle ground" loosely invokes Richard White's characterization (in *The Middle Ground*) of the struggle for accommodation and a sense of common meaning between indigenous peoples and European settlers in the Great Lakes region during the seventeenth and eighteenth centuries. Despite deep reservations about the dynamics of engagement with the liberal settler-state, Simpson treats sovereignty as a "critical language game" that can "signal different processes and intents to others in ways that are understandable" (Simpson, *Mohawk Interruptus*, 105).

4. This spelling, "Dakotah," used here and throughout the book, follows Cook-Lynn's preferred usage.

Chapter 1

1. For good overviews of the Western historical roots and valences of the concept of sovereignty, see Elshtain, *Sovereignty*; Jackson, *Sovereignty*; and Brierly, *Law of Nations*.

2. As Elshtain has argued recently, it is possible to trace the roots of sovereignty in Western thought back as far as the era of Saint Augustine.

3. It is important to note that from a Western legal-political perspective, not every nation-state is, in fact, a *sovereign* state. A sovereign state would be a collective that has a defined and delimited territory and a permanent population, where both are under the formally unrestricted

authority of an autonomous government. A nonsovereign state, in contrast, might take the form of a conquered area or a colonized territory in an empire, a subordinate polity in a federal system (a state like California in the United States), or a semiautonomous (often breakaway) territory of the type often designated an unrecognized state. As Jackson puts it, "a colonial government might be said to possess internal sovereignty without having external sovereignty. But that ignores the profoundly important political and legal fact that differentiates a colonial government from a sovereign government: its internal authority is not held independently" (Jackson, *Sovereignty*, 12). Examples of unrecognized states would include South Ossetia, Northern Cyprus, and Transnistria. On this subject, see Caspersen, *Unrecognized States*.

4. Many contemporary indigenous tribal leaders and political thinkers would reject the absolutist emphasis in this conventional definition of sovereignty. As we will see in chapter 3, John Mohawk argues that sovereignty must be redefined in a way to make the idea of supreme power subordinate to concepts of justice and reciprocity. In this respect, he advocates a shift to something related to the natural-law roots of Western sovereignty discourse.

5. The eventual downfall of the idea of imperial sovereignty was "the liberal idea that there was something inherently wrong about a government that laid claim to foreign territories and populations without their uncoerced consent" (Jackson, *Sovereignty*, 76). Popular sovereignty, in this respect, eventually played a key role in delegitimizing imperial sovereignty. The decolonization process that began in the mid-twentieth century involved imperial sovereignty being replaced by local sovereignty in former colonies. Imperial sovereignty is now unlawful under a range of UN General Assembly resolutions.

6. The following discussion is heavily indebted to Jackson, *Sovereignty*, 49–77.

7. One might note as partial exceptions to this areas that are deemed to have fallen into the condition of a "failed state," though even here, technically, the rubrics of the state system apply.

8. For a sophisticated treatment of the deterritorialization of sovereignty and its extension into New-World contexts through a range of symbolic forms, see Elmer, *On Lingering*.

9. James Anaya describes how this period saw considerable changes in the treatment of indigenous peoples in the framework of international law. As he puts it, "International law . . . shed its naturalist frame as it changed into a state-centered system, strongly grounded in the Western world view; it developed to facilitate colonial patterns promoted by European states and their offering, to the detriment of indigenous peoples" (Anaya, *Indigenous Peoples*, 15).

10. Presented briefly in summary form, the Law of Discovery (or Doctrine of Discovery) is an international-law concept dating back to fifteenth-century canon law, and later refined (particularly by the Marshall Court) to set up mechanisms whereby Western nations might claim uncivilized lands and adjudicate conflicts among themselves over those claims. According to the Law of Discovery, the first (Western) nation-state to explore and lay claim to new territories (non-Christian ones) would be deemed to have the exclusive right of possession over those lands, over and above any claims made by other states. Indigenous peoples living in the newly "discovered" territories were recognized as having some rights to their lands, though said rights were generally defined as those of mere occupancy, as opposed to the firmer, property-centered rights of possession. Under the Law of Discovery the nation-state holding possessory rights over Native territory was deemed the only authority entitled to take full possession of Indian lands, through either conquest or purchase. The Law of Discovery, in this respect, explains why Indian relations in the United States are predominantly a federal matter, unless the federal government has delegated authority to state governments. One can find considerable literature on the subject of Discovery Law. For a more detailed overview, see Carlson, *Sovereign Selves*. For an influential, contemporary indigenous critique of Discovery Law, see Newcomb, *Pagans*.

11. Useful introductions to the construction of racialized discourses surrounding American Indian people can be found in Mihesuah, *American Indians*; Pearce, *Savagism and Civilization*; and Sheehan, *Savagism and Civility*.

12. My use of the concept of interpellation should recall Louis Althusser's formulation of the concept and its relationship to the function of power, particularly in the context of modern states.

13. Frederick Hoxie traces the careers and poses of a number of these individuals in his recent book *This Indian Country*.

14. Other scholars whose work has contributed greatly to our understanding of these processes, in the eighteenth and nineteenth centuries especially, include Hilary Wyss and Lisa Brooks. Frederick Hoxie's *This Indian Country* illuminates the role of print as well in its account of the careers of a number of Indian activists during the nineteenth and twentieth centuries.

15. For one of the most sophisticated and powerful accounts of this process, see Maddox, *Removals*. Also of relevance would be Adams, *Education for Extinction*; Hoxie, *Final Promise*; and Lindsay, *Murder State*.

16. It should be noted that there were Indian citizens of the United States before 1924. For example, the 1817 removal treaty negotiated with the Cherokee Nation included provisions for citizenship. That treaty stipulated that individual heads of families who opted to remain in the east would have the opportunity to receive 640-acre tracts of land and become U.S. citizens (Wilkins and Stark, *American Indian Politics*, 41). The General Allotment Act of 1887 also included citizenship provisions. Indian citizenship has been defined by the Supreme Court (in *United States v. Nice* in 1916) as dualistic: Indians are deemed to be "citizens of their own nations and subject-citizens of the United States." In other words, the granting or acceptance of U.S. citizenship on the part of individual tribal members does not undercut the specific guardian-trust relationship that exists between the U.S. government and tribal governments (Wilkins and Stark, *American Indian Politics*, 45). Finally, we should also note that some members of tribal nations refuse to accept the unilaterally granted status of U.S. citizens. Members of the Haudenosaunee (Iroquois) and Hopi nations often seek to travel using passports issued by their own governments, not the United States.

17. For a discussion of the ongoing significance of the Marshall decisions, see Fletcher, "Iron Cold."

18. The term "Indian country" refers generally to any territories within the borders of the United States where Indian laws and customs and federal laws relating to Indians are applicable. The term also includes any land under U.S. governmental supervision that has been set aside primarily for Indian use. Indian country encompasses Indian reservations, pueblos, individual allotments, and in some cases privately held lands within reservation boundaries. See Wilkins and Stark, *American Indian Politics*, 310.

19. Barsh's piece was originally published in the *University of Michigan Journal of Law Reform*. It has been reprinted in Wunder's collection, *Native American Sovereignty*, and my citations to it are from that text.

20. This is an argument made in various contexts by Mark Rifkin as well in *When Did Indians Become Straight?*

21. For related discussions of tensions between indigenous political models and state sovereignty, see Champagne, Torjesen, and Steiner, *Indigenous Peoples*.

Chapter 2

1. For a consideration of Indian writers and activists engaged directly with claims for legal sovereignty, see Carlson, *Sovereign Selves*, and Hoxie, *Indian Country*.

2. On the current state of that debate, see Velie and Lee, *Native American Renaissance*.

3. The term techne (plural, technai) comes from Greek philosophy, where it refers to the combination of a system of knowledge (an episteme) with specific context-dependent mechanisms for translating that knowledge into practical action. "Techne" strikes me as a suggestive term

of art that I can apply in order to designate the way that particular legal forms deploy the underlying cognitive framework that affects the world in practical ways. For example, the treaty as a legal techne puts into practical effect specific ways of understanding the nature of political polities that come together in a diplomatic context. There is a system of knowledge that is actualized through the treaty, and that system has clearly discernable real-world effects.

4. McNickle also looms large in Hoxie's recent history of American Indian activists and activism. See Hoxie, *Indian Country*, 277–335.

5. For other appreciations of McNickle's literary and political legacy, see Purdy, *Legacy*, and Purdy, *Word Ways*.

6. On the termination policy, see Fixico, *Termination and Relocation*, and Ulrich, *American Indian Nations*.

7. On McNickle's role in the Chicago Conference, see Hoxie, *Indian Country*, 344–51.

8. The discussion that follows draws, in part, on Hauptman and Campisi, "Voice."

9. On the challenges confronted by the numerous unrecognized tribal communities within the borders of the United States, see Den Ouden and O'Brien, *Recognition*.

10. On McNickle's involvement in the founding of NCAI, see Hoxie, *Indian Country*, 316–19. Hoxie reminds us that the NCAI was created precisely at the point when John Collier's resignation from the Indian office removed from view the country's most prominent public voice on Indian affairs. With the emergence of the NCAI, a national body of Indian leaders began to fill that void in a more forceful way than we saw with predecessor organizations like the Society of American Indians (which never credibly aspired to represent Indian people in a collective way).

11. It is worth noting here that in this act of inventing a people, the participants in the Chicago Conference represented slightly less than 10 percent of the total number of recognized and nonrecognized nations and bands in the United States. This is a typical example of how popular sovereignty manifests itself.

12. On Montezuma's career and legacy, see Iverson, *Carlos Montezuma*.

13. It is worth noting that *Wassaja* published poetry, literary reviews and pieces on the arts in addition to hard news and political coverage.

14. One possible exception to this pattern would be his young-adult novel, *Runner in the Sun*, though that book's location in a distant historical past meditates its potential political impact.

15. This is often how traditional law in indigenous communities is encoded within the framework of story and narrative. See Borrows, *Drawing Out Law*, and Llewellyn and Hoebel, *Cheyenne Way*.

16. See Moore, *That Dream*, 77–83, 183–89.

Chapter 3

1. For examples of his other legal writing on these issues, see Deloria and DeMallie, *Documents*; Deloria and Wilkins, *Tribes*; Deloria and Lytle, *American Indians*; and Deloria and Lytle, *The Nations Within*.

2. The relevant provision in article VI of the 1778 Treaty with the Delaware Indians reads as follows: "And it is further agreed on between the contracting parties should it for the future be found conducive for the mutual interest of both parties to invite any other tribes who have been friends to the interests of the United States, to join the present confederation, and to form a state whereof the Delaware nation shall be the head, and have a representation in Congress: Provided, nothing contained in this article to be considered as conclusive until it meets with the approbation of Congress" (quoted in Wilkins and Stark, *American Indian Politics*, 243).

3. On the approaches used by various tribal groups to claim federal recognition, see Den Ouden and O'Brien, *Recognition*.

4. This is not entirely unlike what is going on in Taiaiake Alfred's project, I would submit, and it also resembles Mark Rifkin's notion of "queering" sovereignty.

5. There are similarities between Deloria's vision and the constitutional pluralism imagined in a Canadian context by James Tully and John Borrows. Borrows's work focuses on the ways traditional indigenous law-ways might be integrated into a larger constitutional framework. Tully, working more exclusively from a Western legal perspective, makes a related argument for tolerance of cultural difference in modern multicultural societies. See Borrows, *Recovering Canada*; Borrows, *Canada's Indigenous Constitution*; Borrows, *Drawing Out Law*; and Tully, *Strange Multiplicity*.

6. Deloria's formulation of group politics both intersects with and anticipates certain elements of critical legal studies and critical race studies scholarship. The former takes up the challenge of critiquing the liberal, individualist basis of the American legal system. The latter often draws attention to the need to complement that first project with more complicated theorizations of group political subjectivity and the interactions of groups and the legal system. See Crenshaw et al., *Critical Race Theory*; Peller, "Race Consciousness"; and Cruse, *Crisis*.

7. It is not clear to me whether Deloria's selection of a range of racial groups as parallel examples to Indian tribes (which Indian thinkers and writers generally argue are political groups rather than ethnic ones) represents a potentially problematic turn in his approach or simply a (perhaps ill-chosen) rhetorical gambit. I incline toward the latter view, primarily because I find it hard to see how Deloria himself could be blind to the wide range of problems that would be introduced by incorporating a primarily racial dimension into the corporate political subjectivity he is imagining. Particularly in Indian country, where conflicts surrounding authenticity in personal identity and blood quantum in tribal membership have been so damaging, the theorization of the tribal group needs to proceed very carefully.

8. For a particularly useful discussion of the topic, see Williams, *Linking Arms*.

9. In *God Is Red*, of course, Deloria retreats from his tactical willingness to deterritorialize sovereignty. And in a 1998 essay he expresses disillusionment with the failure of a proliferating discourse of sovereignty to yield practical results: "Self-determination, sovereignty, hegemony, empowerment, and colonialism are nice, big words that philosophers and intellectuals use, but what do they really mean? I often feel they assist us in creating a set of artificial problems, wholly abstract in nature, that we can endlessly discuss without having to actually do something" (Deloria, "Intellectual," 25). It seems to me that part of what Deloria is reacting against here is a problematic reification of sovereignty discourse in a manner that is disconnecting the terms from the realities of political struggle. Here again, the concern that a clear praxis emerges from sovereignty discourse remains. It is also worth noting that even in this more skeptical piece Deloria registers appreciation of his contemporary Jack Forbes's ongoing engagement with the concept. See Forbes, "Intellectual Self-Determination."

10. Four states (the United States, Canada, Australia, and New Zealand) initially refused to sign on to UNDRIP, but by 2010 all had, to some degree, agreed to do so. At the White House Tribal Nations Conference in December 2010 President Obama indicated a shift in American policy, announcing that the United States would be lending its support to the declaration. Subsequent concerns have been raised about this announcement, however, as the United States and other states are attempting to ensure that UNDRIP is read as merely an aspirational document. The U.S. State Department has released a fifteen-page document noting that the declaration is "not legally binding or a statement of current international law" (Toensing, "New Step, 34). From the U.S. government's perspective, the document merely reflects Indian aspirations, and the State Department maintains that those aspirations are to be achieved within the structure of the U.S. Constitution and laws.

11. As Anaya notes, even the early European jurisprudence focused on indigenous peoples that was favorable to their situation (the work of thinkers like Francisco Vittoria) was rooted in "medieval European ecclesiastical humanism," which "perceived a normative order

independent of and higher than the positive law of decisions of temporal authority" (Anaya, *Indigenous Peoples*, 16). The source of that normative order, of course, was the sovereign God of the universal Roman church.

12. These resemblances stand behind much of the longstanding debate about the degree to which the Iroquois directly influenced the form of the United States Constitution, a debate that represents an interesting sidebar to the contemporary discussion of sovereignty. On this discussion, see Johansen, *Debating Democracy*, and Johansen, *Forgotten Founders*.

13. On the political structure of the Longhouse, see Fenton, *Great Law*, and Richter, *Ordeal*.

Chapter 4

1. Here Warrior draws on Frantz Fanon, Edward Said, and a range of feminist political theory in his writings.

2. In aiming to produce such shifts in the critical discourse, we might note, Warrior's work hearkens back to that of Vine Deloria, Jr., another tactical writer whose polemical work is susceptible to being misread as reductive or essentialist.

3. This is a statement clearly congruent with Warrior's emphasis on intellectual sovereignty.

4. This continues to be the core of Womack's stated goals in his work as he expresses them in his more recent book, *Art as Performance: Story as Criticism*.

5. See in particular Waziyatawin, *Indigenous Eyes Only*; Mihesuah, *Natives and Academics*; Mihesuah and Wilson, *Indigenizing the Academy*; and Smith *Decolonizing Methodologies*. Lisa Brooks's afterword to *American Indian Literary Nationalism* also speaks to these issues.

6. Womack's approach to traditionalism resembles the judicial philosophy of Justice Stephen Breyer as laid out in his 2005 book, *Active Liberty*. In that work Breyer advocates applying constitutional principles in a way that adheres to the overarching philosophy of governance embedded in the document as a whole, while also recognizing that the changing needs and conditions of the people require flexibility and adaptation.

7. Womack takes this issue up, to some degree, later on in the book in his discussion of various works that might arguably constitute a Creek literary canon.

8. For a comparable formulation of some of the issues with which Womack is grappling, see Scott Lyons's discussion of the process of modernizing one's ethnie in *X-Marks*.

9. I am using the term "problematic" here in a manner broadly analogous to that of Pierre Macherey's *Theory of Literary Production*. The problematic of a text refers to an internal contradiction or tension within the work that is generative of its overall structure but also is not easily resolved or accessed by the individual producer of the text.

10. Generally speaking, Warrior's critical approach often tilts largely toward intellectual history and biographical study, as opposed to a close attention to textual analysis.

11. On these shifts in autobiography studies, see Carlson, *Sovereign Selves*, and Carlson, "Autobiography."

12. Reprinted in Butler and Scott, *Feminists Theorize the Political*.

13. Warrior deploys the idea of experience in strikingly speculative ways (by his own admission), constructing a hypothetical version of the end of William Apess's life based on his own personal experiences, his knowledge of Clyde Warrior's career, and the assertion of synchronicity among the three of them.

14. Womack sidesteps the work on the oral tradition done by non-Indian scholars like Dennis Tedlock and Dell Hymes, arguing that he is after something different. However, his notion of "unfixing" seems essentially the same as Tedlock's formulation of the difference between text and interpretation in Zuni ritual storytelling.

15. Weaver calls for an end to these debates in his contribution to Velie and Lee's collection, *The Native American Renaissance*.

Chapter 5

1. For one articulation of this initial vision, see Kidwell, "Native American Studies."

2. Here one can discern some distance between Cook-Lynn and Deloria, at least in terms of his theorization of political tactics during the late 1960s and early 1970s. While Deloria would never have embraced an ethnic definition of Indianness, he nevertheless seems to have had, at times, a more flexible notion of how group-based Indian politics might function in an American context.

3. Cook-Lynn registers this skepticism in a number of ways, critiquing, for example, Frank Pommersheim's proposal of a potential amendment to the U.S. Constitution as a vehicle for advancing tribal sovereignty. Pommersheim's political ideas are developed most fully in *Broken Landscape*, but his earlier work *Braid of Feathers* also provides an interesting contrast with Cook-Lynn's thought.

4. For an example of politically engaged NAS criticism that is deeply informed by postcolonialism, see Byrd, *Transit of Empire*.

5. In Cook-Lynn's view, a point of connection between the work of third-world intellectuals and that of American Indian nationalists that is more promising than cosmopolitan aesthetics is the concept of indigeneity. However, she would argue that there is a paradox here, one that lies in the fact that this *general* concept of indigeneity—which references being "aboriginal, inborn, natural, or originating in and characterizing a particular region or country"—can only be made meaningful by particularizing it in its local context. When Indian subalterns speak (to borrow one famous formulation from postcolonial theory), they particularize themselves in a way that makes it misleading to continue to frame them as *the* subaltern. And when that particularizing work is done thoroughly, Cook-Lynn implies, vitally important differences between the Dakotahs and other indigenous peoples will emerge. Thus the real link between Indian writers and third-worldists, she argues, cannot be the notion of aesthetic cosmopolitanism that she sees being employed in too much postcolonial literary theory but rather a set of specific questions derived from the paradigm of indigeneity itself—questions regarding the relationship between fictive mythmaking and the reality of the particular conditions of colonized nations of people (Cook-Lynn, "Fiction Writers," 89).

6. Of course, the "post" in postcolonial need not suggest "after the end of imperialism" but can also speak to scholarship that considers the ongoing implications of colonial structures.

7. I am thinking of the work of Frantz Fanon and particularly Glen Coulthard's deployment of Fanon in a Canadian context.

8. Critiques of Spivak's concept of the subaltern are often developed along these lines, for example.

9. Much literary scholarship on Cook-Lynn has focused on this legal and political history as necessary contexts for interpreting her thought and work. See Stripes, "'We Think.'"

10. Champagne's remarks appear in his essay "American Indian Studies Is for Everyone," in Devon Mihesuah's 1998 collection, *Natives and Academics*.

11. See, for example, Krupat, *Voice*, and Krupat, *Ethnocentrism*.

12. For an example of recent NAS work that addresses the complexity of identity issues while maintaining a focus on political concerns, see Simpson, *Mohawk Interruptus*. Of course, Simpson's home discipline is anthropology.

13. A number of critics have developed arguments along these lines in their interpretations of Cook-Lynn's fiction. See Stripes, "'We Think,'" and to a lesser degree, Hale, "Axiological Dissonance."

14. I would also note that sovereignty reading has a great deal in common with the interpretive practices of New Historicism. We might consider it an indigenized version of that critical methodology.

15. On this relationship between story, place, and territorial claims, see Westerman and White, *Mni Sota Makoce*, and Wilson, *Remember This!*

16. On Dakotah dispossession from Minnesota in the wake of the 1862 war, see Waziyatawin, *Justice*.

17. The material in this prologue has been absolutely central to Cook-Lynn's art throughout her career. She uses the text in prose form as the prologue to the first volume of *Aurelia*, and it previously appeared, also in prose, in her chapbook, *Then Badger Said This*.

18. In her essay "'The Violation of the Earth'" (on the first volume of *Aurelia*) Kathleen Danker maps the novel *From the River's Edge* in precisely the same space.

19. On the effects of federal water projects on Indian lands in this area, see Lawson, *Dammed Indians*.

20. On the ways in which an understanding of oral literary practices can inform the reading of written literary traditions, see Brill de Ramirez, *Contemporary American Indian Literatures*.

21. While the characters are not identified as such, a subsequent reading of the *Aurelia* trilogy might cause some readers to surmise that the grandmother here is the previously imagined version of Grandmother Blue and that the girl is Aurelia herself.

22. On the relationship between place, story, language, and cultural transmission, see Basso, *Wisdom*.

23. The full study guide can be found at http://library.sd.gov/PROG/sdbookbag/Cook-Lynn_Horses.pdf.

24. This issue has been addressed fairly extensively in law and literature scholarship. See Levinson and Mailloux, *Interpreting Law and Literature*.

25. For a version of this origin story and its link to place, see Westerman and White, *Mni Sota Makoce*. For a more general overview of Sioux cosmology, see Goodman, *Lakota Star Knowledge*.

26. For one example of this focused specifically on autobiography, see Lejeune, *On Autobiography*. Lejeune's writings on "the autobiographical pact" offer a clear articulation of this understanding of the interpretive function of genre.

27. For an excellent discussion of these dimensions in *Aurelia*, see Kirwan, *Sovereign Stories*.

Chapter 6

1. A brief list of critics appreciative of Vizenor's work includes Kimberly Blaeser, Elvira Pulitano, Elaine Jahner, and Deborah Madsen. For a good general overview of positive Vizenor criticism, see Lee, *Loosening the Seams*.

2. This constitution was ratified by almost 80 percent of those voting in a referendum on its adoption held on November 19, 2013. See www.whiteearth.com/news/?news_id=95. For a general discussion of the process of drafting and ratification, see Vizenor and Doerfler, *White Earth Nation*.

3. For a discussion of legal themes in Vizenor's work that complements my discussion here, see Rodríguez, "Vizenorian Jurisprudence."

4. Many critics make this point about the intertextual nature of Vizenor's work. See Haseltine, "Voices," and Blair, "Text as Trickster."

5. There are connections between my argument here and Robert Warrior's discussion of reading as a transformative experience in *The People and the Word*. See Warrior, *People*, xiv.

6. In a published conversation with John Purdy and Blake Hausman, Vizenor confirms that often his inventive process involves working one word at a time, stressing the extensive signifying possibilities of those words. "I don't take words as representations," he observes, "but they do have history. And they deserve a greater meaning, many words" (Purdy and Hausman, "Future of Print," 222–23). The implications of this way of thinking about words are readily apparent, too, in Vizenor's poetry—especially his work in haiku. Blaeser has brilliantly

illuminated the way that haiku has informed Vizenor's prose writing as well, showing that a typical Vizenorian sentence often includes hidden haiku lines. On this "haibun" technique, see Blaeser, *Gerald Vizenor*, 133–35.

7. Interestingly (and perhaps influenced by his recent constitutional work), Vizenor uses a legal base definition of survivance more systematically than is typical of him in *Native Liberty*. Even there, though, he continues to stress that the definition varies based on language, usage, and context. The essay "Aesthetics of Survivance" in that collection employs the legal usage, while the essay "Survivance Narratives" offers a different gloss—"the sensibilities of diplomatic, strategic resistance, and the aesthetics of literary irony" (Vizenor, *Native Liberty*, 58).

8. On the relationship between the Lewis and Clark expedition, U.S. law, and colonialism, see Miller, *Native America*.

9. Vizenor regularly employs an iterative strategy in his own prose, reproducing identical passages in a sequence of essays or narratives in such a way that this repetition subtly alters the meaning of the original. See the essays "Aesthetics of Survivance" and "Genocide Tribunals" from *Native Liberty* for an example of this.

10. This notion of the trace is essentially that which Jacques Derrida develops in *Of Grammatology* and later in his landmark essay "Différence" in *Margins of Philosophy*.

11. This critique mirrors Derrida's challenge to what he refers to as the logocentrism of Western philosophical discourse.

12. James H. Cox's discussion of Vizenor draws particular attention to Vizenor's awareness of colonial history and its literary modes/genres. See Cox, *Muting White Noise*, 101–44.

13. See Baudrillard's famous essay, "Simulacra and Simulations," in *Selected Writings*, 166–84.

14. This is precisely the point that Ollman makes in his introduction to *Dance of the Dialectic* in explaining the difficulties of reading Marx accurately: "When I sought to construct my own definitions from the way Marx used his key concepts in his writing, I was shocked to discover that their apparent meanings varied with the context, often considerably" (4).

15. Notably, Vizenor concludes the essay with a series of brief discussions of writers and activists (some Indian, some not), culminating with the phrase, "this portrait is not an Indian" (Vizenor, "Postindian," 44). For a brief discussion of this element in the text, see Mackay, "Ghosts in the Gap."

16. At this point one can easily discern affinities between the postindian and the trickster figure.

17. This is, I would suggest, the central problem with Elvira Pulitano's reading of Vizenor in *Toward a Native American Critical Theory*. While she is, I think, sensitive to much of the linguistic force of Vizenor's trickster discourse, Pulitano's commitment to "identity" as a critical category, along with her tendency to evaluate Indian writers on a continuum in terms of their conscious acceptance of hybrid identity, greatly undermines the effectiveness of her argument.

18. I will be discussing the CWEN's Vizenorian qualities here, an approach I believe to be justified by the official designation of Vizenor as the principle writer of the text. That said, it must be acknowledged that this is not a single-author work. Erma Vizenor (president of the White Earth Nation) designated three persons—Jill May Doerfler (of the University of Minnesota, Duluth), Jo-Anne E. Stately (vice president of development for the Indian Land Tenure Foundation), and Anita Fineday (chief tribal court judge of the White Earth Nation)—to serve as an advisory committee to the principle writer. The final text of the document also involved some alterations and compromises based on the comments of delegates to the three constitutional conventions (October 19–20, 2007; January 4, 2008; and October 24–25, 2008).

19. The literature on the IRA (Indian Reorganization Act) and its relationship to tribal constitutions is voluminous. For a brief introduction, see David E. Wilkins's introduction to his

recently edited volume of Felix Cohen's *On the Drafting of Tribal Constitutions*. For a good overview of contemporary views on constitution drafting, see Kalt, "The Role of Constitutions."

20. I have examined the performative aspects of legal texts elsewhere. See Carlson, *Sovereign Selves*, 4, 36–37.

21. See Kalt, "The Role of Constitutions," 82–83.

22. On this point, see Wilkins's introduction to Cohen's *Tribal Constitutions*, xvi–xviii. It is worth noting that these early tribal constitutions have a truly complicated legacy. On the one hand, in the wake of the disaster that was the allotment policy, tribal communities desperately needed some mechanisms for self-government, even if those mechanisms were initially more municipal than national. It is possible, in this regard, to view Cohen's work in this area as legitimately progressive. At the same time, it is easy to discern real tensions between colonial economic interests and legitimate assertions of sovereignty in the creation of these constitutional documents. For a related discussion of these historical tensions, specifically focused on the Osages, see Warrior, *People*, 49–93.

23. See Kalt, "The Role of Constitutions," 82–83. Vizenor uses the term continental liberty in a similar sense in *Native Liberty*, in which he locates the Civil War as a historical marker that might be seen as having "forever abated an original native sense or presence, cultural sovereignty, and continental liberty" (Vizenor, *Native Liberty*, 57).

We might note, also, that in the Wednesday, September 2, 2009, edition of *Anishinaabeg Today* a series of definitions of selected words from the CWEN (which is also printed in that issue) was published. This list of definitions, most likely written by Vizenor, includes "continental liberty," but the definition offered functions more to expand the meaning of the word than to limit it: "Continental liberty refers to the Continent of North American [sic], and native liberty refers to the natural freedoms and rights of natives before contact with Europeans. Natives had established extensive and active trade routes throughout the continent and hemisphere. Trade routes, and other associations of native communities required a sophisticated sense of rights, travel, trade, and native liberty" ("Constitution: Definitions" 19).

24. See Adkins, "White Earth."

25. Vizenor's frequent comments on his own Crane clan roots legitimize such a reading, of course (as does the definition of the term in *Anishinaabeg Today*). He develops the importance of clan most clearly in *Interior Landscapes*, but one can see the emphasis throughout his recent *Native Liberty*. Vizenor's invocation of his ancestors' editing of the tribal newspaper, *The Progress*, on the White Earth Reservation in the 1880s, interwoven with his reflections on his own newspaper career, is further contextualized by his declaration (authorized by Anishinaabe historian William Warren) that Native Crane leaders traditionally acted as interpreters for the tribe (Vizenor, *Native Liberty*, 90). One suspects that Vizenor views his contribution to the present-day constitution-drafting process as part of the same continuum.

At the same time, though, to reduce "totemic" to a single meaning would surely be a mistake. Vizenor's use of the term in a discussion of Anishinaabe pictomyths and picture writing, for example, associates "totemic" with symbolic "transformations by vision and memory." See Vizenor, "Anishinaabe Pictomyths," 180.

26. The CWEN's innovative move to codify representation for urban and other off-reservation White Earth Anishinaabeg (in chapter 6, article 7) represents another way that the text speaks to the complexities of contemporary Indian life.

27. The civil rights framework that dominates chapter 3 enumerates a number of limitations on Anishinaabe governmental power vis-á-vis its citizens, both collectively and individually. Such a move to foreground limitations on tribal governmental power is somewhat unusual in a contemporary tribal constitution. The St. Regis Mohawk Constitution, which focuses more on assertions of positive rights and power—what people and government *can* do—is perhaps a more typical expression of tribal sovereignty. The emphasis on "negative liberty" and the

limitation of even tribal governmental powers is, however, very much in line with Vizenor's career-long struggle against discursive power.

28. In *Native Liberty* Vizenor echoes the long-standing perception that the risk of democracy is that majoritarianism does not guarantee the respect of individual or minority rights. Nevertheless, the fact that the democratic process requires public debate, public justification of policies, and indeed public *interpretation* of law should not be overlooked.

29. For a good overview of some of the key constitutional terms frequently in play in Indian policy and of the shifting terms of Indian policy, see Deloria and Wilkins, *Tribes, Treaties*. See also Carlson, *Sovereign Selves*, 15–38.

30. A particularly striking and damaging recent example of the latter is the U.S. Supreme Court's reintroduction of the concept of laches (a defense against a legal claim drawn from equity jurisprudence that asserts, essentially, that too much time has passed during which the claimant has "slept on his rights") to decide against the Oneida in the 2005 tax case, *City of Sherrill v. Oneida Indian Nation*. As Kathryn E. Fort of the Indigenous Law and Policy Center at Michigan State University has argued, the disadvantageous application of precedent in *City of Sherrill* has opened up a new move to quash tribal land claims throughout the United States. See Fort, "New Laches."

31. On this issue of the borrowing from state, local, and federal law by tribal courts and legislative bodies, see Fletcher, "A Perfect Copy."

32. See Golding, *Legal Reasoning*, 97–111.

33. In the opening essay of *Native Liberty*, "Unnamable Chance," Vizenor relates himself to Camus through the figure of Ishi, whom he has often cited as an inspirational, "virtual, visionary ancestor." Of Ishi and Camus, he writes, "both lived in exile" (Vizenor, "Unnameable," 28).

34. For an earlier formulation of this concept, see Vizenor, "Native Transmotion."

35. Sarris recounts his discovery of his Indian identity in the final section of *Mabel McKay*, 139–44. Vizenor's essay references a shorter version of that narrative, which was printed in a 1998 issue of *People* magazine.

36. Vizenor notes that his thinking about modernity here is influenced by Louis Dupré, *Passage to Modernity*.

37. This is part of what he was attempting in his juxtaposition of Lewis and Clark and Standing Bear in "Postindian Warriors" as well.

38. One of the novel's three opening epigraphs, from Edmond Jabés's *The Book of Questions*, offers an initial interpretive key to seeing how this might work. "I am in the book," Jabés writes. "The book is my world, my country, my roof, and my riddle." Working in an esoteric tradition of interrogative rabbinical teaching—something analogous in some ways to the use of the koan in Zen tradition—Jabés's expansive, multivolume work seeks to reinvent Jewish identity, law, and literature in the wake of displacement and genocide. Jabés's comment highlights a performative process of identity formation in an intertextual, interlocutional mode, one that Vizenor has clearly found inspirational in his current work. Vizenor's interest in him derives both from the similarity of themes that they treat and from his increased interest since the 1990s in the problem of responses to genocide.

39. The prohibition against banishment appears in chapter 3, article 16, of the Constitution of the White Earth Nation. A history of the drafting of the constitution and a copy of the full text can be found in Vizenor, "Constitution." See also Vizenor and Doerfler, *White Earth Nation*.

40. Marlene American Horse's story is recounted in an abbreviated way by Dogroy in Vizenor, *Shrouds of White Earth*, 98–100. The full story can be found in Vizenor, *Wordarrows*, 38–46.

41. See in particular Vizenor, "Native Liberty."

42. See Vizenor, *Shrouds*, 95–97.

43. See Momaday, *Names*, 22, and Allen, *Blood Narrative*, 1–24.

44. Vizenor's manner of writing, we might note, has the effect of making most of these references feel discrete, new, and initiatory; he tends to employ the full name "Marc Chagall" each time he invokes the painter and often opens a new paragraph in doing so.

45. Specific references to Chagall as the central inspiration for Dogroy appear in the novel on pp. 17, 56, 68, 70, and 105. The novel is also dedicated to Chagall (as well as to George Morrison and Edmond Jabès), and an epigraph from his autobiography, *My Life*, is one of three that open the book.

46. Beaulieu is listed in the 2000 U.S. census as a township with a population of 108. It is located near the border of the White Earth Reservation.

47. For Dogroy's views on casinos, see Vizenor, *Shrouds*, 112. Vizenor's own critical views on casinos have appeared in print in many places. See, for example, Vizenor, "Mercenary Sovereignty."

48. The linkage with Camus is not casually made and is fully authorized by the novel itself, which invokes Camus explicitly. Toward the end of *Shrouds* Dogroy reflects on his experiences as a visiting artist in Paris and comments on Camus's transient artistry before explicitly linking that to the addressee, "Vizenor": "Albert Camus, in fact wrote sections of his novel *L'Étranger* at the Hotel Madison nearby on the Boulevard Saint Germain. . . . Albert Camus was one of the first authors that inspired you to be a writer, a literary artist. Camus inspired me too, but obviously my interests were painterly. I would have done the same, my friend, and registered in his memory at the Hôtel Madison. Yes, *L'Étranger* and *La Chute* are also my favorite novels" (Vizenor, *Shrouds*, 135).

49. The epigraph Vizenor takes from Chagall's autobiography, part of Chagall's discussion of a memory of the Jewish Day of Atonement ritual, appears on p. 41. Later in that discussion he includes one of many resonant comments regarding blue: "If you exist, make me blue, fiery, lunar, hide me in the altar with the Torah, do something, God, for our sake, for mine" (Chagall, *My Life*, 44).

50. A good example of this mode in Chagall's work would be his 1911 painting "I and the Village," but we might also consider his many Christian-themed paintings from this period (such as the 1912 "Adam and Eve"). Chagall's insistence on symbolic/mythic reference in his work was at odds with the tenets of cubism, though his use of techniques (geometric forms and grids to splinter the image in fragments of perception) is clearly cubist influenced. For a good general overview of the work of this period, see Walther and Metzger, *Marc Chagall*, 15–33.

51. Vizenor offers another version of this historical process in "Anishinaabe Pictomyths," where he traces the mediation and reemergence of Native identity through the medium of photography.

52. For good general overviews of this issue, see Wilkins and Lomawaima, *Uneven Ground*, and Deloria and Lytle, *American Indians*.

53. Vizenor has acknowledged the U.S. Constitution and other tribal constitutions, as well as the constitution of Japan, among multiple inspirational sources of the text.

54. The growing and harvesting of wild rice is a central part of traditional Anishinaabe lifeways.

55. See the novel *Chancers* for an example of Vizenor's treatment of repatriation. His various writings on Ishi also address these issues, in part through their treatment of the sordid history of Ishi's stolen remains, specifically his brain, which was stored secretly at the Smithsonian for decades after his death. For a discussion of the eventual repatriation of Ishi's brain, see Starn, *Ishi's Brain*.

56. On the "union of chance" with Chagall, see Vizenor, *Shrouds*, 62, 147.

Chapter 7

1. The most thoroughly documented history of this period can be found in Lindsay, *Murder State*.
2. In this context Ishi would become a celebrated figure of the "last wild Indian" in the years just before the First World War.
3. On the Agua Caliente experience of the claims process, see Garner, *Broken Ring*, 121–51.
4. An example of this would be the San Manuel Band of Mission Indians' lawsuit against the National Labor Relations Board (decided in 2007), attempting to prevent the unionization of its casino workers under U.S. labor law. The tribe asserted that the National Labor Relations Act should not apply to the actions of tribal governments on their reservation lands. The San Manuels lost this bid to assert their sovereignty, and the effects of that loss, of course, will be felt throughout Indian country owing to the precedent of the case.
5. The language appears on the website of the Agua Caliente Cultural and Historical Museum, www.accmuseum.org/About-the-Tribe.
6. Garner, *Broken Ring*, offers a detailed account of the maneuvering surrounding the allotment of Agua Caliente lands. At various times this struggle saw national figures, including John Collier, actively scheming against traditional tribal leaders. Patencio himself was briefly imprisoned in 1937 by the special agent, Harold H. Quakenbush, who had been appointed to administer the Agua Caliente reservation.
7. For the Cahuillas, the category of "people/Nukatem" is a broadly inclusive one encompassing animal ancestors and relatives, stars who once lived among us, monstrous beings, and other more distinctly human figures including the specific ancestors of Patencio's own Fox clan.
8. At this time many California tribes were also pursuing land-claim lawsuits under the auspices of the 1928 Jurisdiction Act. In that act Congress authorized California Indians covered by eighteen unratified treaties negotiated in the 1850s to sue the federal government for compensation.
9. On Cahuilla cosmology and cultural practices, see Bean, *Mukat's People*.
10. Patencio also offers a range of traditional stories that provide precisely those resources. As he notes in another narrative from the first part of the book (about an evil Nukatem called the Devil Woman who nearly destroys a band living near her), no tribe (or clan lineage) will ever be totally wiped out, for even in the worst instance, "Power always saves two" (Patencio, *Stories*, 50).
11. Patencio's use of place-names goes well beyond the use of individual words as "memorials," or markers of a disappearing language, placed in the text, a strategy that Margaret Noori has examined in her scholarship on Simon Pokegon's 1899 novel, *Ogimawkwe Mitigwaki* (*Queen of the Woods*). Patencio does not simply drop into his work the occasional, relatively decontextualized noun. His narrative is full of Cahuilla words—more than two hundred, in fact, and a significant number of these are specific place-names—He also makes use of a handful of Serrano words, a fact that is reflective of the significant amount of cultural sharing (and intermarriage) between these two neighboring groups.
12. See Garner, *Broken Ring*, 123–24.
13. See in particular Basso, *Wisdom*.
14. It is worth noting, in this regard, that Patencio's text is one of the sources cited in a United States Bureau of Land Management report published in 1981 for the purpose of identifying, evaluating, and protecting tribal sites. See Bean, Vane, and Young, *Cahuilla*.
15. For a remarkable overview of the Idle No More movement, see Kino-nda-niimi Collective, *Winter We Danced*.

Bibliography

Adams, David Wallace. *Education for Extinction: American Indians and the Boarding School Experience.* Lawrence: University of Kansas Press, 1997.
Adkins, Jason. "White Earth Delegates Ratify New Constitution." *Indian Country Today,* April 22, 2009.
Alfred, Taiaiake. *Peace, Power, Righteousness: An Indigenous Manifesto.* Oxford: Oxford University Press, 2009.
———. "Sovereignty." In *Sovereignty Matters: Locations of Contestation and Possibility in Indigenous Struggles for Self-Determination,* edited by Joanne Barker, 33–50. Lincoln: University of Nebraska Press, 2005.
Allen, Chadwick. *Blood Narrative: Indigenous Identity in American Indian and Maori Literary and Activist Texts.* Durham, N.C.: Duke University Press, 2002.
Althusser, Louis. *Lenin and Philosophy and Other Essays.* New York: Monthly Review Press, 2001.
Anaya, James. *Indigenous Peoples in International Law.* 2nd ed. Oxford: Oxford University Press, 2004.
Anderson, Benedict. *Imagined Communities: Reflections on the Origin and Spread of Nationalism.* New York: Verso, 1983.
Barker, Joanne. "For Whom Sovereignty Matters." In *Sovereignty Matters: Locations of Contestation and Possibility in Indigenous Struggles for Self-Determination,* edited by Joanne Barker, 1–32. Lincoln: University of Nebraska Press, 2005.
Barreiro, Jose. *Thinking in Indian: A John Mohawk Reader.* Golden, Colo.: Fulcrum Press, 2010.
Barsh, Russel Lawrence. "The Challenge of Indigenous Self-Determination." In *Native American Sovereignty,* edited by John Wunder, 129–57. New York: Routledge, 1999.
Basic Call to Consciousness. Edited by *Akwesasne Notes.* Summertown, Tenn.: Native Voices, 2005.
Basso, Keith. *Wisdom Sits in Places: Landscape and Language among the Western Apache.* Albuquerque: University of New Mexico Press, 1996.
Baudrillard, Jean. *Selected Writings.* Edited by Mark Poster. Stanford: Stanford University Press, 1988.
Bean, Lowell. *Mukat's People: The Cahuilla Indians of Southern California.* Berkeley: University of California Press, 1972.

Bean, Lowell, Sylvia Brakke Vane, and Jackson Young. *The Cahuilla and the Santa Rosa Mountain Region: Places and Their Native American Associations.* Riverside, Calif.: United States Department of the Interior, Bureau of Land Management, 1981.

Bernstein, Bruce, and W. Jackson Rushing. *Modern by Tradition: American Indian Painting in the Studio Style.* Santa Fe: Museum of New Mexico Press, 1995.

Blaeser, Kimberly M. *Gerald Vizenor: Writing in the Oral Tradition.* Norman: University of Oklahoma Press, 1996.

Blair, Elizabeth. "Text as Trickster: Postmodern Language Games in Gerald Vizenor's *Bearheart.*" *MELUS* 20, no. 4 (Winter 1995): 75–90.

Borrows, John. *Canada's Indigenous Constitution.* Toronto: University of Toronto Press, 2010.

———. *Drawing Out Law: A Spirit Guide.* Toronto: University of Toronto Press, 2010.

———. *Recovering Canada: The Resurgence of Indigenous Law.* Toronto: University of Toronto Press, 2002.

Breyer, Stephen. *Active Liberty: Interpreting Our Democratic Constitution.* New York: Vintage Books, 2005.

Brierly, J. L. *The Law of Nations: An Introduction to the International Law of Peace.* 6th ed. Edited by Humphrey Wadlock. New York: Oxford University Press, 1963.

Brill de Ramirez, Susan Berry. *Contemporary American Indian Literatures and the Oral Tradition.* Tucson: University of Arizona Press, 1999.

Brooks, Lisa. "Afterword: At the Gathering Place." In *American Indian Literary Nationalism,* edited by Jace Weaver, Robert Warrior, and Craig Womack, 225–52. Albuquerque: University of New Mexico Press, 2006.

———. *The Common Pot: The Recovery of Native Space in the Northeast.* Minneapolis: University of Minnesota Press, 2008.

Bross, Kristina. *Dry Bones and Indian Sermons: Praying Indians in Colonial America.* Ithaca, N.Y.: Cornell University Press, 2004.

Bruyneel, Kevin. *The Third Space of Sovereignty: The Postcolonial Politics of U.S.–Indigenous Relations.* Minneapolis: University of Minnesota Press, 2007.

Butler, Judith, and Joan W. Scott. *Feminists Theorize the Political.* New York: Routledge, 1992.

Byrd, Jodi. *The Transit of Empire: Indigenous Critiques of Colonialism.* Minneapolis: University of Minnesota Press, 2011.

Camus, Albert. "Helen's Exile." In *The Myth of Sisyphus: And Other Essays,* 185–92. New York: Knopf, 1964.

Carlson, David. "Autobiography." In *Reading Primary Sources: The Interpretation of Texts from 19th and 20th Century History,* edited by Miriam Dobson and Benjamin Ziemann, 175–91. New York: Routledge, 2009.

———. *Sovereign Selves: American Indian Autobiography and the Law.* Champaign: University of Illinois Press, 2006.

Caspersen, Nina. *Unrecognized States: The Struggle for Sovereignty in the Modern International System.* Malden, Mass.: Polity Press, 2012.

Chagall, Marc. *My Life.* New York: Orion, 1960.

Champagne, Duane. "American Indian Studies Is for Everyone." In *Natives and Academics: Researching and Writing about American Indians,* edited by Devon Mihesuah, 181–89. Lincoln: University of Nebraska Press, 1998.

Champagne, Duane, Karen Jo Torjesen, and Susan Steiner, eds. *Indigenous Peoples and the Modern State.* New York: Rowman and Littlefield, 2005.

Cobb, Amanda. "Understanding Tribal Sovereignty: Definitions, Conceptualizations, and Interpretations." *American Studies* 46, nos. 3–4 (Fall–Winter 2005): 115–32.

Cobb, Daniel. *Native Activism in Cold War America: The Struggle for Sovereignty.* Lawrence: University of Kansas Press, 2010.

Cohen, Felix. *On the Drafting of Tribal Constitutions*. Edited by David E. Wilkins. Norman: University of Oklahoma Press, 2006.
"Constitution and By-laws of the Saint Regis Mohawk Tribe ON-KWA-IA-NE-REN-SHE-RA (Our Laws)." *National Indian Law Library*. Native American Rights Fund. www.narf.org/nill/constitutions/saint_regis/index.html.
"Constitution of the White Earth Nation, The." *White Earth Nation*. www.whiteearth.com/programs/?page_id=523&program_id=26.
"Constitution of the White Earth Nation: Definition of Selected Words." *Anishinaabeg Today*. September 2, 2009.
Cook, Ray. "Beware the Voices of Political Assimilation." *This Week from Indian Country Today*. February 12, 2012.
———. "Tribal Citizens and American Elections." *This Week from Indian Country Today*. March 2, 2011.
Cook-Lynn, Elizabeth. "The American Indian Fiction Writers: Cosmopolitanism, Nationalism, the Third World, and First Nations Sovereignty." In *Why I Can't Read Wallace Stegner and Other Essays: A Tribal Voice*, edited by Elizabeth Cook-Lynn, 78–97. Madison: University of Wisconsin Press, 1997.
———. *Anti-Indianism in Modern America: A Voice from Tatekeya's Earth*. Champaign: University of Illinois Press, 2001.
———. *A Separate Country: Postcoloniality and American Indian Nations*. Lubbock: Texas Tech University Press, 2011.
———. *Aurelia: A Crow Creek Trilogy*. Boulder: University of Colorado Press, 1999.
———. *New Indians, Old Wars*. Champaign: University of Illinois Press, 2007.
———. *Notebooks of Elizabeth Cook-Lynn*. Tucson: University of Arizona Press, 2007.
———. *The Power of Horses and Other Stories*. Tucson: University of Arizona Press, 2006.
———. *Then Badger Said This*. Fairfield, Wash.: Ye Galleon Press, 1983.
———. *Why I Can't Read Wallace Stegner and Other Essays: A Tribal Voice*. Madison: University of Wisconsin Press, 1997.
Cornell, Drucilla. *The Philosophy of the Limit*. New York: Routledge, 1992.
Costo, Rupert. "Sovereignty." *Wassaja*. July 1973.
———. "Tribalism vs. Nationalism." *Wassaja*. October 1978.
———. "Wassaja—The Name." *Wassaja*. Jan 1973.
Costo, Rupert, and Jeanette H. Costo. *Missions of California: A Legacy of Genocide*. San Francisco: Indian Historian Press, 1987.
———. *Natives of the Golden State: The California Indians*. San Francisco: Indian Historian Press, 1995.
Coulthard, Glen. *Red Skin, Black Masks: Rejecting the Colonial Politics of Recognition*. Minneapolis: University of Minnesota Press, 2014.
Cox, James H. *Muting White Noise: Native American and European American Novel Traditions*. Norman: University of Oklahoma Press, 2006.
Crenshaw, Kimberle, Neil Gotanda, Gary Peller, and Kendal Thomas, eds. *Critical Race Theory: The Key Writings That Formed the Movement*. New York: New Press, 1995.
Cruikshank, Julie. *Life Lived Like a Story: Life Stories of Three Yukon Native Elders*. Lincoln: University of Nebraska Press, 1992.
———. *The Social Life of Stories: Narrative and Knowledge in the Yukon Territory*. Lincoln: University of Nebraska Press, 2000.
Cruse, Harold. *The Crisis of the Negro Intellectual: A Historical Analysis of the Failure of Black Leadership*. New York: New York Review of Books, 1967.
Danker, Kathleen. "'The Violation of the Earth': Elizabeth Cook-Lynn's *From the River's Edge* in the Historical Context of the Pick-Sloan Missouri River Dam Project." *Wicazo Sa Review* 12, no. 2 (Autumn 1997): 85–93.

Debord, Guy. *Society of the Spectacle*. Translated by Donald Nicholson-Smith. New York: Zone Books, 1995.
Declaration of Indian Purpose: The Voice of the American Indian by the Indians of North America. Chicago. New York: Kessinger, 2010.
Deloria, Vine, Jr. *God Is Red: A Native View of Religion*. New York: Putnam, 1973.
———. "Intellectual Self-Determination and Sovereignty: Looking at the Windmills in Our Minds." *Wicazo-Sa Review* 13, no. 9 (Spring 1998): 25–31.
———. "Self-Determination and the Concept of Sovereignty." In *Native American Sovereignty*, edited by John Wunder, 118–24. New York: Routledge, 1999.
———. *We Talk, You Listen: New Tribes, New Turf*. Lincoln: Bison Books, 2007.
Deloria, Vine, Jr., and Raymond DeMallie. *Documents of American Indian Diplomacy: Treaties, Agreements, and Conventions, 1775–1979*. 2 vols. Norman: University of Oklahoma Press, 1999.
Deloria, Vine, Jr., and Clifford Lytle. *American Indians, American Justice*. Austin: University of Texas Press, 1983.
———. *The Nations Within: The Past and Future of American Indian Sovereignty*. Austin: University of Texas Press, 1998.
Deloria, Vine, Jr., and David Wilkins. *Tribes, Treaties, and Constitutional Tribulations*. Austin: University of Texas Press, 2000.
Den Ouden, Amy, and Jean O'Brien, eds. *Recognition, Sovereignty Struggles, and Indigenous Rights in the United States: A Sourcebook*. Chapel Hill: University of North Carolina Press, 2013.
Derrida, Jacques. *Margins of Philosophy*. Translated by Alan Bass. Chicago: University of Chicago Press, 1982.
———. *Of Grammatology*. Translated by Gayatri Chakravorty Spivak. Baltimore: Johns Hopkins University Press, 1976.
Driskill, Quo-Li, ed. *Queer Indigenous Studies: Critical Interventions in Theory, Politics, and Literature*. Tucson: University of Arizona Press, 2011.
Du Bois. W. E. B. *The Souls of Black Folk*. New York: Dover, 1994.
Elmer, Jonathan. *On Lingering and Being Last: Race and Sovereignty in the New World*. New York: Fordham University Press, 2008.
Elshtain, Jean Bethke. *Sovereignty: God, State, and Self*. New York: Basic Books, 2008.
Fanon, Frantz. *The Wretched of the Earth*. Translated by Richard Philcox. New York: Grove Press, 2004.
Fenton, William. *The Great Law and the Longhouse: A Political History of the Iroquois Confederacy*. Norman: University of Oklahoma Press, 2010.
Fixico, Donald. *Termination and Relocation: Federal Indian Policy, 1945–1960*. Albuquerque: University of New Mexico Press, 1990.
Fletcher, Matthew. "The Iron Cold of the Marshall Trilogy." *North Dakota Law Review*, 82, no. 4 (2006): 627–96.
———. "'Native American Fiction' Tough on Indian Culture." *Indian Country Today*. August 8, 2007.
———. "A Perfect Copy: Indian Culture and Tribal Law." *Yellow Medicine Review* 2 (Fall 2007): 95–118.
Forbes, Jack. "Intellectual Self-Determination and Sovereignty: Implications for Native Studies and Native Intellectuals." *Wicazo-Sa Review* 13, no. 9 (Spring 1998): 11–23.
Fort, Kathryn E. "The New Laches: Creating Title Where None Existed." *George Mason Law Review* 16, no. 2 (Winter 2009): 357–401.
Freud, Sigmund. *Group Psychology and the Analysis of the Ego*. Translated by James Strachy. New York: Norton, 2012.
Garner, Van H. *The Broken Ring: The Destruction of the California Indians*. Tucson: Westernlore Press, 1983.
Gellner, Ernest. *Nations and Nationalism*. New York: Blackwell, 2008.

Golding, Martin P. *Legal Reasoning*. Toronto: Broadview, 2001.
Gonzalez, Mario, and Elizabeth Cook-Lynn. *The Politics of Hallowed Ground: Wounded Knee and the Struggle for Indian Sovereignty*. Champaign: University of Illinois Press, 1999.
Goodman, Ronald. *Lakota Star Knowledge: Studies in Lakota Stellar Theology*. Mission, S.Dak.: Sinte Gleska University, 1992.
Gross, Emma. "The Origin of Self-Determination Ideology and Constitutional Sovereignty." In *Native American Sovereignty*, edited by John Wunder, 125–42. New York: Routledge, 1999.
Habermas, Jurgen. *The Structural Transformation of the Public Sphere: An Inquiry into a Category of Bourgeois Society*. Translated by Thomas Burger. Cambridge: Massachusetts Institute of Technology Press, 1991.
Hale, Frederick. "Axiological Dissonance and Moral Accountability in Elizabeth Cook-Lynn's *From the River's Edge*." *European Review of Native American Studies* 14, no. 1 (2000): 39–44.
Haseltine, Patricia. "The Voices of Gerald Vizenor: Survival through Transformation." *American Indian Quarterly* (Winter 1985): 31–47.
Hauptman, Lawrence, and Jack Campisi. "The Voice of the Eastern Indians: The American Indian Chicago Conference of 1961 and the Movement for Federal Recognition." *Proceedings of the American Philosophical Society* 132, no. 4 (December 1988): 316–29.
Hinton, Leanne. *Flutes of Fire: Essays on California Indian Languages*. Berkeley: Heyday Books, 1994.
Hobsbawm, E. J. *Nations and Nationalism Since 1780*. Cambridge: Cambridge University Press, 1990.
Hooper, Lucile. "The Cahuilla Indians." *University of California Publications in American Archaeology and Ethnology* 16, no. 6 (April 10, 1920): 315–80.
Hoxie, Frederick. *A Final Promise: The Campaign to Assimilate the Indians, 1880–1920*. Lincoln: University of Nebraska Press, 2001.
———. *This Indian Country: American Indian Activists and the Place They Made*. New York: Penguin, 2012.
Indian Country Today. "Renew Sovereignty Lessons for a New Generation," June 24, 2009.
———. "Tribal Sovereignty in the 21st Century." February 6, 2008.
Iverson, Peter. *Carlos Montezuma and the Changing World of American Indians*. Albuquerque: University of New Mexico Press, 1982.
Jabés, Edmond. *The Book of Questions*. Middletown, Conn.: Wesleyan University Press, 1976.
Jackson, Robert. *Sovereignty: The Evolution of an Idea*. Cambridge: Polity Press, 2007.
Johansen, Bruce. *Debating Democracy: The Iroquois Legacy of Freedom*. Santa Fe: Clear Light, 1997.
———. *Forgotten Founders: How the Indians Helped Shape Democracy*. Cambridge: Harvard Common Press, 1982.
Jonaitis, Monique Ramune. "Review: *The Power of Horses*." *American Indian Culture and Research Journal* 31, no. 2 (2007): 147–50.
Justice, Daniel Heath. *Our Fire Survives the Storm: A Cherokee Literary History*. Minneapolis: University of Minnesota Press, 2006.
Kalt, Joseph P. "The Role of Constitutions in Native Nation Building: Laying a Firm Foundation." In *Rebuilding Native Nations: Strategies for Government and Development*, edited by Miriam Jorgensen, 78–114. Tucson: University of Arizona Press, 2006.
Kidwell, Clara Sue. "Native American Studies: Academic Concerns and Community Service." *American Indian Culture and Research Journal* 2, nos. 3–4 (1978): 4–9.
Kino-nda-niimi Collective, The, ed. *The Winter We Danced: Voices from the Past, the Future, and the Idle No More Movement*. Winnipeg: Arbeiter Ring, 2014.
Kirwan, Padraig. *Sovereign Stories: Aesthetics, Autonomy, and Contemporary Native American Writing*. Bern, Switzerland: Peter Lang, 2013.
Konkle, Maureen. *Writing Indian Nations: Native Intellectuals and the Politics of Historiography, 1827–1863*. Chapel Hill: University of North Carolina Press, 2006.

Krupat, Arnold. *Ethnocriticism: Ethnography, History, Literature.* Berkeley: University of California Press, 1992.

———. *For Those Who Come After: A Study of Native American Autobiography.* Berkeley: University of California Press, 1989.

———. *The Voice in the Margin: Native American Literature and the Canon.* Berkeley: University of California Press, 1989.

Kymlicka, Will. *Multicultural Citizenship: A Liberal Theory of Minority Rights.* Oxford: Oxford University Press, 1996.

Lawson, Michael. *Dammed Indians: The Pick-Sloan Plan and the Missouri River Sioux, 1944–1980.* Norman: University of Oklahoma Press, 1982.

Lee, A. Robert. *Loosening the Seams: Interpretations of Gerald Vizenor.* Bowling Green, Ohio: Bowling Green State University Press, 2000.

Lejeune, Phillipe. *On Autobiography.* Translated by Katherine Leary. Minneapolis: University of Minnesota Press, 1989.

Levinson, Sanford, and Steven Mailloux. *Interpreting Law and Literature: A Hermeneutic Reader.* Evanston, Ill.: Northwestern University Press, 1988.

Lindsay, Brendan. *Murder State: California's Native American Genocide, 1846–1873.* Lincoln: University of Nebraska Press, 2012.

Litowitz, Douglas E. *Postmodern Philosophy and Law.* Lawrence: University of Kansas Press, 1997.

Littlefield, Daniel. *Alex Posey: Creek Poet, Journalist, and Humorist.* Lincoln: University of Nebraska Press, 1997.

Llewellyn, Karl, and E. Adamson Hoebel. *The Cheyenne Way: Conflict and Case Law in Primitive Jurisprudence.* Norman: University of Oklahoma Press, 1941.

Lyons, Oren. "Preamble." In *Basic Call to Consciousness,* edited by Akwesasne Notes, 13–25. Summetown, Tenn.: Native Voices: 2005.

Lyons, Scott. "Battle of the Bookworms." *Indian Country Today.* August 15, 2007.

———. *X-Marks: Native Signatures of Assent.* Minneapolis: University of Minnesota Press, 2010.

Lyotard, Jean-Francois. *The Postmodern Condition: A Report on Knowledge.* Translated by Geoff Bennington and Brian Massumi. Minneapolis: University of Minnesota Press, 1984.

Macherey, Pierre. *A Theory of Literary Production.* Translated by Geoffrey Wall. New York: Routledge, 2006.

Mackay, James. "Ghosts in the Gap: Diane Glancy's Paradoxes of Survivance." In *Survivance: Narratives of Native Presence,* edited by Gerald Vizenor, 247–70. Lincoln: University of Nebraska Press, 2008.

Maddox, Lucy. *Removals: Nineteenth-Century American Indian Literature and the Politics of Indians Affairs.* Oxford: Oxford University Press, 1991.

Madsen, Deborah L. *Understanding Gerald Vizenor.* Columbia: University of South Carolina Press, 2009.

Martin, Joel. *Sacred Revolt: The Muskogees Struggle for a New World.* Boston: Beacon Press, 1991.

McNickle, D'Arcy. *Native American Tribalism.* New York: Oxford University Press, 1973.

———. *The Surrounded.* Albuquerque: University of New Mexico Press, 1978.

———. *Wind from an Enemy Sky.* Albuquerque: University of New Mexico Press, 1978.

Mihesuah, Devon. *American Indians: Stereotypes and Realities.* Atlanta: Clarity Press, 2004.

———, ed. *Natives and Academics: Researching and Writing about American Indians.* Lincoln: University of Nebraska Press, 1998.

Mihesuah, Devon, and Angela Cavendar Wilson. *Indigenizing the Academy: Transforming Scholarship and Empowering Native Communities.* Lincoln: Bison Books, 2004.

Miller, Robert. *Native America, Discovered and Conquered: Thomas Jefferson, Lewis and Clark, and Manifest Destiny.* Lincoln: Bison Books, 2008.

Miranda, Deborah. *Bad Indians: A Tribal Memoir.* Berkeley: Heyday Press, 2013.

Momaday, N. Scott. *The Names: A Memoir.* New York: Harper and Row, 1976.

Moore, David L. *That Dream Shall Have a Name: Native Americans Rewriting America*. Lincoln: University of Nebraska Press, 2013.
Morgan, Edmund. *Inventing the People: The Rise of Popular Sovereignty in England and America*. New York: Norton, 1989.
Morrison, George, and Margot Fortunato Galt. *Turning the Feather Around: My Life in Art*. St. Paul: Minnesota Historical Society, 1998.
Newcomb, Steven. *Pagans in the Promised Land: Decoding the Doctrine of Christian Discovery*. Golden, Colo.: Fulcrum, 2008.
O'Brien, Jean. *Firsting and Lasting: Writing Indians Out of Existence in New England*. Minneapolis: University of Minnesota Press, 2010.
Ollman, Bertell. *Dance of the Dialectic: Steps in Marx's Method*. Champaign: University of Illinois Press, 2003.
Ortiz, Alfonso. "D'Arcy McNickle (1904–1977): A Personal Remembrance." *Wassaja*. January/February 1978.
Patencio, Francisco. *Stories and Legends of the Palm Springs Indians*. As told to Margaret Boynton. Los Angeles: Times-Mirror, 1943.
Pearce, Roy Harvey. *Savagism and Civilization: A Study of the Indian and the American Mind*. Berkeley: University of California Press, 1988.
Peller, Gary. "Race-Consciousness." In *Critical Race Theory: The Key Writings That Formed the Movement*, edited by Kimberle Crenshaw et al., 127–58. New York: New Press, 1995.
Penn, W. S. *All My Sins Are Relatives*. Lincoln: University of Nebraska Press, 1995.
Peyer, Bernd. *The Thinking Indian: Native American Writers, 1850s–1920s*. New York: Peter Lang, 2007.
Pommersheim, Frank. *Braid of Feathers: American Indian Law and Contemporary Tribal Life*. Berkeley: University of California Press, 1997.
———. *Broken Landscape: Indians, Indian Tribes, and the Constitution*. New York: Oxford University Press, 2012.
Posey, Alexander. *The Fus Fixico Letters: A Creek Humorist in Early Oklahoma*, edited by Daniel Littlefield. Norman: University of Oklahoma Press, 2002.
Prucha, Francis Paul. *Documents of United States Indian Policy*. 2nd ed. Lincoln: University of Nebraska Press, 1990.
Pulitano, Elvira. *Toward a Native American Critical Theory*. Lincoln: University of Nebraska Press, 2003.
Purdy, John, ed. *The Legacy of D'Arcy McNickle: Writer, Historian, Activist*. Norman: University of Oklahoma Press, 1996.
———. *Word Ways: The Novels of D'Arcy McNickle*. Tucson: University of Arizona Press, 1990.
Purdy, John, and Blake Hausman. "The Future of Print Narratives and Comic Holotropes: A Conversation with Gerald Vizenor." *American Indian Quarterly* 19, nos. 1–2 (Winter/Spring 2005): 212–25.
"Revised Constitution and Bylaws of the Minnesota Chippewa Tribe, Minnesota." *National Indian Law Library*. Native American Rights Fund. www.narf.org/nill/constitutions/minn_chippewa/.
Reynolds, Jerry. "Delegates Announce Pullout from U.S. Treaties." *Indian Country Today*. January 2, 2008.
Richter, Daniel. *The Ordeal of the Longhouse: The Peoples of the Iroquois League in the Era of European Colonization*. Chapel Hill: University of North Carolina Press, 1992.
Rifkin, Mark. *When Did Indians Become Straight: Kinship, the History of Sexuality, and Native Sovereignty*. New York: Oxford University Press, 2011.
Rodríguez, Juana María, "Vizenorian Jurisprudence: Legal Interventions, Narrative Strategies, and the Interpretive Possibilities of Shadows." In *Loosening the Seams*, edited by A. Robert Lee, 246–62. Bowling Green, Ohio: Bowling Green State University Press, 2000.

Round, Phillip. *Removable Type: Histories of the Book in Indian Country, 1663–1880.* Chapel Hill: University of North Carolina Press, 2010.
Sarris, Greg. *Mabel McKay: Weaving the Dream.* Berkeley: University of California Press, 1994.
Schmitt, Carl. *The Concept of the Political.* Translated by George Schwab. Chicago: University of Chicago Press, 2007.
———. *Political Theology: Four Chapters on the Concept of Sovereignty.* Translated by George Schwab. Chicago: University of Chicago Press, 2006.
Scott, Joan W. "Experience." In *Feminists Theorize the Political,* edited by Judith Butler and Joan W. Scott, 22–40. New York: Routledge, 1992.
Sheehan, Bernard. *Savagism and Civility: Indians and Englishmen in Colonial Virginia.* Cambridge: Cambridge University Press, 1980.
Simpson, Audra. *Mohawk Interruptus: Political Life Across the Border of Settler States.* Durham, N.C.: Duke University Press, 2014.
Smith, Linda Tuhiwai. *Decolonizing Methodologies: Research and Indigenous Peoples.* New York: Zed Books, 2012.
Smith, Paul Chaat, and Robert Warrior. *Like a Hurricane: The Indian Movement from Alcatraz to Wounded Knee.* New York: New Press, 1997.
Starn, Orin. *Ishi's Brain: In Search of America's Last "Wild" Indian.* New York: Norton, 2004.
Stripes, James. "'We Think in Terms of What Is Fair': Justice Versus 'Just Compensation' in Elizabeth Cook-Lynn's *From the River's Edge*." *Wicazo-Sa Review* 12, no. 1 (Spring 1997): 165–87.
Strong, William Duncan. *Aboriginal Society in Southern California.* Banning, Calif.: Malki-Ballena Press, 1987.
Tedlock, Dennis. *Finding the Center: The Art of the Zuni Storyteller.* Lincoln: University of Nebraska Press, 1999.
———. *The Spoken Word and the Work of Interpretation.* Philadelphia: University of Pennsylvania Press, 1983.
Teuton, Sean. "Writing American Indian Politics." In *Reasoning Together: The Native Critics Collective,* edited by Craig S. Womack, Daniel Heath Justice, and Christopher B. Teuton, 105–25. Norman: University of Oklahoma Press, 2008.
Toensing, Gale Courey. "Next Step: Implementation." *This Week from Indian Country Today.* January 19, 2011.
———. "Withdrawal from U.S. Treaties Enjoys Little Support from Tribal Leaders." *Indian Country Today.* January 9, 2008.
Treuer, David. *Native American Fiction: A User's Manual.* Saint Paul: Greywold Press, 2006.
———. "Treuer Defends Purpose of 'Manual.'" *Indian Country Today.* August 15, 2007.
Tully, James. *Strange Multiplicity: Constitutionalism in an Age of Diversity.* Cambridge: Cambridge University Press, 1995.
Turner, Dale. *This Is Not a Peace Pipe: Toward a Critical Indigenous Philosophy.* Toronto: University of Toronto Press, 2006.
Ulrich, Roberta. *American Indian Nations from Termination to Restoration, 1953–2006.* Lincoln: University of Nebraska Press, 2013.
United Nations. "United Nations Declaration on the Rights of Indigenous Peoples." *United Nations.* 2008. www.un.org/esa/socdev/unpfii/documents/DRIPS_en.pdf.
Velie, Alan, and A. Robert Lee, eds. *The Native American Renaissance: Literary Imagination and Achievement.* Norman: University of Oklahoma Press, 2013.
Vizenor, Gerald. "Aesthetics of Survivance." In *Native Liberty,* 85–103. Lincoln: University of Nebraska Press, 2009.
———. "Anishinaabe Pictomyths." In *Native Liberty,* 179–90. Lincoln: University of Nebraska Press, 2009.
———. *Chancers: A Novel.* Norman: University of Oklahoma Press, 2000.

———. "Constitution of the White Earth Nation." *Language Value* 1, no. 1 (2009): 51–80.
———. *Father Meme*. Albuquerque: University of New Mexico Press, 2008.
———. "Genocide Tribunals." In *Native Liberty*, 131–57. Lincoln: University of Nebraska Press, 2009.
———. *Interior Landscapes: Autobiographical Myths and Metaphors*. Minneapolis: University of Minnesota Press, 1990.
———. *Landfill Meditation*. Hanover, Penn.: Wesleyan University Press, 1991.
———. *Manifest Manners: Narratives on Postindian Survivance*. Lincoln: University of Nebraska Press, 1999.
———. "Mercenary Sovereignty." In *Native Liberty*, 105–30. Lincoln: University of Nebraska Press, 2009.
———. "Native Liberty." In *Native Liberty*, 35–56. Lincoln: University of Nebraska Press, 2009.
———. *Native Liberty: Natural Reason and Cultural Survivance*. Lincoln: University of Nebraska Press, 2009.
———. "Native Transmotion." In *Fugitive Poses: Native American Indian Scenes of Absence and Presence*, 167–99. Lincoln: University of Nebraska, 1998.
———. "Ontic Images." In *Native Liberty*, 159–78. Lincoln: University of Nebraska Press, 2009.
———. "Postindian Warriors." In *Manifest Manners*, 1–44. Lincoln: University of Nebraska Press, 1999.
———. *Shrouds of White Earth*. Albany: State University of New York Press, 2010.
———. "Unnamable Chance." In *Native Liberty*, 15–34. Lincoln: University of Nebraska Press, 2009.
———. *Wordarrows*. Lincoln: University of Nebraska Press, 2003.
Vizenor, Gerald, and Jill Doerfler. *The White Earth Nation: Ratification of a Native Democratic Constitution*. Lincoln: University of Nebraska Press, 2012.
Vizenor, Gerald, and Jace Weaver. *Bear Island: The War at Sugar Point*. Minneapolis: University of Minnesota Press, 2006.
Walther, Ingo F., Rainer Metzger, and Marc Chagall. *Marc Chagall 1887–1985; Painting As Poetry*. Cologne, Germany: Taschen, 2006.
Warner, Michael. *Letters of the Republic: Publication and the Public Sphere in Eighteenth-Century America*. Cambridge: Harvard University Press, 1992.
Warrior, Robert. "Native Critics in the World: Edward Said and Nationalism." In *American Indian Literary Nationalism*, edited by Jace Weaver, Robert Warrior, and Craig Womack, 179–224. Albuquerque: University of New Mexico Press, 2006.
———. *The People and the Word: Reading Native Nonfiction*. Minneapolis: University of Minnesota Press, 2005.
———. *Tribal Secrets: Recovering American Indian Intellectual Traditions*. Minneapolis: University of Minnesota Press, 1994.
Wassaja. "One Axe to Grind." May 1975.
Waziyatawin, ed. *For Indigenous Eyes Only: A Decolonization Handbook*. Santa Fe: School of American Research Press, 2005.
———. *What Does Justice Look Like?: The Struggle for Liberation in Dakota Homeland*. St. Paul: Living Justice Press, 2008.
Weaver, Jace. *Other Words: American Indian Literature, Law, and Culture*. Norman: University of Oklahoma Press, 2001.
———. "Splitting the Earth: First Utterances and Pluralist Separatism." In *American Indian Literary Nationalism*, edited by Jace Weaver, Robert Warrior and Craig Womack, 1–90. Albuquerque: University of New Mexico Press, 2006.
———. *That the People Might Live: Native American Literatures and Native American Community*. Oxford: Oxford University Press, 1997.

———. "Turning West: Cosmopolitanism and American Indian Literary Nationalism." In *The Native American Renaissance*, edited by Alan Velie and A. Robert Lee, 16–38. Norman: University of Oklahoma Press, 2013.
Weaver, Jace, Robert Warrior, and Craig Womack, eds. *American Indian Literary Nationalism*. Albuquerque: University of New Mexico Press, 2006.
Westerman, Gwen, and Bruce White. *Mni Sota Makoce: The Land of the Dakota*. Minneapolis: Minnesota Historical Society Press, 2012.
White, Richard. *The Middle Ground: Indians, Empires, and Republics in the Great Lakes Region, 1650–1815*. New York: Cambridge University Press, 1991.
Wilkins, David E. Introduction to *On the Drafting of Tribal Constitutions* by Felix Cohen. Norman: University of Oklahoma Press, 2006.
Wilkins, David E., and K. Tsianina Lomawaima. *Uneven Ground: American Indian Sovereignty and Federal Law*. Norman: University of Oklahoma Press, 2001.
Wilkins, David E., and Heidi Kiiwetinepinesiik Stark. *American Indian Politics and the American Indian Political System*. 3rd ed. New York: Rowman and Littlefield, 2011.
Williams, Robert. *Linking Arms Together: American Indian Treaty Visions of Law and Peace, 1600–1800*. New York: Routledge, 1999.
Wilson, Waziyatawin Angela. *Remember This!: Dakota Decolonization and the Eli Taylor Narratives*. Lincoln: University of Nebraska Press, 2005.
Womack, Craig. *Art as Performance, Story as Criticism: Reflections on Native Literary Aesthetics*. Norman: University of Oklahoma Press, 2009.
———. *Drowning in Fire*. Tucson: University of Arizona Press, 2001.
———. "The Integrity of Indian Claims: Or, How I Learned to Stop Worrying and Enjoy My Hybridity." In *American Indian Literary Nationalism*, edited by Jace Weaver, Robert Warrior, and Craig Womack, 92–178. Albuquerque: University of New Mexico Press, 2006.
———. *Red on Red: Native American Literary Separatism*. Minneapolis: University of Minnesota Press, 1999.
———. "A Single Decade: Book–Length Native Literary Criticism between 1986 and 1997." In *Reasoning Together*, edited by Craig S. Womack, Daniel Heath Justice, and Christopher B. Teuton, 3–104. Norman: University of Oklahoma Press, 2008.
Womack, Craig, Janice Acoose, Lisa Brooks, Tol Foster, Daniel Heath Justice, Phillip Carroll Morgan, Kimberly Roppolo, Cheryl Suzack, Christopher Teuton, Sean Teuton, Robert Warrior, and LeAnne Howe. *Reasoning Together: The Native Critics Collective*. Norman: University of Oklahoma Press, 2008.
Wunder, John, ed. *Native American Sovereignty*. New York: Routledge, 1999.
Wyss, Hilary. *Writing Indians: Literacy, Christianity, and Native Community in Early America*. Amherst: University of Massachusetts Press, 2003.
Zah, Erny. "NAC Leaders Spank Council on Fundamental Law Restrictions." *Navajo Times*. April 7, 2010. http://navajotimes.com/politics/2010/0310/0326101aw.php.

Index

aboriginal rights, 4–5
Aboriginal Society in Southern California (Strong), 188
absolutism, 18
aesthetics, 109; liberty, 168–69; Vizenor's, 144, 164–65
"Aesthetics of Survivance" (Vizenor), 173–74
Agamben, Giorgio, 170
Agua Caliente Band of Mission Indians (Cahuilla), 12, 181, 211n7; and Americans, 194–95; constitution of, 187–88; creation cycles, 188–89; on creative and destructive power, 190–91; geography, 192–93; land issues, 189–90, 196, 211n6; migration stories, 193–94
Agua Caliente Reservation, 182; allotment system and, 189–90, 211n6
AIM. *See* American Indian Movement
Akwesasne Notes, 67, 72
Aldama, Frederick Luis, 94
Alexander VI, Pope, *Inter Caetera*, 20
Alexie, Sherman, 89
Alfred, Taiaiake, 59, 72, 91; *Peace, Power, and Righteousness*, 32–33; on sovereignty, 33–34
Allen, Chadwick, *Blood Narrative*, 165
All My Sins Are Relatives (Penn), 162
"All the Children of Mother Earth" (Mohawk), 72–73
alliances, inter-tribal, 45

allotment, 40, 41, 97–98, 138, 186; resistance to, 189–90, 211n6
American Indian Chicago Conference, 9, 45, 48, 58, 202n11; *Declaration of Indian Purpose*, 10, 40
"American Indian Fiction Writers: Cosmopolitanism, Nationalism, the Third World, and First Nations Sovereignty, The" (Cook-Lynn), 109, 110–11, 115–16
American Indian Literary Nationalism (Womack), 78, 97, 99, 111, 117
American Indian Movement (AIM), 37
American Indian Religious Freedom Act, 88
American Indian Studies Consortium, 114
American Revolution, 23, 25, 55
analogical thought, and identity formation, 162–63
Anderson, Benedict, 23, 25
Anishinaabeg, 159, 172, 173, 208n15, 209n27; Constitution of the White Earth Nation and, 152, 155, 156–58; nationhood of, 153–54; in *Shrouds of White Earth*, 163–64
anticosmopolitanism, 135
Anti-Indianism in Modern America (Cook-Lynn), 105, 107
Apess, William, 7, 26, 92, 95, 204n13
Arapahoes, 120
art, 210n50; decolonization and, 168–69; and survivance, 169–70

Art as Performance (Womack), 88, 96, 102
assimilation, 27, 40, 84, 179
Atcitcems clan, 194
Aubid, Charles, 173–74, 177
audiences, non-Indian, 110
Aurelia: A Crow Creek Tragedy (Cook-Lynn), 117, 119, 120, 125, 126–27, 141
authenticity, cultural, 89–90
authority, 16, 17, 22, 108; and natural law, 18, 19
autobiography, 7, 49, 189; as form of thinking, 91–92
autonomy, 16, 90, 98, 146; Indian, 40, 55; political, 107–108

Bad Indians (Miranda), 183
Barker, Joanne, 36
Barsh, Russel Lawrence, 34, 59; "The Challenge of Indigenous Self-Determination," 30–31; self-government, 31–32
Barthes, Roland, 94
Basic Call to Consciousness, 67–69; Great Law of Peace in, 70–71
Basso, Keith, 97
Baudrillard, Jean, 148
Bellecourt, Clyde, 165
BIA. *See* Bureau of Indian Affairs
Big Bend Dam, Missouri River, 123
Big Pipe Case, 111, 122
Bird Is Gone, The (Jones), 135
Black Elk, Nicholas, 116
Black Elk Speaks, 116
Black Hills, S.D., theft of, 111, 119, 120–21, 140
black power/black nationalism, 63
Blanket Dance ritual, 134
blood memory, 165
Blood Narrative (Allen), 165
blood quantum, 153
Bodin, Jean, *De Republica*, 17–18
Book of Questions, The (Jabès), 164, 209n38
Boynton, Margaret, 188, 189
Bozeman Trail, Montana Terr., 120
Brierly, J. L., 17
Brooks, Lisa, 81
Brown, Hank, 194, 195
Brulé Lakota, *Ex Parte Crow Dog* case and, 29
Bruyneel, Kevin, 59; *The Third Space of Sovereignty*, 5
Bureau of Indian Affairs (BIA), 38, 44, 49, 111
Buster and Jones v. Wright, 57

Cahuilla. *See* Agua Caliente Band of Mission Indians
Cahuilla Indians, The (Hooper), 188
California, 44; colonial history, 11–12; Indian Country in, 181–82; mission system, 179, 183–84; U.S. government and, 185–86
California Environmental Quality Act, 196
California Indian Indenture Act, 185
California Indians, 179, 211n4; Catholicism and, 180–81; constitutions, 187–88; Jurisdiction Act, 186–87; land base, 184–85; political sovereignty, 182–83; U.S. government and, 185–86. *See also* Agua Caliente Band of Mission Indians
California Senate Bill 18, 196
Callahan, Alice, *Wynema*, 100–101
Campisi, Jack, 45
Camus, Albert, 209n33, 210n48; "Helen's Exile," 160, 167
Canada, aboriginal rights in, 4–5
Carcieri v. Salazar, 111
Carlisle boarding school, 148
casinos, 167
Catholic Church, 17; and California Indians, 180–81; and Serra's canonization, 179–80
Cayol, Pierre, 175
Chagall, Marc, 164, 210n45, 210n50; and exile consciousness, 166–67; liberty aesthetic, 168–69; survivance art, 169–70
"Challenge of Indigenous Self-Determination, The" (Barsh), 30–31
Champagne, Duane, 38, 113
Cherokee, 29, 55, 56, 77, 201n16
Cherokee Nation v. Georgia, 29, 56, 112
Chicago Conference. *See* American Indian Chicago Conference
Chippewa. *See* Anishinaabeg
Chirac, Jacques, 175
Christianity, 26, 92, 102; Dakotah knowledge and, 133–35. *See also* Catholic Church
Churchill, Ward, 116
citizenship, 28, 40, 185, 201n16
civil jurisdiction, 44
civil rights, 208n27; and Constitution of the White Earth Nation, 155–56
"Clearest Blue Day, The" (Cook-Lynn), 129, 130
Clement, Gilles, 176
Coachella Valley, Calif., Americans in, 194–95
collective survival, McNickle on, 42–43
Collier, John, 40, 42, 202n10, 211n6

colonialism, 5, 11, 19, 22, 23, 37, 68, 84, 109, 118, 155, 169, 180; American, 27, 66, 140, 148, 150; and Native American literature, 80–81; U.S. settler, 41, 111, 145, 146–47, 167, 183
colonial period, 23, 55
community, 42, 128
Constitution Act of 1982 (Canada), 4
Constitution of the White Earth Nation (CWEN), 11, 145, 206n2, 207n18, 208n23, 209n39; as postindian, 158–59; preamble of, 154–55, 172–73; and *Shrouds of White Earth*, 164–65, 172–73; structure of, 156–58; trickster hermeneutics in, 151–53
constitutions, 18; California Indians, 187–88; and human rights, 170–71; tribal, 108, 151–53, 204n12, 208n22, 209n27; Vizenor's criticism of, 144–45, 156–58. *See also* Constitution of the White Earth Nation
Continental Congress, treaties, 55
continental liberty, 171, 208n23
contracts, treaties as, 65
Cook-Lynn, Elizabeth, 6, 9, 34, 48, 51, 66, 81, 88, 93, 102–103, 104, 117, 118, 159, 178–79, 205nn2–3; "American Indian Fiction Writers," 110–11; on Dakotah sovereignty, 10–11, 108, 109; on Dakotah symbolism and story format, 134–37; on Doctrine of Discovery, 112–13; on indigeneity, 107, 126–27, 205n5; on interpretive context, 129–31; on literary representation, 115–16; on nationalism, 105–106, 137–42; on oral tradition, 124–25; on postcolonialism/cosmopolitanism, 109–110; *The Power of Horses*, 121–22; on resistance, 133–34; on sovereignty, 130, 142–43; on Wallace Stegner, 128–29; and symbolism of place, 122–24; on treaties and nationhood, 86, 119–20; treaty reading, 127–28, 153; on tribal nationalism, 125–26, 131–32
corporate identity, 24; of California Indians, 180–81
cosmology, indigenous, 72–73
cosmopolitanism, 109–10
cosmoprimitivism, 169
Costo, Jeannette Henry, *The Missions of California*, 179
Costo, Rupert, 36, 84, 185; *The Missions of California*, 179; *Wassaja*, 10, 48–50
Coulthard, Glen, 5; *Red Skin, Black Masks*, 4
council-fire tradition, 191

court system, 44
Crazy Horse, 163
Crazy Snake uprising, 102
creation cycles, Cahuilla, 188–89, 190
Creek, 87, 102; dialect letters, 97–99; identity, 81–82; literary nationalism, 79, 80; nationalism, 99–101; oral tradition, 96–97; and Red Stick movement, 82–86
crime, 44; federal jurisdiction over, 28, 29–30
criticism, 92, 94, 116, 117; constitutional, 144–45; literary, 78–79, 95–96, 100–101, 178; and story, 101–102
Crow Creek Reservation, S.D., 119–20, 122, 138
Crow Dog, 29
Cruikshank, Julie, 97
cultural autonomy, as sovereignty, 62
cultural integrity, 41, 58
cultural policing, 90
cultural values: constitutional incorporation of, 156–57; traditional, 61
CWEN. *See* Constitution of the White Earth Nation

Dakotah, 108, 111, 131; horses and, 137–38; indigeneity, 126–27; knowledge, 133–34, 139–40; mythic symbolism, 134–36; sovereignty, 11, 105, 109, 118; treaties, 119–20; treaty nationalism, 141–42; tribal lands, 138–39
dams, Missouri River, 123, 129
Dance of the Dialectic (Ollman), 8, 207n14
Dead Voices (Vizenor), 135
Declaration of Human Rights, 68
Declaration of Indian Purpose: The Voice of the American Indian, 10, 40, 43, 45–47, 48
decolonization, 16, 22, 31, 33, 41, 57, 59, 64, 65, 83, 110, 143, 177, 178; art and, 168–69; and Constitution of the White Earth Nation, 158–59
Deganawida, 69
Delaware, 55, 202n2
delegates, Indian, 55
Deloria, Ella, 135
Deloria, Vine, Jr., 4, 5, 8, 18, 34, 39, 125, 203nn5–7, 204n2, 205n2; on indigenous human rights, 58–59; on Marshall Court decisions, 55–57; "Self-Determination and the Concept of Sovereignty," 10, 16–17, 39, 54–55, 59–60; on treaty relations, 63–65; *We Talk, You Listen*, 10, 60–63, 154; on tribal sovereignty, 57–58, 171

Deskaheh, 67
deterritorialization, 22, 64
dialectics, 8, 66, 207n14
dialect letters, 97–99
discourse, 8–9
discrimination, and group identity, 64
Doctrine of Discovery. *See* Law of Discovery
Dog, in Dakotah mythology, 134–35
Drowning in Fire (Womack), 102
Dunn, Dorothy, 168

Eagle Flower people, 193–94
Eastman, Charles, 7, 26
England, 43, 67
environmental impacts, and tribal communities, 196–97, 196
Equalization Act, 190
Erdrich, Louise, 89, 109
Ethnic Studies, 107
Ethnography, Francisco Patencio's, 188
ethno-nationalism, 27
Euro-American Law of Discovery, 38
Europe, 17; sovereignty in, 19–20, 55
exile, 160–61, 162; shared consciousness of, 166–67
Ex Parte Crow Dog, 29–30
experience, 93
"Experience" (Scott), 93
extraconstitutionality, 108

Fall, The (Camus), 160
Fanon, Frantz, 4
Father Meme (Vizenor), 160
federal aid, 47
federal trust responsibility, 29
Federated Indians of Graton Rancheria (Coast Miwok and Southern Pomo), 162
fiction, legal, 149
Firsting and Lasting (O'Brien), 26
Flathead Reservation, 40
Flathead Nation, 44
Fletcher, Matthew, 90; "'Native American Fiction' Tough on Indian Culture," 89
flooding, Lower Brulé Reservation, 123
Florida, termination policy, 44
Fort George Station, 122, 138
Foucault, Michel, 93
Fox clan (Cahuilla), 192–93
France, 17, 18
From the River's Edge (Cook-Lynn), 117
Fus Fixico Letters, The (Posey), 84–85, 98

Galerie Orenda, Paris, 175
Geertz, Clifford, 99
Gellner, Ernest, 23
General Allotment Act (Dawes Act), 28, 138, 201n16
genocide, of California Indians, 179, 186
geography, Cahuilla, 192–93
God Is Red (Deloria), 58, 92, 203n9
Gonzalez, Mario, 112
governance, Haudenosaunee, 67
Great Law of Peace, 70–71
Great Sioux Reservation, 120
Greece, Stoics in, 21
Gross, Emma, 37
guardian-ward relation, 29

Habermas, Jurgen, 26
Hall, Douglas, 165
Harjo, Chitto, 98
Haudenosaunee, 67, 83; as nation, 68–69, 201n16; political theory, 71–72
Hauptman, Lawrence, 45
"Helen's Exile" (Camus), 160, 167
Highwater, Jamake, 116
Hobsbawm, Eric, 23, 25
homeland, separation from, 41
homesteads, California Indian, 186
Hooper, Lucille, 192; *The Cahuilla Indians*, 188
horses: knowledge formation and, 139–40; significance and power of, 137–38, 141
House Made of Dawn (Momaday), 115
Howe, LeAnne, 6
Hoxie, Frederick, 47
humanistic tradition, 43
human rights, 38, 68; constitutions and, 170–71; indigenous, 58–59; in international law, 69–70

identity, 40, 41, 50, 58, 78; Anishinaabe, 173, 208n25; corporate, 180–81; Creek, 81–82
identity formation, Vizenor on, 161–63
imagic moments, Vizenor on, 161–62, 163, 165–66, 173–74
imperialism, 20–21, 31, 43
imperial sovereignty, 22, 200n5
Indian Child Welfare Act, 88
Indian Citizenship Act, 27–28, 185
Indian Civil Rights Act, 28, 157
Indian Claims Commission, 187
Indian country, 201n18; in California, 181–82

Indian Country Today, 15, 37, 38, 89
Indian nations, 55, 56
Indianness, 41, 205n2
Indian New Deal, 108
Indian people, invention of, 26
Indian publics, 26
Indian Removal Act, 28
Indian Reorganization Act (IRA), 42–43, 47, 108, 138
Indian Self-Determination and Education Assistance Act, 38
Indian Trade and Intercourse Acts, 27, 28; and *Ex Parte Crow Dog*, 29–30
Indians Tribal Government Tax Status Act, 88
Indian Tribes of the United States, The (McNickle), 42
indigeneity, 107, 118, 176, 205n5; Dakotah, 126–27
indigenization, of sovereignty discourse, 54, 69
indigenous activism, 106
Indigenous Law Institute, 38
indigenousness, 114
indigenous peoples, 20, 22, 68, 71; global struggles, 30–31; political subjectivity and, 72–73; U.S. legal system and, 173–74
indigenous sovereignty, 73–74
Institute for the Development of Indian Law, 16
intellectualism, Native, 95
intellectual sovereignty, 103; Robert Warrior on, 77–78, 103
intellectual traditions, 9, 26, 80
Inter Caetera (Alexander VI), 20
internationalization, of sovereignty, 67–68
international law, 21, 69–70
international treaty council, 68
interpretive context, Cook-Lynn on, 126–27, 129–31
intertextuality, Vizenor's, 146, 154
IRA. *See* Indian Reorganization Act
Iroquois, 33, 204n12; natural law, 70–71
Iroquois Confederacy, 69
isolationism, U.S. Indian, 30–31

Jabès Edmond, 210n45; *The Book of Questions*, 164, 209n38
Jackson, Robert, 17
Johnson, Joseph, 26
Johnson and Graham's Lessee, 120

Johnson v. McIntosh, 112
Jonaitis, Monique Ramune, 133
Jones, Stephen Graham, *The Bird Is Gone*, 135
Juaneño Band of Mission Indians, 182
judicial system, U.S. federal, 29
jurisdiction, Native literature, 117
Jurisdiction Act, 186–87, 195
justice, 117, 200n4
Justice, Daniel Heath, *Our Fire Survives the Storm*, 77

Kelsey, Harry, 180
keyapi stories, 136, 140
king, as head of state, 17
kinship, 73
Kirwan, Padraig, *Sovereign Stories*, 5–6
Klamath Nation, termination, 44
knowledge: Dakotah, 133–34; horses and, 139–40; traditional, 156, 196
Konkle, Maureen, *Writing Indian Nations*, 26

Lakotahs, 120
land base, 37, 40, 41, 138, 196, 209n30; Black Hills, 111, 120–21; Cahuilla, 189–90, 192–93, 211nn6–7; California Indians, 181, 182, 184–86
Land Claims Act, 185–86
landscape: Dakotah, 122–23; mythic consciousness of, 123–24, 129
language(s): California Indian, 183; and settler-colonialism, 145, 183
law, 7, 18, 21, 118, 203n11; interpretation of, 158–59; and literature, 90–91, 117, 172; U.S. Indian, 19, 22, 27, 29, 33. *See also* natural law
Law of Discovery, 22, 56, 68, 119, 180, 200n10; and U.S. Indian law, 111–13, 120, 132
Law of Nations, 68
League of Nations, 67
Lee, A. Robert, *The Native American Renaissance*, 12
legal fiction, 149
legal sovereignty, 7, 37, 38, 55
legal status, of indigenous people, 22
legal system, "Other" in, 173–74; U.S., 158, 173–74, 187
Lewis and Clark expedition, 145, 149; settler-colonial experience and, 146–47, 148
liberty: continental, 171, 208n23; native, 165
Lincoln, Kenneth, 12

228 INDEX

linguistic competence, 126
listening, and meaning, 147
literacy, alphabetic, 26
literary canon, tribal, 115–16
literary criticism, 78–79, 89, 116, 178; Womack's, 95–96, 100–101
literary nationalism, 77, 91, 117; Creek, 79, 80, 96
literary scholarship, and politics, 114, 115–16
literary theory, postcolonial, 112
literature(s), 7, 96; as cultural repositories, 89–90; and law, 11, 90–91, 172; Native American, 77–81, 84–85; sovereignty and, 86–87
Little Crow War, 120
lobbying, California Indians, 187
Lone Wolf v. Hitchcock, 30, 113
Lower Brulé Reservation, 122, 123
Lyons, Scott, *X-Marks*, 6, 24, 90, 132

Mabel McKay: Weaving the Dream (Sarris), 161–62
"Mahpiyato" (Cook-Lynn), themes in, 119, 121, 125–28
Major Crimes Act, 28, 30, 112
Manifest Manners (Vizenor), 145, 146
Maori, 67
maps, Patencio's book as, 191–92, 194
Marshall, John, 112, 120
Marshall Court, 29; decisions by, 55–56, 112, 120
mass culture, 23; Indian, 24–25
Mathes, Michael, 180
Mathews, John Joseph, 40, 135
McLean, John, 56
McLuhan, Marshall, 60
McNickle, D'Arcy, 9–10, 36, 39, 40, 135; collective survival, 42–43; on *Declaration of Indian Purpose*, 45–46, 48; fictional works, 51–53; nonfiction, 41–42; on tribalism, 44–45
meaning, listening and reading and, 147
media, retribalization, 60
melting-pot ideology, Deloria on, 62–63
memories, native, 165–66
Menchú Túm, Rigoberta, 116
Menominee Nation, termination, 44, 57
Menominee Tribe of Indians v. United States, 3
"Mercenary Sovereignty" (Vizenor), 170, 171
Merriam Report on Indian Affairs, 45, 47

metafiction, 164
Mexico, and California Indians, 184–85
migrations, in Cahuilla history, 192–94
Mihesuah, Devon, 81
military strength, 55
Minnesota, termination policy, 44
Minnesota Chippewa Tribe, 155
Minnesota River, 120
Miranda, Deborah, *Bad Indians*, 183
Missions of California: A Legacy of Genocide, The (Costo and Costo), 179
mission system, missions: California, 179, 180, 183–84; divestment of, 184–85
Missouri River dams, 123, 129
modeling, Creek context, 81–82
modernity: identity formation and, 162–63; industrial, 23
Mohawk, John, 83, 200n4; "All the Children of Mother Earth," 72–73; on Haudenosaunee natural law, 70–72; on self-determination, 67–69
Mohawk Interruptus (Simpson), 7
Mohawk Nation, 67
Momaday, N. Scott, 92–93, 115, 165
Montevideo Convention of the Rights and Duties of States, 3
Montezuma, Carlos, *Wassaja*, 49–50
Moore, David, 51–52; *That Dream Shall Have a Name*, 5
moral foundation, 18
Morgan, Edmund, 25
Morrison, George, 164, 210n45
Mourning Dove, 40
multiethnic states, 27
municipalities, tribes as, 43
Musée du Quai Branly, Paris, consciousness of, 175–77
museums, 175–77
Muskogee Creeks, 97
My Life (Chagall), 167
mythic consciousness, of landscape, 123–24
mythic experience, 104
mythology, creation, 134–35

NAISA. *See* Native American and Indigenous Studies Association
Names, The (Momaday), 165
NAS. *See* Native American studies
National Congress of the American Indian (NCAI), 45, 115, 202n10
National Indian Youth Council, 45

nationalism, 12, 23, 64, 104, 107, 114, 128; Cook-Lynn on, 137–42; Creek, 99–101; literary, 77, 78, 96; Red Sticks and, 82–83; tribal, 24, 37, 105–106, 125–26, 131–32
national organizations, 45
national sovereignty, Red Stick criticism and, 85–86
nation-building, horses and, 139
nationhood, 107, 108, 131; Anishinaabe, 153–54; Haudenosaunee, 68–69; indigenous, 77, 85, 86–87
nations, 19; peace of, 71–72
nation-states, 3, 19, 20, 34, 107
Native American and Indigenous Studies Association (NAISA), critique of, 113–15, 133
Native American Fiction (Treuer), 89–90
"'Native American Fiction' Tough on Indian Culture" (Fletcher), 89
Native American Graves Protection and Repatriation Act, 88, 196
Native American Renaissance, The (Velie and Lee), 12
Native American Sovereignty (Wunder), 3
Native American studies (NAS), 197; Cook-Lynn on, 104, 105, 106, 107, 109, 113–15, 130, 139, 143
Native American Tribalism (McNickle), 42, 43, 51
Native Liberty (Vizenor), 160, 165, 168, 173–74
natural law, 19, 21, 22, 43; Bodin on, 17–18; in international law, 69–70; Iroquois, 70–71
natural reason, 149
natural rights law, 68
NCAI. *See* National Congress of the American Indian
Nebraska, termination policy, 44
Newcomb, Steven, 38
New Indians, Old Wars (Cook-Lynn), 104, 105
New York, termination policy, 44
New Zealand, Maori sovereignty, 67
Nixon administration, 47
nonfiction: indigenous, 78; native, 92–93
nongovernmental organization (NGO), Haudenosaunee forum, 67, 68–69
non-nationalist critics, 12
Northern Cheyennes, 120
Novel, Jean, 176
novels, 90; as form of thinking, 91–92
Nukatem, 188–89, 190, 211n7, 211n10
Nunis, Doyce B., 180

O'Brien, Jean, *Firsting and Lasting*, 26
Occom, Samson, 26
Oklahoma, Alexander Posey's support for, 97
Oliphant v. Suquamish Indian Tribe, 111
Ollman, Bertell, *Dance of the Dialectic*, 8, 207n14
"Ontic Images" (Vizenor), 161–62, 163
oral tradition/culture, 87; Creek, 96–97, 98–99; reading in, 124–25; Warrior on, 94–95
Oregon, termination policy, 44
origin/migration stories, and political history, 83
Osage, identity formation, 162
other, in U.S. legal system, 173–74
Our Fire Survives the Storm (Justice), 77
ownership, and private law, 21

Palm Springs, as Cahuilla territory, 182, 188, 189–90, 193, 195
papal authority, 17
Pass Cahuilla, creation narratives, 188–89
Patencio, Alejo, 194
Patencio, Francisco, 211nn10–11; *Stories and Legends of the Palm Springs Indians*, 12, 181, 188–89, 190–96
peace, real nations and, 71–72
Peace, Power, and Righteousness (Alfred), 32
Penn, Albert, 162
Penn, W. S., *All My Sins Are Relatives*, 162
People and the Word, The (Warrior), 78, 91, 92–93, 94, 95
peoplehood, 8, 39, 72, 134; Creek, 83–84
performative texts, 9
Peyer, Bernd, *The Thinking Indian*, 26
Pico, Pio, 185
Pine Ridge Reservation, 43, 50
place, place-names, 139, 181; Cahuilla and, 192–93, 196, 211n11; symbolism of, 122–23
plenary power, 29
poetics, 96
poetry: Cook-Lynn's, 121–24; as form of thinking, 91–92; Vizenor's, 206n6
political activism, and literary study, 181
political consciousness, 45
political history, and origin/migration stories, 83
political powers, Deloria on, 56–58
political question doctrine, 29
political rights, 30, 55

political sovereignty, 37, 38
political subjectivity, 25, 27, 40, 52, 60, 62, 102; indigenous model of, 72–73
politics, 36; European, 17; indigenous, 32, 34; and literary scholars, 114–16
Politics of Hallowed Ground, The (Cook-Lynn), 112
popular sovereignty, 23–24, 27
Portolá, Gaspar de, 183
Portugal, Treaty of Tordesillas, 20
Posey, Alexander, 84; dialect letters, 97–98
positivism, 18
postcolonial theory, 205n6; Cook-Lynn on, 109, 110–11
postindian, 11, 148, 150–51; Constitution of the White Earth Nation and, 158–59
"Postindian Warriors" (Vizenor), 145, 148, 150–51; simulation in, 148–49
postmodernism, 135
post-structuralist theory, 147
Potawatomi Nation, termination, 44
poverty, as theme, 140–41
Powder River War, 120
power, 18, 13, 25; as creative and destructive, 190–91; horses and, 137–38
Power of Horses, The (Cook-Lynn), 120; themes in, 121–24, 129–30, 137–42
primitivism, 169, 176
print culture, 51; Creek, 84–85; Indian, 25–27, 36, 48
Progress, The (newspaper), 165
property ownership, 21; in U.S. Constitution, 65–66
Public Law 280 (1953), 28, 44, 112
public sphere, Natives in, 26
Pulitano, Elvira, *Toward a Native American Critical Theory*, 111, 207n17

Quechan, 183
queer experience, 102, 203n4

racialized discourse, 24
railroads, and treaties, 120
rancherias, California, 182, 186
Ratana, T. W., 67
ratio scripta, 21
REA. *See* Rural Electrification Agency
reader-response criticism, 94
reader-response theory, 128
readers, role of, 93–94

reading, and meaning, 147
real estate, 22
realism, structural and magic, 135
reason, 18, 21
Reasoning Together (Womack), 88
reciprocity, 171, 200n4
recognition, 171, 174
Red on Red (Womack), 10, 77, 85, 86, 88–89, 96, 100, 156; dialect letters in, 97–98; literary criticism in, 79–81, 100–101; Red Stick consciousness, 81–82; on traditionalism, 82–83
Red Skin, Black Masks (Coulthard), 4
Red Stick criticism, 80, 81, 84; national sovereignty and, 85–86; print culture and, 84–85
Red Sticks, 102; Creek identity and, 81–82, 96; tribal nationalism and, 82–83
Reformation, and papal authority, 17
relocation, 41
Removable Type (Round), 26
removal, 28, 29
represented people, 24
Republica, De (Bodin), 17–18
reservations: in California, 182, 186; state jurisdiction over, 44
resistance, 48; to allotment, 189–90; to Christianity, 133–34
respublica Christiana, 17, 20
retribalization, 60
Revised Constitution and Bylaws of the Minnesota Chippewa Tribe (Chippewa Constitution), 151–53, 154, 155
revolutionaries, as outlaws, 55
Riding, James, 114
Rifkin, Mark, 154, 203n4; *When Did Indians Become Straight*, 6, 102
ritual of condolence, Iroquois, 33
Rome, property rights in, 21
Rosebud Reservation, Spotted Tail's murder on, 29
Round, Philip, *Removable Type*, 26
Rural Electrification Agency (REA), 123

Sacred Dog, 134–35, 139
Santa Fe Indian School, 168
Santee Sioux: treaties and land, 119–20; uprising, 141
Sarris, Greg, *Mabel McKay: Weaving the Dream*, 161–62
Scott, Joan W., "Experience," 93

self-determination, 4, 8, 32, 33, 37–38, 39, 40, 41, 47, 52, 57, 59, 78, 88; Chicago Conference on, 9–10; in *Declaration of Indian Purpose*, 10, 43; John Mohawk on, 67–68; sovereignty as, 66–67; as *Wassaja* theme, 48–49
"Self-Determination and the Concept of Sovereignty" (Deloria), 10, 16–17, 39, 54–55, 59–60
self-governance, 36, 37
self-government, 16, 23, 28, 29, 47; Barsh on, 31–32
sense of place, California Indians, 181
Separate Country, A (Cook-Lynn), 105, 113, 117, 119, 127
separatist-nationalism, 118
Serra, Junipero, 183; canonization of, 179–80
Serrano, 183
settler-colonialism, 60, 111, 145, 167, 183; and Lewis and Clark expedition, 146–47, 148; and Western narrative, 138–39
sexual normalization, 102
Shrouds of White Earth (Vizenor), 11, 160, 210n45, 210n48; aesthetics and politics in, 168–69; aesthetics of survivance in, 171–72; and Constitution of the White Earth Nation, 172–73; exile/transmotional theme in, 163–65, 166–68, 169–70; imagic moments in, 165–66; museums in, 175–76
Shubsda, Thaddeus, 179
Simpson, Audra, *Mohawk Interruptus*, 7
simulation, 148–49
Singer, Peter, 170
Sioux: creation, 134–35; on Pine Ridge Reservation, 43. *See also* Dakotah
Smith, Linda Tuhiwai, 81
Snake faction (Creeks), 98
Society of American Indians, 40, 49
sociopolitical structure, California Indians, 180–81
Sovereign Stories (Kirwan), 5–6
sovereignty, 15, 114, 199n1, 200nn4–5; on Alfred, 32–34; California Indian, 182–83; Cook-Lynn's focus on, 142–43; Dakotah, 109; Deloria's definitions, 61–62; in Europe, 19–20; fluidity of, 197–98; history of concept, 16–17; internationalization of, 66–67; mercenary, 170; popular, 23–24; postindian, 158; treaty-based, 118; and tribal nationalism, 107–108; U.S. Congress on, 112–13. *See also* tribal sovereignty

"Sovereignty and the Problem of Self-Determination" (Deloria), 62
sovereignty discourse, 56, 58, 69
sovereignty reading, 117
Spain, 20, 43; colonial system, 180, 183–84
spiritualism, 72–73
Spotted Tail, murder of, 29
Squirrel, John, 173
Stafford, Barbara Maria, *Visual Analogy*, 162
Standing Bear, Luther, 148, 149
stare decisis, in U.S. Indian law, 158–59
Stegner, Wallace, 105, 119; Cook-Lynn's criticsm of, 128–29
state(s), 17; Indian nations as, 55–56; and power, 25; sovereign, 19, 199n3; termination policy, 44
Statute of Secularization, 184
Stephen Mission, Crow Creek Reservation, 138
Stijaati Thlaako, 101; on storytelling, 98–99
Stoics, 21
Stories and Legends of the Palm Springs Indians (Patencio), 12, 181, 188–89, 190–91; on American-Cahuilla shared history, 194–95; as map, 191–92, 193–94; sovereignty in, 195–96; territory defined in, 192–93
storytelling, 73, 90; and Constitution of the White Earth Nation, 154; Creek, 98–100, 101–102; keyapi, 136, 140; McNickle's, 52–53; Vizenor's work, 150
storyway, Cahuilla, 12
Strong, William Duncan, 192, 194; *Aboriginal Society in Southern California*, 188
study guides, *The Power of Horses*, 130
subjectivity, model of, 73
Surrounded, The (McNickle), 40, 52
survival, collective, 42–43
survivance, 42, 124, 146, 147, 148, 154, 163, 187, 207n7; aesthetics of, 171–72, 173–74; art and, 169–70
symbolism, 73; Dakotah, 133–35; of place, 122–23

Talton v. Mayes, 56–57
Tax, Sol, 45, 46
TCPs. *See* Traditional Tribal Cultural Places
Tedlock, Dennis, 95, 97, 99, 204n14
termination policy, 3, 28, 37, 41, 43–44, 48, 57, 61

territories: Cahuilla, 192–93; California Indians, 182; Doctrine of Discovery and, 112; European vs. Native, 22–23; rights over, 21, 55
Texas, termination policy, 44
texts, formal and performative, 9
That Dream Shall Have a Name (Moore), 5
thinking, forms of, 91–92
Thinking Indian, The (Peyer), 26
Third Space of Sovereignty, The (Bruyneel), 5
This Is Not a Peace Pipe (Turner), 4–5, 199n2
This Week from Indian Country Today, 37, 38, 51
Thomas Aquinas, 21
totemic associations, 154
Toward a Native American Critical Theory (Pulitano), 111, 207n17
trade, regulating, 28
traditionalism, 82, 204n6
Traditional Tribal Cultural Places (TCPs), 197
transmotion, 160–61, 171, 173; in *Shrouds of White Earth*, 163–65, 166–68, 169–70
transnationalism, of tribal peoples, 163
treaties, 28, 37, 48, 55, 65, 117, 185, 195, 202n2; and Jurisdiction Act, 186–87; literary contexts of, 127–28; and nationalism and, 141–42; and tribal nationalism, 86, 131–32; and tribal sovereignty, 102, 118, 119–20; violations of, 120–21
Treaty of Fort Laramie, 120–21, 131, 140
Treaty of Guadalupe Hidalgo, 185
Treaty of Mendota, 119–20
Treaty of Prairie du Chien, 131, 132
Treaty of Tordesillas, 20
Treaty of Waitangi, 67
treaty reading, 117; Cook-Lynn's work and, 124–25, 127–28, 153
treaty relations, 87; Deloria on, 64–65; termination of, 63–64
treaty rights, 38, 62
Treuer, David, 91; *Native American Fiction*, 89–90
tribalcentrism, 7
tribal consciousness, 147
tribalism: McNickle on, 44–45; new, 60–61
tribal nationalism, 24, 37, 125–26; treaties and, 131–32
tribal nations, 19, 28, 106
Tribal Secrets (Warrior), 40, 78, 81, 92, 103
tribal sovereignty, 15, 27, 30, 36, 102, 132–33, 158, 205n3; Deloria on, 54–55, 57–58; nationalism and, 104, 107–108; *Wassaja* on, 50–51
tribes: autonomous, 45; and land base, 41; as municipalities, 43
trickster hermeneutics, 11, 145; in Constitution of the White Earth Nation, 151–53, 165; Vizenor's, 149–50
trust lands, 29, 44
Turner, Dale, *This Is Not a Peace Pipe*, 4–5
"Turning West: Cosmopolitanism and American Indian Literary Nationalism" (Weaver), 12
Turtle Mountain Chippewa Nation, termination, 44

Udall, Stewart, 44–45
UNDRIP. *See* United Nations Declaration on the Rights of Indigenous Peoples
United Nations Convention on Genocide, 170
United Nations Declaration of Human Rights, 68
United Nations Declaration on the Rights of Indigenous Peoples (UNDRIP), 38, 59, 67, 68, 70, 72, 74, 107, 170, 172, 196, 199n2, 203n10
United Native Americans, 37
U.S. Congress, 44, 131; land claims, 185–87; legislation passed by, 27–29, 30; and tribal sovereignty, 112–13
U.S. Constitution, 62, 88, 153, 154, 157, 204n12; property ownership in, 65–66
U.S. Department of the Interior, 108
U.S. Indian law, 19, 22, 27, 55; decolonization and, 158–59; and Doctrine of Discovery, 111–13, 120, 132; tribal constitutions and, 152–53, 154–55; and tribal sovereignty, 29–30
U.S. Supreme Court, 3, 29–30, 111, 209n30; on Black Hills, 120–21; under Marshall, 55–56, 120; on political powers, 56–57
United States v. Kagama, 30
United States v. Sioux Nation of Indians, 121
urban Indians, 41

Velie, Alan, *The Native American Renaissance*, 12
"Visit from Reverend Tileston, A" (Cook-Lynn): Dakotah symbolism in, 133–36, 139; keyapi format in, 136–37
Visual Analogy (Stafford), 162
Vitebsk, 166, 167

Vizenor, Gerald, 9, 10, 11, 34, 42, 51, 66, 86, 93, 102–103, 135, 177, 178–79, 206n6, 210n44, 210n52; "Aesthetics of Survivance," 173–74; on aesthetics and politics, 164–65, 168–69; constitutional criticism by, 144, 154, 170–71; Constitution of the White Earth Nation, 151–53, 155–56, 157–58, 159; on exile/transmotion, 160–61, 166–68; on identity formation, 161–63; on imagic moments, 165–66; on museums, 175–76; "Postindian Warriors," 147–49, 150–51; survivance, 124, 207n7; on transmotional consciousness, 163–64, 169–70; trickster hermeneutics, 145, 149–50
vox populi, 24, 34, 45, 51

Wakpala, S.D., International treaty council at, 68
Warner, Michael, 26
Warrior, Clyde, 45, 95
Warrior, Robert, 26, 88, 91, 204n13; on intellectual sovereignty, 77–78, 103; literary criticism of, 95–96; on Native nonfiction, 92–93; on oral tradition, 94–95; on role of reader, 93–94; *Tribal Secrets*, 40, 81
wars, 120, 180
Wassaja (newspaper), 10; and Carlos Montezuma, 49–50; political stance of, 50–51; self-determination in, 48–49
Way to Rainy Mountain, The (Momaday), 115
Weaver, Jace, 78; "Turning West," 12
We Talk, You Listen (Deloria), 10, 60, 154; on melting-pot ideology, 62–63; on property rights, 65–66; sovereignty in, 61–62; on treaty relations, 63–65

When Did Indians Become Straight (Rifkin), 6, 102
White Earth Reservation, *The Progress*, 165
Why I Can't Read Wallace Stegner (Cook-Lynn), 105
Wicazo Sa Review (journal), 114
wild rice harvest, 174, 210n54
Williams v. Lee, 112
Wilson, Dick, 50
Wind from an Enemy Sky (McNickle), 40, 52
Wisconsin, termination policy, 44
Womack, Craig, 6, 9, 34, 51, 66, 93, 102, 104, 178–79; on Creek nationalism, 99–100; dialect letters, 97–99; literary criticism of, 95–96, 100–101; on literary nationalism, 86–87, 111, 117; *Red on Red*, 10, 77, 79–82, 88–89, 156; on Red Stick criticism, 83–85; on traditionalism, 82–83, 204n6
Worcester v. Georgia, 29, 56
world, interrelatedness of, 72–73
worldview: indigenous peoples, 72–73; traditionalism, 82
Wounded Knee massacre, 40; memorial for, 112
Writing Indian Nations (Konkle), 26
Wunder, John, *Native American Sovereignty*, 3
Wynema (Callahan), Womack's critique of, 100–101

X-Marks (Lyons), 6, 24, 90, 132

Zuni, 99

www.ingramcontent.com/pod-product-compliance
Lightning Source LLC
Chambersburg PA
CBHW020811230426
43666CB00007B/955